Contents

Foreword

As Chairman of the *Irish News*, I am both pleased and privileged to commend this volume of essays, reviewing events and developments in the north of Ireland over the past century, to the widest possible readership.

These essays have been specially commissioned to mark the birth in 1891 of the *Irish News* which has served as a reflector of the changing fortunes and aspirations of an important section of the community. Since its foundation, the *Irish News* has never deviated from the twin objectives laid down by its founders. It has remained faithful to its role as the responsible voice of constitutional Irish nationalism, firmly renouncing violence and injustice. Moreover, it has consistently sought to promote reconciliation and constructive dialogue in our sadly divided society.

There is an ancient Chinese proverb which reads: 'May you not live in exciting times'. For over a century now, the *Irish News* has been chronicling one of the most exciting, yet tragic phases in Irish history. This book is a tribute to the men and women who have shown skill, courage and objectivity in recording the crucial events which have shaped all our lives. They have set standards and established a tradition of which we may be justly proud.

For the *Irish News*, the early 1990s were a climactic moment in which the press became a key factor in orchestrating the demands of ordinary people, Protestant and Catholic, for an end to violence and a new beginning. As the *Irish News* enters its second century, it is my fervent hope that the years ahead will see the creation of a society where reconciliation and prosperity will replace violence and division. By contributing to a greater understanding of our shared past, this volume will make a positive contribution to that peace process.

Jim Fitzpatrick
Chairman, *Irish News Ltd*

Acknowledgements

The editor would like to express his sincere thanks to a number of individuals whose assistance was invaluable in the preparation of this book. Mr Jim Fitzpatrick, Chairman of the *Irish News Ltd* was most generous in his support, as were Mr Tom Collins, editor of the newspaper and Mr Dominic Fitzpatrick, Deputy Chief Executive. I am also greatly indebted to Mrs Kathleen Bell, librarian at the *Irish News* for her invaluable assistance and unchanging good humour in tracing archive photographs, newspaper articles and historical sources.

I thank also Mr James Kelly, Mr Edward Gallagher, Mr Paddy Scott, Mr Brendan Murphy, Mr Hugh Russell, Mr Jimmy McKinney, Mr P.J. McKeefry, Mr Seaghan Maynes, Mr Alfie Woods, Mr Jim Creagh, Mr Pat Carville, Mr Paddy O'Flaherty, Mr Nick Garbutt, Mr Terry McLaughlin, Mr John Foster, Mr Sam Simpson, Mr Sean Tracey, Mr Rory Fitzpatrick, Mr Noel Doran, Mr Jack J. Magee, Mr Seamus Boyd, Mr William Graham, Mr Tommy McIlveen, Mr Fabian Boyle, Mr Peter O'Reilly, Mr Paddy Meehan, Mr Matt Browne, Mr Norman Ling, Mrs Mary McNeill, Mrs Maeve McGill, Dr Mary Leavy, Mrs Jo McClean, Mrs Margaret Thompson, Mrs Ita Hughes, Mrs Monica Davey, Mr Frank Hennessy, Mrs Sheila Hennessy, Mrs Kathleen Conlon, Mr Malachy McSparran, Mr William McCormick, Mr Patrick Hamill, Mrs Deirdre Larkin and Mr Trevor Parkhill.

A special word of thanks is due to Very Rev George O'Hanlon, diocesan archivist of Down and Connor for drawing my attention to documentary material and to Mr Roger Dixon, formerly Irish Studies librarian at the Belfast Central Library.

Mr Shane McAteer and Dr Brian Trainor of the Ulster Historical Foundation provided valuable suggestions and encouragement. For her patient typing of numerous drafts I am grateful to Mrs Geraldine Harvey and to Miss Elizabeth Belshaw for the typesetting.

Mr greatest debt is to my wife, Alice, without whose love and support this project could not have been undertaken.

Eamon Phoenix

Introduction
A Century of Change

EAMON PHOENIX

This book takes as its starting point the birth of the *Irish News* in August 1891. Founded at a time of deep political crisis in Irish nationalism following the fall of Parnell, the *Irish News* gave expression to the views of the only recently emancipated Ulster Catholics, who then numbered just under half of the province's population. Over the next 100 years, the *Irish News* was to reflect the changing fortunes and aspirations of the northern Catholic minority through the Home Rule crises, partition and the 'Troubles' of 1969-94. The history of the *Irish News* is explored by Eamon Phoenix in the first chapter of this book while James Kelly provides a graphic insight into a reporter's life in the late 1920s.

The century from the 1890s to the 1990s has been a momentous one in the history of the north of Ireland, politically, economically, socially and culturally. The launch of the *Irish News* occurred at a time when Irishmen and women were more highly politicised than ever before. The Third Reform Act of 1884 had extended the vote to the agricultural labourer and manual worker alike, thus paving the way for both an Orange and a Green political resurgence. The emergence of the Home Rule issue in the 1880s sounded the death-knell of the agrarian-based Ulster Liberal Party as the province divided along hard sectarian lines. Ulster Unionism, as a major political force, has its origins in the crisis surrounding Gladstone's abortive First Home Rule Bill of 1886. Bonded together by the social cement of Orangeism, the new movement reflected the determination of the mass of Ulster Protestants to maintain the union. Ulster Catholics, on the other hand, looked to the Irish Parliamentary Party, led from 1900 to 1918 by the imperialistic John Redmond and his northern associate, Joseph Devlin, to achieve self-government for an undivided Ireland.

The decision of Asquith's Liberal government in 1912 to introduce a third Home Rule measure raised the political temperature in the north of Ireland to fever pitch as the Unionists, led by the 'quintessential Southern Unionist', Edward Carson and his lieutenant, James Craig, formed their own private army, the Ulster Volunteer Force to oppose 'Rome Rule' by force, if necessary.

The 'Ulster crisis' saw the crystallisation of partition as a fixed idea in British politics while the 1916 rising and the subsequent executions radicalised Irish nationalism, north and south, and set in train the revolutionary events of 1919-22.

The Government of Ireland Act (1920), which partitioned Ireland and Ulster and established a Unionist government for the six counties of Northern Ireland, marked a major triumph for Ulster Unionism. Northern Nationalists, for their part, felt demoralised and abandoned by the Anglo-lrish Treaty of 1921 which confirmed partition. Excluded from the effective political influence within the new state and subjected to systematic discrimination and gerrymandering, the one third minority quickly formed 'a state within a state', identifying with the religion, politics and culture of their southern neighbours in the fleding Irish Free State. This situation continued until the rise of the civil rights movement in the late 1960s, in itself a product of the post-war welfare revolution. Though few anticipated it at the time, the civil rights campaign and the explosive reaction to it unleashed the longest period of sustained violence in Northern Ireland's history – the recent 'Troubles' which lasted for 25 years from August 1969 to October 1994 and claimed 3,168 lives. Happily, as this book goes to press, the IRA and Loyalist paramilitary ceasefires of August and October 1994 and the publication of the Anglo-Irish *Framework Document* of February 1995 have ushered in a more hopeful climate for all the people of Northern Ireland. Agreement and consent, it is hoped, have replaced violence and confrontation as the political *leitmotifs* of Irish politics.

The political events of the tumultuous period from home rule through partition to the imposition of Direct Rule in 1972 is traced by Eamon Phoenix in two chapters in this volume. Martin O'Brien analyses the significance of the Anglo Irish Agreement of November 1985 and the achievement of peace in 1994, while Tim Pat Coogan casts a critical eye over the changing policies of successive Dublin governments towards Northern Ireland from 1921 to the present day. Bob Purdie provides a succinct account of the civil rights campaign of the 1960s and the failure of Terence O'Neill's attempt at reform.

Economically, the past century has been one of contrasts for the north of Ireland. The period opens with north-east Ulster at the zenith of its industrial power – an Irish outpost of the industrial 'black country' of northern England and lowland Scotland. This prosperity was based on the north's two major industries, linen and shipbuilding. By 1900, Belfast had become the world's 'Linenopolis' with some 70,000 hands, while linen villages, such as Donaghcloney, Sion Mills and Bessbrook, dotted the rural landscape. Shipbuilding developed rapidly from the 1850s, assisted by the genius and enterprise of its two founders, Edward Harland and Gustav Wolff, an excellent site and easy access to British raw materials and imperial markets. By 1912, Belfast was the largest shipbuilding centre in the world. The growth of linen and shipbuilding stimulated other industries, notably engineering and rope-making. Yet the inexorable decline of traditional industries in the 1920s and 1930s hit Northern Ireland hard though the economy has benefited from boom periods during the war years and the more buoyant economic climate of the 1960s. Today, as Peter Collins argues in this volume, the inauguration of peace and the real prospect of inward investment provide grounds for cautious optimism. In another chapter, Eddie O'Gorman focuses on the spectacular success of the Belfsas aircraft manufacturers, Shorts Brothers.

One of the side-effects of industrialisation and the growth of Belfast, in particular, was the development of sectarianism. In the wake of the Great Famine, thousands of Catholic migrants from rural Ulster settled in the expanding industrial town while Protestant fears of 'engulfment' were inflamed by the rise of nationalism and by a series of anti-Catholic demagogues. As Andrew Boyd explains, the resultant tension and antagonism between the Catholic navvies and the Protestant weavers and artisans found bloody expression in a series of major sectarian riots in 1857, 1864, 1886, 1920-22 and 1935. The outbreak of 1920-22, in which 450 people died, further polarised the two communities at the inception of the new state and bequeathed a legacy of bitterness and distrust.

After the 1860s, Irish Catholic migrants tended to prefer Britain or North America to Ireland's only industrial city. Many emigrated to Scotland where they made the slow transition from 'exile politics', best expressed in their support for Home Rule and Irish independence, to assimilation in the British political system. This aspect is the subject of a chapter by Tom Gallagher.

It is hardly surprising, therefore, that the existence of a large unionised labour force in Ulster did not translate itself into a strong class-based labour movement. As Peter Collins shows in his chapter on labour, the establishment of labour as a cohesive political force was constantly stymied by working-class differences on the 'National question'. Apart from a few brief moments of working-class solidarity, notably in 1932, when Protestant and Catholic workers rioted in unison against inadequate unemployment relief, the period of Stormont rule was dominated by the border issue. This is not to minimize the significant contribution made by the trade union movement during the long years of the Troubles to the eradication of sectarianism and discrimination in the work place.

The last century has also witnessed revolutionary changes on the land where the influence of the landlord was steadily eroded from 1870 onwards. As Frank Thompson shows in his chapter, the most important land reform was the Wyndham Land Purchase Act of 1903. By enabling the tenants to buy out their farms, this measure amounted to a bloodless social revolution in Ireland and finally solved the vexed land question which had inflamed landlord-tenant relations in the late Victorian era.

The century after 1891 was also a period of wide-ranging social, educational and legal change in the north of Ireland. The evolution of popular education 'from National Schools to national curriculum' is carefully analysed by the late John Magee in his chapter. The old national schools system, established in 1831 for the whole country, was superseded in Northern Ireland after 1923 by a dual system of state schools and voluntary (mainly Catholic) schools which largely obtains to the present day. A major landmark in the provision of equality of opportunity for all children was the 1947 Stormont Education Act. This shadowed the Butler Act (1944) in its radical provision for free secondary education and a generous system of university grants. The full implications of this Act for Northern Ireland politics and society would only become apparent twenty years later in the 1960s. By the 1980s, however, the traditional framework of denominational education was being challenged by the emergence of a movement towards integrated education amongst a section of middle-class parents.

Educational reform was paralleled by vast improvements in public health and welfare, the focus of E. Margaret Crawford's chapter. In 1948, the archaic Poor Law system, first introduced in Ireland in 1838, was swept away and replaced by a new 'welfare state', in which free medical and social services were guaranteed to the public 'from the cradle to the grave'. As a result of new medical discoveries, improvements in health care and the eradication of slum-housing conditions, the death rate in Northern Ireland was reduced from being the highest to the lowest in the United Kingdom.

The advent of partition also heralded major administrative change in the legal system, as John Larkin reminds us in his survey. Until 1921, the whole of Ireland was a legal and administrative unit but, under the 1920 Act, Northern Ireland obtained a separate Supreme Court of Judicature. Interestingly, Sir Denis Henry (1864-1925), who has a unique distinction of being the only Catholic ever to serve as a Unionist MP, became the first Lord Chief Justice of Northern Ireland in 1921. Henry's fascinating political and legal career is examined by A. D. McDonnell in this volume.

As Philip Ollerenshaw points out in his chapter, the growing prosperity and self-confidence of Ulster in the late nineteenth and early twentieth centuries was reflected also in the rapid expansion of banking before the First World War. The banking industry survived the challenges of Home Rule and the 'Belfast boycott' of the 1920s to undergo a major period of structural change in the 1960s.

Few social institutions in the north of Ireland have been as influential over the past one hundred years as the churches. On the Protestant side, the disestablishment and disendowment of the Church of Ireland in 1869 helped to strengthen still further the incipient alliance between Ulster Anglicans and Presbyterians. The cooperation of the two denominations in the anti-Home Rule struggle and the tendency of Protestant church leaders to depict the UVF as a religious crusade against 'Rome Rule' consolidated this movement, although several Church of Ireland prelates recorded their hostility to partition. After 1921, cooperation was necessary to secure Protestant interests in the vital area of state control over education.

For the Roman Catholic church, the 1890s and early decades of the twentieth century marked the growth of a new self-confident spirit, associated with church-building and a major expansion of Catholic activity in the educational sphere. During the Parnell split of 1890-91, the hierarchy and many priests opposed 'the fallen despot and discredited leader'. However, the Church was sympathetic to the popular demand for Home Rule and Bishop Patrick O'Donnell of Raphoe was a vigorous supporter of Redmond and the Nationalist pressure group, the Ancient order of Hiberians.

As Oliver Rafferty relates in his chapter on Catholicism, the Ulster bishops mirrored the distaste of ordinary Catholics for partition but were quick to exhort their flock to 'organise along constitutional lines' for the redress of their grievances and the defence of Catholic education.

As John Barkley points out in his chapter on the Protestant churches, however, inter-church relations remained frigid until the Decree on Ecumenism of Vatican Two in 1964 created a more liberal spirit. One positive effect of the 'Troubles' was to bring the main Christian church leaders together to condemn violence and sectarianism and to exercise a moderating influence at moments of communal crisis.

What, then, of those other aspects of society – sport, culture and the arts? One of the most striking characteristics of urbanization in the late-nineteenth century was the popularity of soccer and the north of Ireland was no exception. As Peter Finn shows in his chapter on sport, by the 1890s, soccer was well established in the working-class districts of Belfast, Derry and other towns where it was rivalled only by boxing. Amongst the middle classes, rugby, cricket, golf, cycling and yachting had become popular by the turn of the century.

The Gaelic Athletic Association (GAA) was established by the County Clare schoolmaster, Michael Cusack, in 1884 to foster native games and pastimes. As Brendan Harvey describes in his chapter on the GAA, the organisation quickly took root in rural Ulster and, following a dip in the troubled 1920s, Gaelic games underwent a dramatic revival in the north. In

1960, Down made sporting history by becoming the first northern team to win an all-Ireland Gaelic football final. It was to be the first of many triumphs for Ulster teams although the GAA's 'ban', excluding members of the security forces from GAA activities, has continued to generate controversy.

In the field of culture and the arts, the last century has not been a stagnant one, notwithstanding St. John Ervine's gibe that Ulster's 'artistic activities were sporadic'. The *Shan Van Vocht,* edited by Alice Milligan and `Ethna Carbery' between 1896 and 1899, was a high quality 'political and literary magazine' of nationalist views. Its ideals were reflected later in the Ulster Literary Theatre, established by Francis Joseph Bigger and the talented Morrow brothers in 1902. By 1939, people's leisure activities were much more varied. Cinema-going proved a great draw with all social classes, as did radio, after the opening of the BBC's Belfast transmitter in 1924. In the field of visual arts, William Conor emerged as the representative painter of the depression years of the 1930s through his graphic images of shawled mill girls and shipyard workers.

As John Gray points out in his chapter, the 1950s and 1960s were to produce a galaxy of Ulster-born literary talent: playwrights such as Brian Friel, novelists such as Brian Moore and Sam Hanna Bell and poets such as Seamus Heaney and John Hewitt. Indeed, the award of the 1995 Nobel Prize for Literature to Heaney, a small farmer's son from south Derry, was a signal reminder of the massive contribution which the north of Ireland has made to international letters and the arts.

No survey of Ulster history since 1891 would be complete without reference to that intrinsic part of the province's cultural heritage, the Irish language. In 1891, at the beginning of the century under review, Irish, while in full retreat since the Famine, could claim over 6,600 speakers in Tyrone, 2,700 in Derry and 3,500 in Armagh, as well as smaller concentrations in the Antrim Glens and south Down. It was precisely to arrest the decline of the language and to restore it as a living tongue that Douglas Hyde, the son of a Roscommon rector, and Eoin MacNeill, a native of Glenarm, founded the Gaelic League in 1893. As Roger Blaney reveals in his chapter on the Irish language, its *renaissance* in Ulster owed much to a group of Protestant middle-class enthusiasts, amongst them F. J. Bigger and Dr John St Clair Boyd of Holywood. In many ways, these men were the spiritual heirs of the Belfast poet, Sir Samuel Ferguson (1810-86) whose career is traced by his biographer, Greg Ó Dúill, in an Irish language contribution. The language received no encouragement from the Unionist government during 1921-72 but underwent a resurgence in the 1970s and 1980s with the establishment of a 'mini-Gaeltacht' in Belfast as well as Irish medium schools and a local daily newspaper. This 'language revolution' is one of the most striking aspects of the cultural scene in Northern Ireland as the 1990s draw to a close.

In a final chapter, Frances Garbutt revisits the world of fashion a century ago.

The chapters in this book have been written by leading experts in their fields. They seek to explore the rich tapestry of life in Ulster since the establishment of the *Irish News* in 1891 in a readable style, while incorporating the fruits of recent historical research. Central to our story is the history of the newspaper itself and its perspectives on the unfolding dramas of the period spanning the late Victorian era to our own day.

1

The History of a Newspaper
the *Irish News*

1855-1995

EAMON PHOENIX

Founded at a time of great political crisis among the forces of Irish nationalism, the *Irish News* traces its ancestry to the old *Belfast Morning News*, established in 1855 by the Read brothers as Ireland's first penny news-sheet. Robert and Daniel Read had left their home in Antrim in the 1820s to seek their fortune in Belfast where their older brother, Patrick, had entered the retail tobacco business. Robert and Daniel were both apprenticed to the printing trade in the expanding industrial town. The family letter-press printing firm seems to have been set up at 12, Crown Entry shortly after 1840. The *Belfast Directory* for that year records the following entries:

> Robert Read, Letterpress Printing, 12 Crown Entry.
> Patrick Read, Writing Clerk, 12 Crown Entry.
> Daniel Read, Gentleman, 12 Crown Entry.

The fact that Daniel is described as a gentleman suggests that their business had already brought the brothers prosperity. By 1845, the firm was now styled Letterpress Printers and Lithographers and was sufficiently buoyant to acquire additional premises next door at number 10. During the next ten years the most important productions of the Read Printing Press were Catholic prayer books and devotional tracts which found a ready market amongst Belfast's rapidly-growing Catholic population. Such was the response that the Reads were encouraged to print an edition of the Douai Bible, with the *imprimatur* of Dr Cornelius Denvir, the Bishop of Down and Connor. The work sold widely throughout Ulster.

It was not until 1855 that the Reads turned their genius to the publication of a morning newspaper, calculated to appeal to a broad readership in the northern half of Ireland. The new paper, a tri-weekly, was to be known as the *Belfast Morning News* and first appeared on the streets on 2 July, 1855. At this time, Belfast had only one daily newspaper, the *News Letter* (founded in 1737) and five tri-weeklies — the Presbyterian *Banner of Ulster*, the

Morning Post, the *Northern Whig*, a radical voice under F.D. Finlay, the nationally-minded Ulsterman and the *Belfast Mercury* — as well as two weekly journals, the *Ulster Adviser* and the *Mercantile Journal*. The Reads made two innovations when they launched the *Morning News*. It was Ireland's first penny newspaper and it was to become the first successful penny newspaper in the British Isles.

The *Morning News* expanded its sales dramatically, not merely in Belfast but throughout the entire northern half of Ireland, 'from Belfast to Sligo and from Glenties to Longford'. Its very success, however, provoked the unremitting wrath of the long established *News Letter*. In a bitter attack on 16 August, 1856, the *News Letter's* editor reminded the people of Belfast that its soaring competitor emanated from the same press which had printed the heretical Douai Bible. Moreover, he sneered at it as having been established on the street-hawking system and appealing to a readership composed of 'servants, street-sweepers, pedlars and pot-boys.'

The reason for such an unpredecented and violent outburst is easily found in the stamp returns for July 1856 which confirmed that the *Morning News* was selling a staggering 7,000 copies throughout the north of Ireland — some 2,000 more than the total sales of all other Belfast papers put together.[1] The *Morning News*, though Catholic-owned, remained cautiously neutral in politics, a factor which, together with its cheapness, commended it to readers of all creeds and political hues in Ulster.

There was little notable change in the Reads' newspaper until 1872 when a new editor, J.P. Swann, arrived from England. Shortly afterwards, on 20 August, 1872, the *Morning News* became a daily paper. The reasons for the more frequent issue were given in the editorial of that day. The circulation had risen to 12,500 copies daily, spread throughout Ulster and a large portion of the west and midlands. Advertising had also grown apace and was placing severe demands on the four-page journal.

Undoubtedly, however, a major catalyst in the decision to 'go daily' was the growing interest in popular politics. Two years earlier in 1870, Isaac Butt, an Ulster Protestant barrister and former Unionist, had launched the Home Government Association, aimed at the establishment of a devolved parliament in Dublin with control over Irish domestic affairs. The Secret Ballot Act of 1872 had banished landlord influence in Irish elections and greatly increased public interest in the events on the hustings. At the same time, Joseph Biggar, the little Belfast pork butcher, soon to win fame as the father of obstructionism in the British House of Commons, was forming branches of the new association in the north-east. Belfast was the centre of intense political activity and the public appetite for news and views seemed insatiable. The week which saw the change to a daily print was marked by a rash of rioting and destruction in Belfast, Lurgan and Portadown, in the wake of the annual nationalist Lady Day processions. With reports coming in of street battles, assaults and looting, there was no scarcity of news for the first daily issues of the *Morning News*.[2]

By far the most gifted member of the *Morning News* staff, and its editor in the last 14 months of his life, was Robert A Wilson — better known by his pseudonym 'Barney Maglone'. From his first association with the paper in 1865 until his untimely death a decade later, 'Maglone' was the most widely-read journalist in Ireland. Indeed his racy contribution — a series of letters 'To My Cousin in Amerikay' — served to increase the circulation of the issues containing them by up to 6,000 copies. Wilson was born the son of a coastguard, in Dunfanaghy, County Donegal around 1820. After a brief sojourn as a schoolteacher near Ballycastle, he emigrated to America where he became a journalist on the staff of the *Boston Republic*. Returning to Ireland in 1847, he worked on the *Impartial Reporter* in Enniskillen and on the *Nation* newspaper in Dublin under Gavan Duffy, before joining the *Morning News* in Crown Entry. As Barney Maglone, he quickly established an eager following amongst the sweated workers of the Belfast linen mills and foundries whose claims he stoutly defended. The 'most original Irish pressman of his day', Maglone was a familiar figure in the streets of Belfast, dressed characteristically in a slouch hat, a voluminous cloak worn like a Roman toga and flamboyant necktie. He would appear to have been a Home Ruler in politics, a factor which precipitated his premature death. He was found dying in his garret in Wesley Place, Belfast on 10 August 1875, a few days after he had returned from a too-vigorous participation in the O'Connell Centenary celebrations in Dublin.

In the light of his tragic end, one of Barney's last poems, 'Hallow'eve Complaint' has a bathetic significance, prefiguring his own demise. Its devil-may-care quality helps to explain the popularity which this Donegal Dissenter brought to the old *Morning News*:

> Other people have homes of their own, Maglone,
> But your share of the world's to have none, Mavrone:
> As you lived you must die.
> An' your last gasp or cry
> Will be heard, very likely, by none — not one:
> You unfortunate divil, Maglone.

The death of Daniel Read in 1881 marked a major turning point in the history of the *Belfast Morning News*. In 1882 the paper was acquired by Edmund Dwyer Gray, the proprietor of the nationalist *Freeman's Journal* in Dublin, and a leading Parnellite. The Grays were a far more important family than the Reads had ever been. Edmund's father, Sir John Gray (1816-75), a

Protestant Nationalist from County Mayo, had been a close political ally of Daniel O'Connell, Member of Parliament for Kilkenny and sole proprietor of the *Freeman*. Edmund, like his father a Nationalist MP and Lord Mayor of Dublin, had presided over the historic meeting of 17 May, 1880 when Parnell was elected chairman of the now powerful Irish Parliamentary Party.

From this point on, the *Morning News* gave unflagging support to Parnell in his efforts to achieve a Home Rule parliament. In this policy, it reflected the views of the great mass of Ulster Catholics, especially after the 1885 'Invasion of Ulster' when the Home Rule Party swept a majority of the province's 33 seats. The politicising effects of the Third Reform Act of 1884, which gave the vote to the masses, together with the increase in popular literacy, ensured that the nationalist daily commanded a wide circulation throughout the nine counties, even if its more partisan line alienated unionist and Protestant readers.

A particularly successful venture was Gray's acquisition of the *Ulster Examiner*, a weekly journal founded in 1868 with Dr Dorrian, the Catholic Bishop of Down and Connor as its chief promoter. The office of the *Examiner* was at the corner of Donegall Street and Union Street, directly opposite the present site of the *Irish News*. Gray amalgamated the *Examiner* with the weekly edition of the *Morning News* and for the rest of the 1880s both papers were published from new offices in Commercial Court, off Lower Donegall Street.

Under the Gray regime, the *Morning News* enjoyed a succession of able editors. When the first of these, William J. McDowell, left to join the Dublin *Freeman* in 1883, he was succeeded by Patrick J. Kelly, a native of County Derry and a man of 'keen intellect and unclouded judgment'. Like many newspapermen of that day, Kelly interrupted his journalistic career in 1885 to study for the Bar. His successor in the editor's chair was the colourful Dan McAleese, a former shoemaker from Randalstown, Co Antrim and future Home Rule MP. After editing the *Morning News* for just a year, McAleese left for Monaghan to found the *People's Advocate*. The vacancy was filled by the previous editor, Kelly, now a member of the Irish Bar. The blunt Derry man remained editor until the shock waves generated by the tragic Parnell split disrupted the affairs of Gray's Belfast organ during the winter of 1890-91.

The 1880s witnessed a resurgence of nationalist fervour in Belfast as Gladstone's conversion to Home Rule and Parnell's success in creating a powerful pledge-bound Irish party raised public excitement to fever pitch. A group of young men, mostly associated with the *Morning News*, were responsible for setting up the Belfast Young Ireland Society in 1883 as a focus for nationalist discussion and propaganda.

The Society, which met in St Mary's Hall, was addressed by a galaxy of Irish political and literary figures. The first secretary was William McGrath, a young reporter on the *Morning News* from Portaferry, Co Down. He was later to become a leading King's Counsel until his assassination by armed men in Dublin in 1920. McGrath was succeeded as secretary by the popular Belfast journalist Jeremiah ('Jerry') MacVeagh, another young staffman on the *Morning News*. MacVeagh was later to become Nationalist MP for South Down (1902-22) at Westminster and one of the most effective pamphleteers in the cause of all-Ireland Home Rule. MacVeagh migrated to London in 1890 and was replaced as Secretary of the Young Ireland Society by the nineteen-year-old Joseph Devlin, already on the threshold of a meteoric political career.[3]

Edmund Dwyer Gray died in 1888 and the *Morning News* was acquired by a limited liability company. His son, a headstrong young man in his early twenties, became controller of the Gray family interest in the paper. However, the young Gray's interests were even further removed from Belfast than his father's and the next two year's found him cruising extensively in the Southern Pacific.

These were the conditions under which the *Belfast Morning News* was directed when the Parnell split erupted on the political scene. The *Morning News* and its editor, P.J. Kelly, had strongly supported the Irish leader during the crisis of 1887-89, caused by the attempt by *The Times* newspaper to prove a connection between Parnell and agrarian outrages during the Land War. When a Special Commission, in February 1889, found that the incriminating letters had been forged by the renegade Irish nationalist (and former Belfast journalist) Richard Piggott, Parnell's popularity reached its zenith on both sides of the Irish sea. The Home Rule leader's advantage, however, was wiped out in the divorce court in November 1890 when Captain William O'Shea filed his suit against his wife, citing Parnell as co-respondent. The ensuing scandal was to signal a watershed in the history of Irish nationalism and, locally, of the *Belfast Morning News*.

Gladstone made it clear that Irish Nationalists must make a straight choice between Parnell and Home Rule. Almost overnight, the Home Rule Party and practically every nationalist organisation split along pro- and anti-Parnellite lines. In Belfast, Joe Devlin could lament that the seminal Young Ireland Society had been 'almost destroyed by the heat and conflict', unleashed by the 'unfortunate crisis'.[4] Throughout the country the Church followed the lead of the majority of the Parliamentary Party and threw its weight in the scales against 'the fallen despot and discredited leader'.[5] When the crisis broke, the young Dwyer Gray was travelling in the Antipodes and could not be contacted. However, while his Dublin organ, the *Freeman* reflected the strong Parnellite allegiance of the capital, the *Morning News* swiftly struck an anti-Parnellite stance. Kelly, the editor, with 16 years' experience in northern journalism behind him, was well aware that the vast majority of northern Catholics, led by their bishops and clergy, were arrayed on the anti-Parnellite side.

When Gray returned to Ireland, however, he showed a strong sympathy with the 'uncrowned king', now struggling for his political life in a series of hard-fought by-elections. One of the proprietor's first executive acts on his return was to journey to Belfast and dismiss Kelly from his post. The vacancy was filled by one of the sub-editors, Michael J. Callen and, thereafter, the *Morning News* defended the indomitable Parnell against his detractors.[6]

Hostility to Parnell had already led to the formation of a clericalist press in Dublin as a rival to the *Freeman*. The northern bishops felt that a similar course should be adopted in Belfast. The proposal to launch a new paper, *The Irish News*, which would more authentically mirror Catholic and nationalist opinion was floated by Dr Patrick McAlister, Bishop of Down and Connor, and actively promoted by two of his ablest and most energetic priests, Father James Hamill, the parish priest of Whitehouse and Rev. Dr Richard Marner, a former president of St Malachy's College, Belfast and parish priest of Kilkeel.

By the end of April 1891, a new company had been established with Cardinal Logue, the Ulster bishops and leading Catholic businessmen as its main shareholders. In a circular letter outlining the proposal, dated 27 April, 1891, Bishop McAlister underlined 'the great necessity which exists at the present time for a really Catholic and nationalist daily journal in Ulster'. In a clear allusion to Parnell and his supporters, the bishop referred to 'the most insidious methods' being adopted 'to mislead the people from the plain duty they owe to themselves and their country'. 'Almost every day', he declared, 'truth itself is misrepresented for no better purpose than that a miserable and misguided faction may prolong its existence even at a sacrifice of the best interests of our country. If the Catholics and nationalists of Ulster are to discharge their duty in such a crisis, it behoves them to do what in their power lies to put an end to such an unsatisfactory state of things'. Northern Catholics, Bishop McAlister continued, had an obligation to support a journal which would both form a sound public opinion on the great issues of the day and, more importantly, 'represent correctly, and guide in a legitimate way, the views of the people of Ulster'.

The promoters of the new *Irish News* could also point out that of the 48 newspapers published in Ulster in 1891, only four could be described as Catholic or nationalist in outlook. 'Should this monopoly be permitted to continue?' the bishop asked leading Catholics. After all, Catholics comprised nearly half of the province's population and had advanced dramatically in terms of education and social status in the late nineteenth century. It was obvious that such a powerful and politicised section of opinion should be provided with a daily paper 'which they can call their own and on which they can rely to advocate their political and religious rights,' declared Dr McAlister.

The bishop, clergy and laity of Down and Connor had already advanced a large proportion of the required capital. However, the promoters of the new press were adamant that the viability of the venture could only be ensured if shares were taken up 'in every town and district in Ulster' by priests and laymen alike. The bishop and his fellow-promoters expressed particular satisfaction that the clericalist *Irish National Press*, launched in Dublin after the split, was enjoying steady success.

The new company, The Irish News Ltd, was registered on 30 April 1891. Its Articles of Association declared its object: 'to print, publish and circulate daily and weekly and other newspapers in Ireland and elsewhere.' The capital of the company was set at £20,000, divided into £1 shares. The first meeting of the directors was held on 4 May 1891. The first chairman of the Board was Edward Hughes, the owner of one of Belfast's largest bakeries and the son of the town's leading Catholic industrialist and public figure, Bernard ('Barney') Hughes. His fellow-directors, each of whom held over one hundred shares in the new company, were William J. Reynolds, William McCormick, Edward McHugh, Dr Michael Reeves O'Malley, Patrick Dempsey, William H. Campbell and three clerics, Rev Dr Marner, Father James Hamill and Rev Dr John O'Brien, the parish priest of Banbridge.[8]

The lay members of the board together represented a cross-section of the most prosperous Catholics in the north-east. Reynolds was a Dungannon solicitor and the anti-Parnellite Nationalist MP for East Tyrone. William McCormick, one of the largest share-holders in the new paper, and its chairman from 1892 until 1905, was a leading Belfast rent agent and accountant. One of the wealthiest Catholics in the city and amongst the first Catholic representatives on Belfast Corporation in the 1890s, McCormick was possessed of a sharp business acumen which helped to ensure the early commercial success of the *Irish News*.

Patrick Dempsey was a member of a distinguished north Antrim family of Coldagh, near Ballymoney. (His brother, Sir Alexander Dempsey was a leading Belfast medical practitioner). Patrick was a founder of the Irish Whiskey Company and owner of the old Linen Hall Hotel, long a nationalist rendezvous in Donegall Square East. Edward McHugh was a Belfast linen manufacturer who sat as anti-Parnellite MP for South Armagh from 1892 until his death in 1900. Of the remainder, O'Malley was a prominent Catholic doctor while William H. Campbell, a contractor, was the father of the Belfast poet, Joseph Campbell (1879-1944).

The sacked editor of the already flagging *Morning News*, P. J. Kelly, was appointed secretary of the company and editor of the *Irish News*. Throughout that summer, canvassers went around the north of Ireland selling shares in the new paper. Though the prospect of immediate profit seemed remote, their efforts met with unexpected success. Soon 11,000 £1 shares were sold through the nine Ulster counties, Leitrim and Sligo. Among the leading shareholders were parish priests, 'strong farmers' and shopkeepers.

In Belfast, the directors, heartened by the response to the venture, moved to expedite the establishment of the new paper. Initially the company had offices in Queen's Buildings on the corner of Royal Avenue and Berry Street. By August 1891, larger premises had been leased at 121 and 123 Donegall Street (next door to the present site) and on Lady Day, 15 August 1891, the first edition of *The Irish News*, appeared. It cost one penny and had as its motto, *Pro Fide Et Patria* —'For Faith and Fatherland'.

The dramatic circumstances which gave birth to the new paper and the programme it intended to pursue were spelled out in the first leading article. The editor referred tartly to 'the lamentable and painful crisis' unleashed by the O'Shea divorce case the previous November. The Ulster Catholics, declaimed the *Irish News*, had joined with the mass of their fellow-countrymen in rebelling against 'the un-Catholic, unnational, intolerant and grossly insulting sentiments which were flung at them' by the forces of Parnellism. The *Irish News* was confident, however, that 'the cause of Fatherland' had triumphed. Ireland, the editorial averred, would 'advance to future victories when measures, not men, will be the ruling policy'. The new daily paper saw the question of national self-government as the overriding objective for nationalist Ireland. However, it committed itself strongly to a wide-ranging reform programme including the removal of educational inequalities, a more equitable system of taxation and the development of Irish railways, harbours and resources.

Whilst declaring that the *Irish News*' motto epitomised its outlook, the editor was at pains to stress that the paper would respect the deeply-held conviction of others, namely the large Protestant and unionist population of the north-east. 'If we are determined to uphold our own principles, we can at the same time, respect the honest men who differ from our religiously, and who, sustaining their position by argument, live according to their convictions'. The same edition of 15 August 1891 carried letters of support for the paper from Bishop McAlister and Archbishop Kirby, president of the Irish College in Rome. Kirby conveyed the Pope's 'cordial approbation' of the establishment of a journal which might defend Catholics against 'the calumnies...with which they are so continually assailed.'[9]

From the time the *Irish News* was founded, the *Morning News* ceased to advocate the Parnellite cause. It soon became clear, however, that Gray's Belfast organ could not hope to compete with its locally-owned and clerically-supported rival. The *Irish News* had the additional advantage that it was pledged to support the anti-Parnellite section of the Irish party, to which the bulk of Ulster Nationalists had given their allegiance. *Morning News* reporters found themselves barred from important nationalist meetings; throughout the north, resolutions were passed urging Catholics and nationalists to boycott the Gray journal and purchase the *Irish News*.[10] The *Irish News* continued to harry the ailing Parnell until his sudden death on 6 October 1891. The young Thomas J. Campbell, then a book-keeper on a new paper, recalled 'the deep hush in the office when a director, Edward McHugh MP, brought word of the Chief's tragic end. It was felt to be more than an event — to be the close of an epoch.'[11]

So strong was the tide of nationalist opinion in favour of the *Irish News* that in July 1892 the new paper was sufficiently robust to buy out the flagging

The editoral staff of the *Irish News* in the early 1900s. Seated left to right – C. Rogers, J.A. Power & Thomas O'Donaghue. Standing – Billy Duggan (Chief Reporter), T.J. Campbell (editor 1895-1906) and W.J.Flanagan
Irish News

Morning News. On the morning of 29 August 1892, there was no *Morning News* on sale. It was merged with the *Irish News* and the new mast-head — *The Irish News and Belfast Morning News* — was the first public intimation of what had occurred. Gray lost about £20,000 in his Belfast venture. Within four years, however, the *Irish News* had recouped the losses sustained during the year of rivalry and won its way back to a profit-making position. At this time also, the Irish News Ltd subsumed the old *Ulster Examiner* in a new weekly paper, the *Irish Weekly*. This continued in business until 1982.[12]

The early editorial staff of the *Irish News* numbered several figures who were destined to play leading roles in Irish or British public life. The chief sub-editor was Thomas J. Hanna, a young County Down man who later served as private secretary to John Redmond, the leader of the Irish Parliamentary Party. Other young staffmen included the 19 years old Joe Devlin, already renowned for his oratorial powers, and T. J. Campbell who transferred to the editorial staff in 1892. Campbell was appointed editor of the paper in 1895, a post he held until 1908 when he abandoned journalism for a distinguished legal and political career. He became a K.C. in 1918 and represented the Nationalist Party in both Houses of the Northern Ireland parliament after 1929 ending his career as a county court judge. Campbell's *Fifty Years of Ulster*, published as a series by the *Irish News* during the Second World War, remains the best contemporary account of the fortunes of the nationalist minority in the turbulent early decades of this century.

Two talented journalists who joined the staff during Campbell's editorship were the brothers Thomas and P. J. O'Donoghue. Tom O'Donoghue reported from the trenches of the Western Front as the paper's Chief Reporter in 1915. He was later to join the Hansard staff of the British parliament, while his brother P.J. was called to the Irish Bar. Many years later, in 1924, he was responsible for sentencing Eamon de Valera to a month's imprisonment for breaching an exclusion order.

No sooner had the *Irish News* established itself, however, than it became the cockpit of bitter antagonism due to a split among the Belfast Catholics. Like the Parnell split, the rift was a reflection of political events at national level where three different factions, the Dillonites, Redmondites, and Healyites were locked in a bitter power struggle for Parnell's mantle. The new Bishop of Down and Connor, Dr Henry Henry, was an ardent supporter of Tim Healy, the maverick Home Rule politician and leader of the clericalist wing of the movement. Henry was opposed, however, in Belfast by the former *Irish News* reporter, Joe Devlin, the vice-president of the local branch of the Irish National Federation, the organisation of the anti-Parnellite leader, John Dillon. Devlin was a sworn enemy of the acid-tongued Healy who was resisting Dillon's efforts to keep the Party subject to an iron discipline. As early as 1894, the *Irish News*, under the influence of its director, Edward McHugh, a Healyite MP was supporting the Healy faction to the consternation of Devlin and his friends. During the early years, the paper's London editor was Vesey Knox, a leading Healyite MP.[13]

The difference between the Devlinites and the bishop first erupted into the open in 1896 over the decision of the local Catholic Committee to accept an offer from the unionist-controlled Belfast Corporation to establish two exclusively Catholic wards in the city. To Devlin and his supporters, such an arrangement would give an edge to sectarianism in Belfast by equating Nationalism with Catholicism. Bishop Henry, repelled by the unedifying Parnell split, had now decided that a Catholic party under his personal control could best serve Catholic interests in the northern capital. As relations between the two men worsened, the young Falls politician, supported by Dillon and Michael Davitt, determined to challenge Henry for control of the two new Catholic wards.

To ensure his success, Devlin realised the need to get control of the *Irish News* which was giving grudging support to the bishop's new Belfast Catholic Association. However, in a letter to John Dillon in July 1897, a dispirited Devlin was forced to concede that it was 'absolutely impossible to get hold of the *Irish News*'. Even strong supporters of Dillon on the board, such as Dempsey and Rev Dr O'Brien, had been 'frightened' into permitting the paper to launch scathing attacks on Devlin and the mainstream Nationalists. But he added: 'The shopkeepers are almost to a man in our favour, and as these are the people who buy the *Irish News*, the change of policy won't do any harm'.[14]

The chairman of the paper, William McCormick, was a close confidant of the bishop who denounced Devlin as a dangerous demagogue in the columns of the *Irish News*. To counter this onslaught, Devlin was able, with the support of his friends, to launch his own weekly newspaper, the *Northern Star* in October 1897. The paper vigorously denounced Bishop Henry and his Association, accusing them of 'clerical dictation' while Devlin attacked the *Irish News* as a 'jellyfish newspaper'. In the local elections that November, however, the bishop's followers led by McCormick inflicted a decisive defeat on the Devlinites. McCormick himself became the first Catholic Alderman of Falls Ward.

The bitter rancour in Belfast nationalist politics was to fester until 1905. Devlin, for his part, continued to propagate his views through the *Northern Star* which 'twinkled furiously' down to 1908 with a circulation of 3,500. By 1905, however, Bishop Henry had been outflanked by the emergence of a powerful reunited Irish Parliamentary Party.[15] The new Home Rule leader, John Redmond, recognised Devlin — now elevated as Nationalist MP for

North Kilkenny — as the official nationalist spokesman in Belfast. At the same time, the bishop found himself isolated from his brother-bishops and leading clergy over his use of the Catholic Association and was forced to abandon the political arena.

The last act in the drama involving Devlin and the bishop's friends was played out for control of the *Irish News*. Devlin, with the support of the national Home Rule leadership, wished to harness the major organ of Ulster Nationalism firmly to the official Party and the Home Rule cause. At a meeting of the *Irish News* directors early in 1905, a resolution recommending that Devlin should be elected to the board was carried by four votes to two against. Devlin's supporters were led by Patrick Dempsey. Ranged against the 'pocket Demosthenes' — as Healy dubbed Devlin — were two powerful figures, Alderman McCormick and Rev. Dr Henry Laverty, Vicar General, both close associates of Bishop Henry.

The matter was finally resolved at a stormy and protracted meeting of the paper's shareholders on 30 June 1905. Interestingly, the only detailed account of the meeting appeared in the strongly unionist *Northern Whig*. Devlin and

The *Irish News* marks the death of its managing director, Joe Devlin MP in 1934

THE IRISH NEWS AND BELFAST MORNING NEWS, FRIDAY, JANUARY 19, 1934.

IRELAND LOSES ONE OF HER NOBLEST SONS

MR. JOSEPH DEVLIN, M.P., PASSES AWAY

The End Comes Peacefully after a Trying Illness

LAST OF THE GREAT LEADERS OF THE HOME RULE MOVEMENT

The Story of His Electoral Triumphs and His Fights for His Country and the Workers

his supporters in the new Home Rule machine, the United Irish League (UIL) had spared no effort to acquire sufficient proxy votes to gain control of the *Irish News* for the Home Rule Party. McCormick and the bishop's friends, however, had countered with an unsigned circular exhorting the shareholders 'to support the men who had been associated with the conduct of the *Irish News* in past years.' The atmosphere at this critical meeting can be gauged from the *Whig* report: 'The meeting lasted from twelve o'clock until half-past six in the evening. Many speakers were of a very lengthy character, Dr Laverty holding the floor for nearly an hour. Mr Joseph Devlin MP also occupied considerable time in the delivery of his speech.'[16] The thrust of Devlin's argument was that his election to the Directorate would enhance the standing of the *Irish News*. He now held the key post of general secretary of the United Irish League (UIL) and had the confidence of the nationalist leaders in Dublin.

In the upshot, after an adjournment to enable a thorough scrutinising of the poll of shareholders, a motion electing Devlin and his close associate, Thomas Maguire, solicitor (and secretary of the local UIL) was carried out by 2,005 to 1,901 — a narrow margin of 104 votes. The *Irish News* announced this revolutionary change in its direction in a terse notice on 5 July 1905.[17] However, the significance of the result was quickly grasped by the unionist press. As the *Whig* reported on the same date: 'The result is a conspicuous victory for the leaguers who have now a clear majority on the directorate of the journal and is certain to be followed by other changes of a far-reaching character in Nationalist and Roman Catholic circles in the city.' Within the *Irish News*, the effects of the policy change were immediately felt. McCormick at once resigned from the board of directors and was replaced by Patrick Dempsey. Dempsey had contested West Belfast unsuccessfully as a Nationalist candidate in the 1904 by-election.[18]

Over the next few years other leading Home Rulers were elected to the board. Of these the most prominent was Daniel McCann, a leading Belfast fish and poultry merchant. A passionate Parnellite, McCann later joined with Devlin in opposing the Catholic Association and was the chief architect of his dramatic victory in West Belfast in 1906 when the Home Rule 'captain' captured the former Tory seat by the narrow margin of 16 votes. A founder member of the National Club — the Nationalists' social headquarters in Belfast — McCann was for almost twenty years chairman of Belfast Celtic Football Club. He sat on the *Irish News* board from 1916 until his death in 1923.[19]

The UIL take over of the paper was swiftly followed by a change of editor. In August 1906, T J Campbell who had edited the paper during the difficult decade of political rivalry, resigned. Essentially 'a bishop's man', he was replaced by Devlin's close associate, the polemical County Cork journalist, Tim McCarthy who had earlier edited the *Northern Star*.[20] In the same year, the *Irish News* removed a few doors from its former site near the corner of Donegall Street and York Street to the present building, designed by the Belfast architect, J. J. McDonnell.

Under the direction of Devlin, and McCarthy's stern tutelage, the paper became undeviating in its support for the official Home Rule Party. However, its markedly sympathetic attitude towards the strikers during the 1907 Belfast dock strike and the city police mutiny of the same year drew sharp criticism from Bishop Henry's embittered supporters. In a private letter circulated to *Irish News* shareholders, they accused the new board of directors of 'disseminating Socialist propaganda' and having 'blotted out the name Catholic' from the newspaper. Attempts, however, to force a special meeting of shareholders to consider the 'alarming' financial position of the company in 1907 failed.[21]

McCarthy was to become almost an institution in the story of the *Irish News*. His editorship lasted until his death in 1928 and spanned the dramatic period which saw the tense anti-Home Rule campaign in the north, with its threat of civil war, the Great War, the Irish revolution, partition and the eruption of violence north and south in the early 1920s. T. P. O'Connor ('Tay Pay'), the prominent Irish Nationalist MP and editor and pioneer of the 'new journalism', once described him as 'the greatest political and most versatile journalist in the country.'

McCarthy was born into a farming family at Cloghroe, Inniscarra, County Cork in the 1860s and educated at the local national school. He began his career on the *Cork Herald* and served his apprenticeship during Land League days when public meetings were proclaimed and agrarian crime and eviction widespread. He was present at the celebrated political meeting in Ennis in the 1880s when William O'Brien and Michael Davitt were 'dragooned' by the military and 'the street ran red with blood'. McCarthy later recalled how his silk hat was severed by a sword slash during a cavalry charge that day. Leaving Cork in 1893, McCarthy worked for a time on the Dublin *Freeman's Journal*, before moving to London where he became chief assistant to T. P. O'Connor on *The Evening Sun* and later to W. T. Stead, another brilliant journalist, on *The Daily Paper*.

'Intensely patriotic', he returned to Ireland in 1897 to edit first Devlin's *Northern Star* in Belfast and, in 1899, the *Irish People*, the Home Rule journal of — William O'Brien, the leading Nationalist MP. While directing the paper in 1900, the Corkman served a three months term of imprisonment for a written attack on the Wyndman Coercion Acts.[22] His last position before beginning his twenty-two year editorship of the *Irish News* was in

Omagh as editor of the *Ulster Herald* group of publications. As editor, McCarthy was supreme, gifted with a facile pen, an incisive mind and a sound grasp of Irish history with brilliant recall. 'The young journalist under McCarthy', wrote a comtemporary, 'found in him.... a guide, a philosopher and a friend'.[23]

Like most observers in the run-up to World War One, the *Irish News* confidently expected the granting of a Home Rule Parliament for an undivided Ireland by 1914. McCarthy, in common with the nationalist and liberal press, ridiculed the threats of resistance by Carson and the UVF and delighted in caricaturing 'Carson's Army' as 'paper tigers with dummy rifles'. Any thought of partition, declared an editorial in April 1912, was 'plainly absurd'. With the outbreak of the Great War in August 1914, the paper, following the lead of Redmond and Devlin, fully supported the British war effort and carried regular reports on the heroic sacrifices of Irish volunteers, both nationalist and unionist, in the fight for 'the freedom of small nations'.

While sympathetic to the first stirrings of the Gaelic Revival in the north, the *Irish News* firmly rejected the physical force tradition of the Irish Republican Brotherhood. Nor was it encouraging to the tiny non-violent Sinn Fein movement, led by Arthur Griffith in the early years of the century. Such political manifestations were roundly condemned as 'factionist' and calculated to weaken the Home Rule struggle. Instead, the *Irish News* lent consistent support to Devlin's political machine, the Ancient Order of Hibernians (AOH) which spread dramatically throughout Ulster during 1904-15. From 1904 until the 1940s, the paper carried a weekly column on Hibernian activities by the mysterious 'Rory Oge'.

To the Tyrone IRB leader, Dr Patrick McCartan, writing after the 1916 rising, the *Irish News* was 'vicious and unscrupulous' in its treatment of the insurgents.[24] In common with most Home Rule organs, the paper condemned the rising as a 'wicked German plot'. To Joe Devlin and Tim McCarthy, Pearse and his fellow-insurgents were nothing more than 'the unhappy instruments of German duplicity and treachery who have fought Germany's battle in the capital of this country'.[25] Real Irish heroism was to be witnessed in the trenches of northern France and at the Dardanelles. But while McCarthy condemned the 'mad venture', pointing out that the rising had been staged 'without the knowledge or sanction of the Irish nation', he realised that the execution of the leaders was generating a wave of public sympathy for the rebels. Thus, on 6 May 1916, after the first eight executions, the *Irish News* called for an end to the policy, warning: 'The Government will be wise if they reject the advice of ... the ghoulish papers and individuals ... who are clamouring for more blood. These ... are (as) reckless, short-visioned and foolish as the Sinn Fein leaders themselves.' It was too late, however, to halt the swing of the nationalist pendulum towards republicanism and the Home Rulers' involvement in the abortive Lloyd George scheme for 'temporary partition' in June 1916 helped to seal their fate. As 'Mr. Devlin's organ', the *Irish News* exerted all its influence to ensure a majority for the Lloyd George proposals at the crucial conference of northern Nationalists in St.Mary's Hall on 'Black Friday', 23 June 1916. When the government declared the partition scheme permanent, McCarthy mirrored the sense of outrage and betrayal of the Home Rule leaders who now denounced the scheme as a trap.[26]

With the rise of Sinn Fein and the Irish Republican Army in the wake of the executions, the *Irish News* strenuously opposed the revolutionary and physical force movements, warning — with much accuracy — that any attempt to set up an Irish Republic would mean permanent partition. Instead, the paper urged a Home Rule settlement within the British Empire with special safeguards for Ulster. The rising and the Lloyd George scheme, in particular, caused a major split in northern Nationalism. Thus, while the *Irish News* remained the voice of a significant Irish Party rump, especially in east Ulster, the growing Sinn Fein section in rural Ulster found expression in the *Herald* group of newspapers, published by Michael Lynch of Omagh, a leading Sinn Fein advocate. In the 1918 election, which signalled the ascendancy of Sinn Fein, the paper continued to advocate the 'sane policy of

The *Irish News* reports the end of the 1916 Rising, April 1916

constitutionalism', maintaining that an abstentionist tactic would only play into the hands of the Carsonites in their demand for partition.[27]

The bloodshed of the Anglo-Irish war in the south during 1919-21 was matched by unremitting sectarian violence in Belfast and the six counties. Following the brutal expulsion of Catholic workers from the shipyards in July 1920, McCarthy added a new word to the Irish political vocabulary when he characterised the Belfast attacks as a concerted 'pogrom' against the Catholic minority in the city. Partition and the establishment of a separate northern parliament in May 1921 came as a bitter draught to the *Irish News* which stigmatised the Government of Ireland Act of 1920 as 'a plan devised by unscrupulous politicians to assassinate Ireland's nationality'.[28]

The Treaty and, in particular, the outbreak of the civil war in the south completed the demoralisation of the minority. Their feelings were graphically reflected in the *Irish News* at the time and in the subsequent years and decades. McCarthy spoke for the bulk of northern Nationalists when he welcomed the ratification of the Treaty by the Dail in January 1922 in the hope that it might pave the way for Irish unity and an end to the Belfast bloodshed. The only regret of Ulster Nationalists, he declared, was that the pro-Treaty majority in the Dail was 'not 107, but merely 7'.[29]

Many northern Nationalists, especially in border areas such as Fermanagh and Tyrone, looked to the promised Boundary Commission to restore the unity of Ireland. But the *Irish News*, fearing the reduction of the minority to a still more powerless faction in a smaller Northern Ireland, opposed the Commission, urging instead a federal arrangement between north and south. To this end, the paper welcomed the Craig-Collins pact of March 1922 as the basis of a new Ireland.[30] At the same time, the *Irish News* castigated de Valera and his anti-Treaty republicans as the 'apostles of dissension' charging the former president with responsibility for the civil war.[31] As the full scale of the hostilities became obvious on 6 July 1922, an editorial captured the prevailing sense of frustration of the beleaguered northern minority: 'Mr de Valera has insisted on a grim sacrifice from the Irish people. Nothing can be done for any part of Ireland until peace has been established again'.

In the early 1920s, northern Nationalists remained divided between former Sinn Fein supporters and the supporters of Joe Devlin, who became managing director of the *Irish News* in 1923, on Patrick Dempsey's death. As partition hardened into permanency, the *Irish News* began to exhort the two sections of nationalism to join their forces in a new constitutional movement, pledged to defend the rights of the minority within the new northern state. By 1923, the paper was calling for the abandonment of the Boundary Commission and declaring bluntly that owing to their internal divisions, the northern

sparks to his frequent expletives as he groaned over the shorthand outlines of a Joe Devlin speech. Billy was a legendary character whose mastery of journalese impressed even parish priests with his liberal use of such pearls as 'sacred edifice' to describe some modest chapel, 'ad multos annos' or 'catafalque' at a funeral.

His waxed-moustache would bristle at those 'clerical errors' with dog-collars who dared offend him. Others in the room were Paddy Davey, sports doyen, chronicler of famous Belfast Celtic under the *nom de plume* of 'Parkite' and making a name for himself in the new sport of the electric hare; reporters Jimmy McElroy and Paddy Donaghy, who years later went to the 'Indo' (*Irish Independent*) in Dublin.

In those years the *Irish News* was virtually the nursery of journalists who graduated to the Dublin press, one of them, Mick Rooney, from Ardglass becoming editor of the *Independent* and my boss. Donaghy, a handsome blonde youth in his early twenties, owned a high-powered motor-bike and lived near Trinity Street. Later he was able to keep us up to date about the latest activities of the apparition known as the 'Trinity Street Ghost', a story which lasted up to the 1941 blitz when Trinity Street and, presumably, its phantom were buried in the rubble by a German bomb.

Local news from all parts of the north passed through the Reporters' Room, some telephoned in by the country correspondents and the rest contributed by the staff from 'markings', courts, meetings, Parliament, shows, dinners, luncheons, inquests, City Hall, etc. Editorials were contributed by Paddy Fennessy, a Clonmel man, who came north after covering the civil war, and Bob Kirkwood, later to become Editor, a cultivated Belfast man with experience of newspapers in the west of Ireland. One of Fennessy's duties was to watch out for the latest edition of the *Gazette* published by the Ministry of Home Affairs. Frequently buried away in an inconspicuous page was the latest exercise of the notorious 'Special Powers' Act by the equally notorious Sir Dawson Bates, who as Minister of Home Affairs was said to sleep with the Special Powers act and a revolver under his pillow. Sometimes it was a nationalist meeting banned, or another local anti-unionist served with an 'exclusion order' or more hilariously an obscure publication or patriotic gramophone record banned! Under Bates — 'Ulster's Iron man' — the bans and prohibitions fell like snowflakes.

The routine introduction for the fledgling reporter was to make him responsible for what was termed 'Night-town', in other words take over the coverage of untoward happenings in the city between the hours of 7.00 pm and 3.00 am. This was certainly throwing you in at the deep end, a nerve-racking experience until you knew the ropes. My particular mentor was a tall young man named Brian Riordan, my predecessor on Night-town. First he took me on a conducted tour of the other newspaper offices to meet my colleagues-to-be, a cheerful and friendly lot whose camaraderie in later years provided much of the fun behind the daily grind.

As the reporters' room emptied before midnight, Riordan, in between phoning the police, fire brigade and hospitals, and taking country corrs' copy over the phone, — Paddy O'Hare from Enniskillen, BertieTroy of Coleraine, whose deep chiming clock could be heard in the background, Joe Connellan, MP from Newry, and a host of others — immersed himself in the musical critics' long screeds in *The Times*, *Morning Post* and *Manchester Guardian*. Soon I was on my own as Night-townman in sole possession of the Reporters' room with the weight of responsibility for coverage of the deeds and misdeeds of rowdy old Belfast on my shoulders. Riordan went to London, not to Fleet Street but to join a religious order as a priest. My stint on 'Town' ended after six months, I was lucky.

James Kelly in conversation with Eamon de Valera and Peter Robinson of the *Daily Mail* in Belfast, 1960
Irish News

It was a quiet period at home but less so elsewhere with the 'Roaring Twenties' coming to an end with the emergence of Prohibition, Al Capone, gang-warfare in Chicago, and in London, poor old Ramsey MacDonald burbling on about a 'World Economic Blizzard'. The Stormont government here were conspiring to end Proportional Representation, gerry-mander Derry, and perpetuate itself. But that was not my responsibility or my successor's, Jack Flanagan from Omagh.

Spot-news was our job, fires, shootings, road accidents, arrests and all happenings not covered in Bob Hayes' 'markings' in the office diary where Joe Devlin, MP and managing director of the paper, was so revered that the reporter marked for his meetings was notified to go to St Mary's Hall and report the speech by 'Mr D.'

If I was lucky Jack Flanagan was not. All hell seemed to break loose during his sojourn on the night shift. He was hardly familiar with the lay-out of the city when, late one night, a huge blaze occurred on the £2 million luxury liner 'Bermuda' which was being refurbished at Workman and Clarke's shipyard. Jack was so appalled at the sight of the great ship ablaze from stem to stern that he stood paralysed to the spot and was eventually 'rescued' by the senior sub-editor, Paddy Kelly, who helped to turn out one of the biggest splash stories of the year.

The editor, a tough-talking Englishman, Sydney Redwood, who at that time was transforming the paper into an up-and-coming modern daily was not told and Jack survived to rise in the journalistic hierarchy to succeed me as staff reporter for Dev's new *Irish Press*, and later, like me, to move to, the 'Indo', in his case as assistant news editor.

From night-town the next stop was the police courts where a knowledge of your native city took on a new slant, the seamy side of life, some of it so shocking that it could not be reported. There was hilarity in the 'abusive language' cases where the rival solicitors put on an act for warring clients and a weary Resident Magistrate usually ended by putting both sides under a rule of bail. Afterwards the solicitors and journalists enjoyed the humour of it all around a blazing coal-fire in the room across the corridor, with the leading *personae*, Barney Campbell, the Tughans and an eccentric Mr Pickwick look-alike named Johnny Beggs, whose seedy clients were picked up in pubs by his clerk nicknamed 'The Mouse'.

With such a small staff, reporters in the *Irish News* in the those days obtained more experience in a short space of time than was possible elsewhere. If not rich in financial terms, you became rich in experience in a hectic whirligig in which time never seemed to stand still. Every day brought a new challenge, a new experience, meeting new people, high and low. The press-pass was 'open sesame' everywhere, and everybody in the public domain inflated your ego in their grateful anticipation of a 'good show' in tomorrow's edition!

Some entrusted their manuscripts to you hoping that the 'gentlemen with the blue pencils', meaning the subs, would be gentle with them. Reporters too hoped they would, for they blessed those who prepared their speeches thus, and cursed those who insisted on the old fashioned *extempore* oratory, straining your ability to record it all in shorthand. You had to get it right, for everyone read your report, MPs, Lord Mayors, bishops, parish priests, judges, learned lecturers, cabinet ministers. A complaint from one of those about being 'misquoted' and you landed in Redwood's room with threats of the sack just as you were plucking up courage to ask for a salary rise.

Redwood, who looked like a Burmese with his dark skin, tortoise- shell specs and black hair, was a barking tyrant but a damned good newspaperman and years later those who suffered under his whiplash had to admit that he had taught them a thing or two about their craft. He had guts too and took on the powers-that-be with his revelations about Craigavon's government's 'squandermania'. They were not prepared for his onslaughts, being used to a more docile local press, and eventually took him to court for alleged seditious libel. A fine was imposed but there was more embarrassment for government ministers in the spirited defence by William Lowry KC, later to join the government he had slated to become Minister of Home Affairs.

All that was a long time ago, a different world, now only a memory of times past. Stormont had not been built and the High Court sat in makeshift accommodation at the old Crumlin Road Courthouse where learned counsel warmed their backsides at a roaring fire surmounted by a regimental drum while the affairs of Chancery were conducted at a long table in the centre of a room marked 'Dining Room'. Judge Wilson presided at the head of the table and reporters craned their ears to catch the words of wisdom from a nearby half-moon table.

At Assize Courts in Downpatrick and Armagh death sentences were still being imposed, necessitating the appearances of hangmen from England to carry out the sentence. The first time I heard a judge, wearing the traditional black cap, pronouncing the barbaric words 'hanged by the neck until your are dead. And may the Lord have mercy on your soul', I felt physically sick. Flogging was still inflicted on unfortunate prisoners. One day in the well of the Crumlin Road courthouse I was shown the prison warder who wielded the dreaded 'cat' across the prisoner's marked back. He was a burly, sadistic-looking individual with thick blood-flecked lips, an ex-member of the Royal Navy where he no doubt obtained his experience. I must say he looked the part. What kind of man, I wondered, would volunteer for such a job?

Courts, inquests, City Council meetings, riots, sectarian outbursts, all soon became part of the daily round which sometimes extended until midnight. Only senior men were entrusted with the reporting of parliament but Bob Hayes on the spur of the moment decided to send me to the old parliament at College Green — to try me out, no doubt. The northern Commons and Senate were then conducted in the old Presbyterian Assembly's College at the rear of Queen's University. I did not know it then but this was to be the beginning of a long association with the Partition Parliament until its abolition by Westminster in 1972.

As I look back over those years there is one thought which strikes me. I feel that the northern community has not perhaps realised how much it owes to that long line of almost unknown editors and their staff at Donegall Street who stood up for civil rights for all with courage and integrity. Politicians aside, do they not deserve a chapter to themselves in the annals of our history?

3

The Political Background

from Parnell to Partition

1890-1921

EAMON PHOENIX

The foundation of the *Irish News* in 1891 occurred at a time when Irishmen and women, regardless of political outlook, were more highly politicised than ever before. The Third Reform Act of 1884 had extended the vote to the agricultural labourer and urban worker alike. This act, and the creation of elected county councils in 1898, were to pave the way for both an Orange and a Green political resurgence in Ireland.

Until the emergence of Home Rule in the 1880s, Protestant voters in the north had been divided into Conservative and Liberal. Most Ulster Catholics, on the other hand, tended to support the Home Rule Party of Charles Stewart Parnell, particularly from 1885 when the Parnellites captured 17 of the province's 33 seats. But as the tar-barrels blazed in nationalist strongholds at this signal triumph, the mass of Ulster Protestants were determined to thwart any attempt by the Liberal Prime Minister, William Gladstone, to grant Ireland self-government.

Parnell's dramatic electoral victory finally convinced the 'Grand Old Man' of the essential justness of the Home Rule cause. His first Home Rule Bill of 1886 failed, however, in the teeth of a combined unionist opposition in the House of Commons. A second bill in 1893 was thrown out by the Tory-dominated House of Lords which now became the greatest obstacle to nationalist aspirations.

The more dramatic result of the Home Rule crisis in the north of Ireland was the revival of the Orange Order. Formed in north Armagh in 1795 against a background of sectarian faction-fighting, the order's anti-Catholic overtones had tended to repel the better-off during the nineteenth century. From the 1880s, the gentry and middle-classes returned to its banner, realising its potential as a powerful cross-class alliance against an all-Ireland Home Rule scheme. In their campaign against an Irish parliament, the northern loyalists were assured of the powerful support of the British Conservative Party for which the union became 'almost a sacred thing'. From 1885, therefore, until the Treaty settlement of 1921, the union was the single dominating issue in Irish politics.

The Parnellite split of 1890-91 led to the dramatic break-up of the party he had welded into a disciplined phalanx. The next decade was to witness a bitter 'civil war' within the Home Rule movement. Such internecine feuding, together with the Conservatives' long ascendancy at Westminster (from 1895-1905) relegated Home Rule to the 'back burner' of British politics.

The ending of the period of Conservative rule coincided with the reunification of the antagonistic strands of constitutional Nationalism under the chairmanship of John Redmond. Redmond, a Wexford barrister and ardent imperialist, believed passionately in the concept of 'Home Rule within the Empire'. As such, he was strongly opposed to the separatist stirrings which marked the dawn of the new century. The Gaelic League had from the 1890s steadily promoted the idea of a separate Irish cultural nation. Of a similar stamp was Arthur Griffith's tiny Sinn Fein party, whose novel policy of an Anglo-Irish 'dual monarchy' even attracted some northern Protestants like the essayist Robert Lynd. In the background, too, flickered the 'Fenian Flame' of the militantly separatist Irish Republican Brotherhood.

The Irish Parliamentary Party, however, still reigned supreme, led in the north by the young Belfast barman turned journalist, 'Wee Joe' Devlin. Born in 1871 into a working-class family in Hamill Street, he rose from humble beginnings to become a Home Rule MP and finally, in 1903, general secretary of the United Irish League (UIL), the main Home Rule organisation. For the next thirty years, this 'pocket Domosthenes' (as the acid-tongued T.M. Healy once dubbed him) dominated the nationalist scene by the sheer weight of his personality and consummate political intellect.

Charles Stewart Parnell (1846-91) pictured in 1880. His downfall led to the founding of the *Irish News*

Devlin's control of the sectarian Ancient Order of Hibernians (AOH) has led to the somewhat distorted image of the Ulster Home Rule leader as a 'ghetto boss', assiduously cultivating an atavistic sectarian vote. But this view is unfair to a politician who did much to improve the lot of the Catholic and Protestant working classes of Belfast. His successful exposure of the sweated conditions in the city's linen mills led to the application of the Trade Boards Act to the industry with a consequent improvement in working conditions.

The Liberal landslide of 1905 and the subsequent constitutional crisis in Britain over the powers of the House of Lords, conspired by 1911 to force the Prime Minister, Herbert Asquith, back to the 1886 position of reliance on the votes of the Irish nationalists. One immediate result was the removal of the veto power of the House of Lords. Nationalist Ireland confidently predicted that 1914 would be the 'Home Rule Year' and that John Redmond would preside over an all-Ireland parliament in Dublin's College Green.

But the wheel of political fortune had not yet come to rest and the two years between the introduction of the third Home Rule Bill and the outbreak of the Great War were to see the emergence of determined unionist resistance to the Liberals' policy. The leaders of Ulster Unionism at that time were Sir Edward Carson, a Dublin lawyer and compelling orator, and Capt. James Craig, a Belfast stockbroker whose massive, blunt features seemed to personify 'the very soul of Ulster intransigence'. Carson's aim however was not to get special treatment for the north, but rather to see Ulster resistance maintain intact the union of Britain and Ireland.

From the outset the unionist campaign was supported by powerful interests in British society, in the Conservative Party — now led by Bonar Law, a ruthless political opponent of Ulster stock — in the army, the aristocracy and big business. 'There are things stronger than parliamentary majorities,' declared Law darkly in 1912, underlining the extra-parliamentary nature of the Unionist campaign.

Tension rose in Ulster with the introduction of the Third Home Rule Bill in April 1912. The climax and supreme demonstration of Protestant feeling was the public signing by over 200,000 loyalists of the Solemn League and

Sir Edward Carson inspecting the Ulster Volunteer Force in Belfast, 1914
Irish News

Covenant that September. In January 1913, the Ulster Volunteer Force (UVF) was formed with the leading Presbyterian journal, *The Witness*, asserting that resistance to Home Rule, even in arms, was 'a sacred duty'.

At first, the UVF was dismissed by the Home Rulers as 'Carson's Comic Circus'. But the Larne gun-running of April 1914, together with such coincidental factors as the 'Curragh Incident' and the transparent weakness of the Asquith government, brought about a radical change in the balance of power in Ireland. Military supremacy now lay with 'Carson's Army'. This factor, more than any other, was to ensure that the British government would introduce some form of 'exclusion' or partition to deal with the 'Ulster problem'.

The impact of the UVF was no less dramatic on Irish Nationalism. As one historian has put it, by re-introducing the gun as the final arbiter in Irish politics, 'Carson rekindled the Fenian Flame'. The revolutionary Irish Republican Brotherhood, watching in the wings, was quick to take advantage of the situation and, by late 1913, had called into existence a nationalist counterweight in the shape of the Irish Volunteers, initially under Redmond's nominal control. The nationalist army's main concern was to ensure the implemenation of all-Ireland Home Rule and by June 1914, it had swollen to some 170,000 men, a quarter of them concentrated in Ulster. The Buckingham Palace Conference in the last days of peace failed to resolve the Ulster impasse, and in Churchill's colourful phrase, it became bogged down in 'the muddy byways of Fermanagh and Tyrone.'

The outbreak of war was marked by what the RIC termed 'a mutual cessation of political strife' as both Redmond and Carson pledged unequivocal support for Britain's war effort. As the storm clouds gathered, the Irish leader's success in forcing a reluctant Asquith to place the Home Rule Act on the statute book proved something of a hollow victory. Not only was its operation suspended for the duration of the war, but Asquith made it clear that any final settlement must include partition.

In a desperate effort to win British goodwill for the future, Redmond — ever the imperialist — was to make his great mistake in September 1914 in urging Irishmen to enlist in the British army and 'go wherever the firing-line extends'. The immediate effect of Redmond's speech was to split the Irish Volunteers. A small radical section — by far the most active militarily — broke away under Professor Eoin MacNeill, Antrim Glensman and Gaelic Leaguer. This section now passed into the hands of the IRB which was to use it as the strike force of the 1916 Rising.

Thousands of Irish Volunteers joined the rush to the colours in the first years of the war and fought bravely alongside their former UVF adversaries on the battlefields of Europe. Amongst the Irish contingent were several thousand members of Devlin's National Volunteers from west Belfast. 'We have succeeded in making national self-government the law of the land', Devlin assured them as they marched off to the front in November 1914.

James Connolly, the Belfast-based leader of the Irish Citizen Army and a supporter of a separatist uprising, expressed a rather different view in his paper, the *Worker's Republic*:

> 'Full steam ahead, John Redmond said,
> and everything is well chum.
> Home Rule will come when we are dead
> and buried out in Belgium'.

The 1916 Rising caused major devastation in the heart of Dublin
Irish News

Redmond's political standing was further weakened by the formation of a coalition government in 1915 which included Carson and Bonar Law. In such circumstances, it required only the 'blood sacrifice' of the Easter Rising and the crop of martyrs it produced to seal the Home Rule Party's fate.

The Rising was originally intended as a successful national revolt by the Volunteers and *élite* Citizen's Army. But, in the event, with the struggle narrowed to Dublin, Pearse and the secret *cadre* of revolutionaries realised that they had no prospect of military success. However, they calculated that an armed stand — however futile — would almost certainly provoke the British into harsh reprisals; by their 'martyrdom', they might give their cause — an Irish Republic instead of anaemic Home Rule — its elixir of life.

The insurgents judged accurately. The Rising had at first engendered feelings of strong hostility. But its aftermath — internment, martial law, and above all, the execution of 16 of the leaders — worked a sea change in Irish public opinion. As one observer wrote: 'A few unknown men, shot in a barrack yard, had embittered a whole nation'.

In a final effort to salvage the Home Rule Act, the Nationalist leaders allowed themselves to be stampeded in May 1916 into the disastrous Lloyd George scheme for six-county partition. The resourceful 'Welsh Wizard' led Redmond to understand that 'exclusion' would be temporary whilst giving Carson cast-iron guarantees that it would be permanent. The proposals fell through, sabotaged by the southern Unionists in the cabinet, but not before the Home Rulers, and Devlin in particular, had become tarred by the brush of partition in the Irish Nationalist mind. The 'Black Friday' conference in St Mary's Hall, Belfast, which endorsed the Lloyd George scheme in June 1916, was to split northern Nationalism irrevocably and paved the way for Sinn Fein in the north.

Support of the insurgents and their cause soon crystallized around a new republican Sinn Fein party led by Eamon de Valera and dedicated to a policy of abstention from the British parliament. In the north, however, the burning issue for Nationalists remained partition rather than 'Home Rule v Republic'. Many Ulster Catholics opposed the abstentionist tactic, arguing, with much force, that such a policy would make the 'naked deformity of partition' more likely. This underlay the Home Rule victories over Sinn Fein in the South Armagh and East Tyrone by-elections in the spring of 1918.

Events during the last months of the war, and particularly the British government's threat to impose conscription in April 1918, brought an accession of strength to the revolutionary party. This was the background to the post-war general election of 1918. Sinn Fein, pledged to an all-Ireland republic, swept 73 of the 105 Irish seats. The old Home Rule party was reduced to half a dozen seats in Ulster — thanks to a 'green pact' with Sinn Fein brokered by the Roman Catholic Primate, Cardinal Logue.

Carson, bent on a policy of partition for the north-east, now led the largest Irish grouping at Westminster with 26 seats, 23 of them in north-east Ulster. In the Falls Division, however, Joe Devlin humiliated the Sinn Fein leader, de Valera, by a margin of almost three to one. It was a slight which the republican leader would never forgive.

Few periods in modern Irish history have been as momentous as the three years which elapsed between the 'Khaki Election' of 1918 and the Anglo Irish Treaty of 1921. This brief period was to witness the establishment of Dail Eireann, partition and the conferring of dominion status on 26 Irish counties. In accordance with their election manifesto, the Sinn Fein MPs, meeting as Dail Eireann, set up an alternative government to that of Dublin Castle, headed by President de Valera, But while the new cabinet achieved striking success in several areas, its hopes of raising the question of Irish self-determination at the Paris Peace Conference came to nought. As the peace strategy faded, an astute Devlin could predict starkly: 'Things must come to a fierce conflict between the government and Sinn Fein'.

Indeed, that conflict slowly crytallized into an Anglo-Irish war between the Volunteers, re-styled the Irish Republican Army (I.R.A.) and the Royal Irish Constabulary (R.I.C.), soon to be reinforced by the notorious 'counter-terror' forces, the Auxiliaries and Black and Tans. Though the relationship between the Dail and the I.R.A. was a confused one, the Volunteers might claim a certain legitimacy as the military arm of a democratically-elected order.

In Britain, meanwhile, the return of a coalition government, headed by Lloyd George, ensured that partition would become a 'fixed idea' of British policy. Sinn Fein's 'blessed abstention' from Westminster — to borrow Churchill's phrase — meant that the balance of power now shifted from Irish nationalists to the Ulster Unionists.

The cabinet committee which drew up the Partition Act in late 1919 was tempted to include the historic nine-county province in the new 'Northern Ireland'. Liberals argued that the large Catholic population (43 per cent) might make eventual Irish unity more probable. In the end, however, the Lloyd George cabinet gave way to Craig's pragmatic view that a six county *bloc* would provide a more 'viable' area for permanent unionist control. The scattered Unionists of Cavan, Monaghan and Donegal felt 'betrayed and deserted' at this breach of the 1912 Covenant.

The Government of Ireland Act (1920), as finally passed, divided Ireland into two areas, each having its own regional parliament and government with control over domestic affairs. At the same time, the measure seemed to envisage Irish unity by providing 'a bond of union' in the shape of a low-powered Council of Ireland. The 1920 Act represented a major triumph for Craig. On the nationalist side, only Joe Devlin, a solitary figure at Westminster, saw the dangers of the 'Partition Act'. He railed against it as portending both 'permanent partition' and 'permanent minority status' for northern Catholics. Not without justification, the West Belfast MP attacked the glaring lack of safeguards in the act for the minority. The need for such safeguards, he told the Commons, was underlined by the tragic sectarian bloodshed in north-east Ulster in the summer of 1920 against the backcloth of the Anglo-Irish war. The worst episode occurred in the mass expulsion of some 8,000 Catholic workers from the shipyards and other industries. These events were a foretaste of the serious sectarian disturbances which were to scar the face of Belfast, Lisburn and other northern towns during the next two years. The Dail responded with the 'Belfast boycott', but this tended merely to reinforce the embryonic border.

It was not until late 1922 that murder, arson and expulsion from home ceased to be a daily occurrence. Over 450 people, the majority of them members of the minority community, died violently during the black days of 1920-22. In a reference to these events, Lloyd George was to admit to Churchill: 'Our Ulster case is not a good one'. The upsurge of violence had two important effects. First, it seemed to confirm nationalist fears of being subjected to the rule of the Unionist majority in a separate state. Secondly, the mounting unrest led Lloyd George to endorse Craig's scheme for a new auxiliary police force, the Ulster Special Constabulary, formed in October 1920. In nationalist eyes, however, this sectarian force was viewed, in the words of a British official, 'with a bitterness exceeding that which the Black and Tans inspired in the south'.

In May 1921, following elections in the six counties, the new northern parliament was established with Sir James Craig as its first prime minister. 'From that moment', wrote Churchill perceptively, 'Ulster's position was unassailable'. During those vital years, the Sinn Fein leadership failed, in the words of one northern Sinn Fein leader, 'to grapple with the Ulster question'. Partition came a poor second to national status in the revolutionary scheme of things. This was certainly the case during the Treaty negotiations of 1921. Arthur Griffith and Michael Collins, the leaders of the Irish delegation, tried to secure the 'essential unity' of Ireland, but were forced in the end to settle for dominion status for the 26 counties. A Boundary Commission was to revise the disputed 1920 border. The prospect of the commission and the belief that it would so reduce the north's territory and produce Irish unity by 'contraction', largely explains why the Sinn Fein leaders signed the treaty of 6 December 1921.

Northern nationalists were shocked and bitterly disappointed by the Treaty terms. Most supported them, however, in the hope that some form of 'essential unity' might yet be achieved. For the border nationalist majorities, the fatally flawed Boundary Clause was the crucial article. Four years later, in 1925, the much-vaunted Boundary Commission collapsed, leaving the Northern Ireland state intact and partition more deeply entrenched.

For the northern nationalists, the disunity and disenchantment of the Parnell split had been replaced 30 years later by an even deeper sense of isolation and betrayal. For the Ulster Unionists, their new state and administration had survived despite Nationalist non-recognition, I.R.A. attacks and British pressure. The minority problem, however, remained unaddressed and would continue to fester in the years ahead.

4

Bigotry and Politics in Belfast
from the Victorian Era
to the Twentieth Century

ANDREW BOYD

The Victorian Background

When the first edition of the *Irish News* rolled off the presses in 1891, Belfast was already well known as a city of clerical agitators, sectarian violence and political intolerance – a city of tormented people. The first Home Rule crisis had passed with the defeat of Gladstone's bill in June 1886 and in the midst of prolonged sectarian disturbances during that summer. The second Home Rule crisis and more urban violence lay only seven years ahead, in the year 1893.

In those days the predominant industries in Belfast were linen and shipbuilding, along with tobacco, ropemaking, and several branches of

Riots in Belfast, June 1886, following the rejection by Westminster of Gladstone's first Home Rule Bill
Illustrated London News

general engineering. In those industries, and indeed in most industries until the end of World War Two, the working day and the working week were long, tiresome and exhausting, and it is likely that the psychologists – if the science of psychology had been as advanced in the nineteenth century as it is today – would have attributed the frequent outbursts of communal violence in the city of Belfast to pent-up industrial frustration. The most dangerous times seem to have been the weekends when the shipyards and the factories were closed.

By 1891 Belfast's inner-city Catholic and Protestant ghettos were well-defined, though not so exclusively defined as they are today. Nonetheless, the Falls was known throughout the British Isles as a Catholic ghetto and the Shankill as a Protestant one. Sandy Row was mainly Protestant but the Catholic enclave known as the Markets was not far away. Across the Lagan, in Ballymacarrett, the small Catholic community was confined within a few streets between Short Strand and St Matthew's Church. All the rest of east Belfast was Protestant.

But people and institutions did then cross the borders of the ghettos. There were Protestant churches on the Falls Road and in the Short Strand. Catholic churches such as St Brigid's in Derryvolgie Avenue, St Columbcille's at Ballyhackamore and Holy Family at Newington were built originally for the Catholic domestics, mostly girls from outside Belfast, who worked in the houses of the comfortably-off middle classes.

Sectarian violence was something unknown in the suburbs of the 1890s. The Protestant middle classes and their Catholic domestics lived their different lives side by side, but separated by the barriers of class and religion. Whatever bigotry prevailed in the suburbs would have been expressed – if expressed at all in front of the servants – in polite and restrained terms. But in the working-class ghettos of inner Belfast there was an entirely different atmosphere. In those parts of the city sectarianism was raw and unrestrained. This is amply verified in the several official inquiries into urban disturbances in nineteenth century Belfast. The first of these inquiries was in 1857, a year of prolonged and sustained sectarian riots during the months of July and August. Those, however, were not the first outbreaks of such violence.

The records show that a Catholic man was shot dead after an Orange procession through Millfield in 1815. There was an especially serious outbreak in 1833 on the boundary line of what was then called The Pound, a Catholic district in the Lower Falls, and Sandy Row, near Christ Church in Durham Street.

The 1830s was a particularly disturbed decade all over Ireland. Catholic rights – Catholic Emancipation – had been granted in 1829, much to the dismay and chagrin of the more militant Protestants. The tithe war in southern

Ireland, soon after Emancipation, was considered a direct Catholic attack on the rights of the Protestant Established Church. The Orange Order came under official scrutiny and did not emerge unscathed from a parliamentary inquiry. The first Party Processions Act sought to curtail all sorts of sectarian demonstrations, including Orange demonstrations.

The Protestants of Belfast also witnessed, with growing concern, the steady increase in the proportion of Catholics in the town's population. Most of those Catholics were migrants who came to work in Belfast's linen mills and as navvies on the construction of Belfast Harbour. The geographer Emrys Jones associates this growth in Belfast's Catholic population with a revived interest in Orangeism, the appearance of clerical agitators like Henry Cooke, Thomas Drew and Hugh Hanna and the subsequent escalation of communal disorder. In July 1843, for example, the *Northern Whig* reported 'much excitement and rioting' between the Catholics of the Pound and the Protestants of Sandy Row. After that the resident magistrates, the police and the newspapers were to note that the month of July, when the Orangemen celebrated the Battle of the Boyne, had become the most dangerous month in the year. Samuel Tracey, who was one of Belfast's RMs in the 1850s, said he could not remember a July when there had not been sectarian trouble.

The 1850s was also the decade when the Belfast shipyards 'took off' – to use the terminology of economists – to become one of the most important industries in the world. The success of shipbuilding in Belfast was due to the enterprise, the technical knowledge and the energy of Edward Harland, a Yorkshireman, and his partner Gustav Wolff of Liverpool. It was due also to the skill of the engineers and shipwrights from Harland and Wolff brought to Belfast from the Clyde, from the Tyne and from Merseyside.

The migration of these cross-channel craftsmen introduced a new element into the population of Belfast. The new migrants were invariably skilled, craft protective like all nineteenth century artisans, and probably entirely Protestant. Soon afterwards, in the summer of 1864, there was what amounted almost to war between the Catholic navvies excavating Belfast Harbour and the Protestant shipwrights in Queen's Island. Once again the disturbances were the subject of an inquiry by government-appointed commissioners and the Queen's Island was identified, almost from the beginning, as a centre of sectarian proletarian power.

Entry into the skilled trades was more restricted in the nineteenth century than it is today and the pattern of industrial employment was different. There were, for example, very few of what are classified as semi-skilled workers in modern industry. Furthermore the trade unions tried, where they could, always to maintain an agreed ratio of apprentices to journeymen, that being the term then applied to the fully-trained artisan. To be apprenticed in the reign of Queen Victoria was a privilege.

In addition to that there was the tendency for established craftsmen to secure apprenticeships for their own sons and family relatives. This tended to exclude the sons of the unskilled outsider and may partly explain why skilled labour in nineteenth century Belfast appeared to be mainly Protestant with a corresponding preponderance of unskilled labourers among the Catholics.

That is not to say that all skilled workmen were Protestants or that all Protestants were skilled, nor does it mean that all Catholics were unskilled. There were probably as many Protestants unskilled as skilled, and there were undeniably many skilled Catholics, especially in the building trades. But generally speaking Protestants of the working class had more chance of entering the skilled occupations and of thus enjoying what was then a moderately better standard of living than their Catholic fellow-citizens. Once established, this sectarian segregation of the skilled and the unskilled lasted for generations. It has been noted even in recent times by the Fair Employment Agency (now the Fair Employment Commission). So there would probably have been occupational segregation to some extent, considering the origins of the migrations into industrial Belfast, irrespective of the ill-feeling generated by the Orange Order and exploited by anti- Catholic clergymen. Orangeism and clerical agitation merely reinforced industrial segregation in terms of religion and politics.

But it was not until the Home Rule crisis of 1886, six years before the *Irish News* appeared, that the English Conservative Lord Randolph Churchill showed how Orange prejudice could be adapted to the advantage of politicians who had little else to offer the Protestant electors of Belfast. When he first decided to 'play the Orange Card' – on behalf of the British Tories – Churchill hoped it would be the ace of trumps and not the deuce. And who would say, looking back over more than 100 years, that the Orange Card has not been the ace of trumps, at least for the Unionist parties?

There were at least two really serious periods of rioting in the 1890s, in 1893 when the Second Home Rule Bill was presented to parliament and in 1898 when the nationalists paraded on the centenary of the rebellion of United Irishmen. The Second Home Rule Bill was passed in parliament with a majority of 70 on Friday 21 April 1893 and when the news reached Belfast that afternoon loyalist crowds gathered in the centre of the town and demonstrated outside the premises of well-known Catholic businessmen. That was the prelude to riots that were sporadic and violent that summer and to attacks upon Catholic workers in the shipyards and in the linen factories.

Then, as today, Catholic spokesmen protested to London about the violence of the loyalists and about the evident partiality of the police and the local magistrates. John Morley, the Liberal Home Secretary, was inclined to blame the Catholics as much as the loyalists, but that was probably because he allowed himself to be misled by reports from the unionist-controlled Corporation in Belfast.

It was then that Belfast Chamber of Commerce drew up what many historians believe to have been the most reasonable case ever made against Home Rule, the fact that the north of Ireland and especially the city of Belfast had prospered industrially under the union and feared that whatever economic progress had been made would be reversed under Home Rule. The statistics presented by the Chamber of Commerce were impressive. Prime Minister Gladstone said so himself when he read the submissions from Belfast. Statistics, however, or fluctuations in the value of Irish company shares meant nothing to the loyalists in the Belfast shipyards or in the factories. They had been told that Home Rule would be Rome Rule. That is what they believed then. It is what they believe to the present day.

Sectarian Violence Since the 1890s

*Looting, arson, terror and murder, `savage, repeated and prolonged' –
Winston Churchill*

The misfortune of modern Ireland is that the Ulster Unionists continued to exploit Orange susceptibilities even when they could have opposed Home Rule with perfectly reasonable economic arguments, which is what the Belfast Chamber of Commerce tried to do in its submission to Gladstone in 1893.

Non-sectarian opposition to Home Rule would undoubtedly have attracted support from Catholics of all classes, both in the north of Ireland and in the south. Indeed at the time of the unionist conventions against Home Rule in 1892 it was obvious that many eminent Catholics in southern Ireland were as much unionist as the Protestants of the north.

Unfortunately that was not the strategy of the Ulster Unionists. In their campaign against Home Rule they relied almost completely on the 'Orange Card', thus dividing Unionists north and south, dividing all Ireland and generating sectarian hatred and sectarian violence that continues to the present day.

Orange demonstrations, the fear that a Home Rule Bill would be passed by parliament in London, and nationalist demonstrations, either commemorative of some historical event or concurrently political, were the three principal occasions on which there was always the danger of sectarian unrest. And on all these occasions the people most vulnerable were Catholics who lived isolated from the ghettos or who worked in firms and factories where the workforce was predominantly Protestant and loyalist.

It was so in 1912, when the third and last Home Rule Bill was being processed in parliament, and when Winston Churchill, who was then a minister in the Asquith Liberal Government, came to Belfast at the invitation of the local Liberal Home Rulers. Although Churchill was to become in later years, and especially after Ireland was partitioned, a staunch defender of Northern Ireland he probably never forgot his February 1912 visit to Belfast.

The Nationalists and Liberal Home Rulers had booked the Ulster Hall – some would say rather too brashly – for Churchill's rally. Had they decided on some other venue there would probably have been little or no trouble. But booking the Ulster Hall in order to promote the objectives of the Nationalists was an open challenge to unionists and Orangemen. They had come to regard the Ulster Hall as their own political citadel for it was there in 1886 that Lord Randolph Churchill (Winston's father) had declared that 'Ulster would fight and that Ulster would be right'. To allow the Ulster Hall to be a venue for rebels – as the Unionists and Orangemen would have put it – would have been something tantamount to surrender. And so on the eve of Churchill's arrival in Belfast the Ulster Hall was occupied overnight by loyalists, probably armed; Dublin Castle was warned to expect trouble; more troops and Royal Irish Constabulary were drafted in, as on so many other similar occasions, to keep the peace in Belfast.

However reinforcements of soldiers and policemen were no protection for the small numbers of Catholics working in places like the Belfast shipyards or in those linen factories situated in mainly Protestant parts of the city. Once again they were the victims of what had become a recurring cycle of industrial intimidation. They were forced by threatening mobs of their fellow-workers to flee from their jobs.

Meanwhile Churchill, having crossed by the Stranraer-Larne route, found himself surrounded by hostile loyalists in York Street and was lucky, it was revealed years afterwards by a Unionist who was there, not to have been shot dead when his car was blocked by the mobs in Royal Avenue. But all danger of further trouble was avoided, it would seem, when the Nationalists and Home Rule Liberals were diverted into Divis Street and the Falls to hold their Home Rule rally in the comparative safety of Celtic Park. That evening Churchill left Belfast under military protection and got safely back to England.

Eight years afterwards, in July 1920, Queen's Island (the Belfast shipyards) became the flashpoint of the prolonged disturbances or pogrom that continued until the late autumn of 1922. Just as the inauguration of the Irish Free State was marked by the civil war between the Irregulars of the IRA and the armed forces of the new Irish government, the inauguration of Northern Ireland was marked by 'the pogrom'. But there was one dreadful difference between the civil war in southern Ireland and the sectarian war that was waged in Belfast. In the civil war most of the casualties were military belligerents, soldiers of the Free State Army or members of the anti-treaty IRA. In Belfast, the people who suffered and died were ordinary men, women and children, most of them non-belligerents.

There is no doubt that Belfast with its unhappy long history of community discord was always on the very verge of violence, but even so the violence of 1920-22 might not have occurred had it not been deliberately incited by unionist politicians, among them the Unionist leader Sir Edward Carson. According to 'G B Kenna' (Fr John Hassan) in his *Facts and Figures Belfast Pogrom 1920-22*, Carson's inflammatory speech at the Orange rally in July 1920 incited sectarian feelings in Queen's Island when work resumed after the brief summer break. Gangs of aggressive loyalists roamed the shipyards in search of Catholics.

Sectarian rioting in York Street, Belfast in August 1920
Irish News

The violent expulsion of the Catholics from Queen's Island, on the grounds that they were all 'Sinn Feiners' and therefore all traitors, was the beginning of a wave of intimidation that spread almost immediately to other firms and workplaces, and before long something like 10,000 Catholic workpeople, men and women, had been forced to flee from the places where they had been employed.

During the next two years Belfast was wrecked from one side to the other. Damage amounting to many millions of pounds was caused by the arsonists, by violent mobs, and by gangs of looters. The newly-established authority, the government of Northern Ireland, was either unable or unwilling to control those who expressed their loyalty to crown and constitution by destroying the homes and taking the lives of their fellow-citizens. Even the agreement signed by Michael Collins, on behalf of the government in Dublin, and by Sir James Craig, the Prime Minister of Northern Ireland, in March 1922 failed to bring the Belfast pogrom to an end or to have the expelled workers reinstated in their jobs. The pogrom continued until, it is believed, somebody in the Belfast IRA shot and killed Councillor W. J. Twaddell, a leading unionist politician. By the late autumn of 1922 Belfast had returned, more or less, to something like normality.

Under the terms of the 1920 Government of Ireland Act Home Rule devolved on the Ulster Unionists in a form which they eventually found convenient. But instead of accepting this settlement graciously, and encouraging the Catholic minority within Northern Ireland also to accept it, the unionists adopted measures and attitudes that perpetuated and aggravated deep-rooted sectarian differences.

Meanwhile the British having settled, as they thought, the troublesome Irish Question, elected not to interfere further in the internal affairs of Northern Ireland, no matter how much the Catholic minority might complain or how justified the complaints. That was certainly the attitude of Stanley Baldwin, the British Prime Minister, during the 1935 riots in Belfast. Those riots had their origins back as early as 1931 when a movement known as the Ulster Protestant League attracted the more intolerant sort of loyalist politicians and sustained an anti-Catholic campaign that reached a climax during the year of the Eucharistic Congress, a major event for Catholics in Ireland, and proceeded from that to hostile demonstrations in the centre of Belfast and to the riots of 1935.

The immediate occasion of the riots was the firing of a pistol shot on July 12 either by an Orangeman in the procession or by someone who wanted to provoke the Orangemen. Nobody was ever able to establish who actually fired that shot. The Orangemen and the Unionists blamed the Catholics of east Belfast. More reasonable people, like Ronald Kidd, Secretary of the

National Council for Civil Liberties, (an eye-witness) thought the shot could have been fired, as an act of bravado, by one of the Orange marchers.

A report in the *Capuchin Annual* for 1943 detailed the consequences of the riots of 1935. Between July and September that year eleven people were killed in the disturbances; 514 Catholic families were evicted from their homes by aggressive mobs or by threats of violence; seventy-three houses were destroyed by sectarian incendiaries.

So, no matter what British politicians might have wanted to think, the so-called Irish Question had not been settled at all. The Government of Ireland Act which had been described as a measure 'for the better government of Ireland' had and has created more problems, for everybody in the British Isles, than it was assumed to have solved. That was made abundantly clear, even to Britain's usually smug and indifferent Labour politicians, when the most prolonged cycle of violence began in August 1969.

5

Tracing the History of a Troubled Society
Northern Ireland Since Partition
1921-79

EAMON PHOENIX

The 1921 Treaty, setting up a twenty-six county Free State and including a commission to revise the border, failed to pacify Ireland. President de Valera's swift repudiation of its terms as including both crown and empire led directly to the ugly rancour of the Treaty split. The agreement was ratified narrowly by the Dail on 7 January 1922 and Michael Collins became chairman of a new pro-Treaty government. But the split in the Sinn Fein movement proved irreparable and, with the subsequent split in the IRA in March 1922, the south began a rapid descent into civil war.

The drift towards anarchy in the south had a profound effect on the already unstable situation in the north. Two major problems confronted Craig's administration in 1922: the attitude of the minority towards the state and the continuing problem of IRA and sectarian violence, especially in Belfast. The northern Nationalists refused to recognise the new state and were now supported in this policy by Collins. For a ten month period, Catholic teachers refused to accept their salaries from the Craig government and were paid by Dublin; some 25 nationalist councils pledged their allegiance to the Dail and were dissolved for their pains; and Nationalist and Sinn Fein MPs enforced a strict boycott of the new parliament.

Secondly, the northern IRA, secretly armed by Collins in defiance of the Treaty, continued its campaign of burning and disruption within the six counties in an effort to undermine the Unionist government's authority. This was matched by an upsurge of sectarian warfare in Belfast where 147 Catholic and 73 Protestant civilians were killed between the Treaty and May 1922. The Unionists responded with the draconian Civil Authorities (Special Powers) Act, internment, and the expansion of the Ulster Special Constabulary.

It was against this background that two agreements were signed by Craig and Collins in 1922. Both men had much to gain from the restoration of settled conditions north and south while Craig recognised the need to conciliate his own resentful minority. The first pact, signed in January 1922, broke down almost at once over the Boundary Question. The rift was followed in the spring of 1922 by what Churchill was to describe as 'a return to the hideous bog of reprisals' both in Belfast and along the border. As Tim Pat Coogan has shown, Collins was to operate a twin-track approach to the northern problem in the last ten months of his life, alternating attempts at conciliation with a policy of coercion.

In Belfast the IRA raids and kidnappings along the border came as a match to a powder-keg. In February 1922 alone 43 were killed in the city. The Catholic bishop, Joseph MacRory, demanded military protection for nationalist districts. In March 1922, the murder of two Specials in the city by the IRA was to provoke one of the most repellent atrocities of the 1920-22 'Troubles' – that of the Catholic MacMahon family in north Belfast. The ferocity of the crime moved Churchill, as the British minister in charge of Irish affairs, to summon Collins and Craig to London. The upshot was the wide-ranging Craig-Collins Pact of 30 March 1922 with its over optimistic assertion, 'Peace is today declared'. It contained radical proposals for the recruitment of Catholic special police to protect nationalist areas from attack and the prospect of a *rapprochement* between the two Irish states.

Almost at once, however, the pact's prospects of success were blighted by the violent activities of the anti-Treaty IRA in the south and by the hostile attitude of the sectarian Unionist Minister of Home Affairs, Dawson Bates.

Lord Craigavon (centre) with Cabinet colleagues from left:
Sir Richard Dawson Bates (Home Affairs); the Marquis of Londonderry (Education); Sir James Craig (PM); Hugh Pollock (Finance); Edward Archdale (Agriculture) and John Andrews (Minister of Labour and PM 1940-43)
Irish News

The pact was soon submerged in a sea of blood. As anti-Catholic attacks intensified in May, Collins ordered a renewed IRA offensive in the north-east. This reached its pitch at the end of May but provoked a merciless sectarian backlash.

It was not until the outbreak of open civil war in the Free State and Dublin's adoption of a 'peace policy' towards Craig that the violence which had scourged the north for two years finally ended. By then, however, the shifting southern policy towards partition, the failure of the pacts with Craig and the intensity of the sectarian onslaught had broken the nationalist population's spirit of resistance. The tragedy of the civil war merely completed the minority's sense of despondency and betrayal.

It was during these first years that the basic local government and educational framework of Northern Ireland was laid down, without, it must be admitted, any constructive criticism from the nationalists. But the fact remains that on all matters over which the Unionist parliament had real control – especially education, representation and law and order, policy in Professor Buckland's words, 'was determined by the majority with scant regard for the susceptibilities of the minority.'

The 1923 Londonderry Education Act did provide for a non-denominational system of schooling but, by 1930, under pressure from Protestant Church interests, the Act had been amended to produce 'the virtual endowment of Protestantism by the state'. Nowhere was the Unionist government's insensitivity to minority interests more glaring than in the field of local government. In 1922, Proportional Representation (PR) – seen by nationalists as a major safeguard – was abolished for local elections and whole areas such as Derry City and Fermanagh were flagrantly gerrymandered to ensure loyalist control. Nationalist charges of gerrymandering were to be upheld by the Cameron Commission almost 50 years later.

Nationalist resentment was also sharpened by the adoption of a sectarian security policy during the troubles of the early 1920s. Floggings and internment were directed only at the 'disaffected and disloyal' section convincing many that they could not expect impartial treatment from the new regime. One-third of the places in the new Royal Ulster Constabulary were reserved for Catholics, but its Catholic membership was to decline from an initial 16 per cent to less than 10 per cent by the 1960s.

Nationalist hopes that the Boundary Commission might produce Irish unity by 'contraction' were dashed by the leak of the Commission's award in November 1925 which revealed that only minor changes were contemplated. By the resulting Boundary Agreement, the Free State government finally recognised the 1920 border, while Craig scored a major victory in having the

1920 Council of Ireland – the last bridge between the north and south– dissolved by consent.

The 1925 pact came as a bitter disappointment to the border Nationalists – mostly former supporters of Sinn Fein – and by 1928 this section, led by the old Sinn Feiner, Cahir Healy, joined with Joe Devlin and the constitutional Nationalists in a new united movement, the National League. It was dedicated to pursue Irish unity by peaceful means. Devlin's appeals for the redress of nationalist grievances were repeatedly rejected by the unionist majority. His hopes that stability would bring about a new political orientation in the north along class lines were finally dashed by the abolition of PR for parliamentary elections in 1929. Here, however, Craig's object was to thwart the threat posed to Unionists by the fledging Northern Ireland Labour Party. In the Prime Minister's words, there was room for only two political parties in Northern Ireland, 'men who are for the Union ... or who are against it and want to go into a Dublin Parliament...'.

'Wee Joe' Devlin died in 1934 and for the next decade his followers largely abstained from Stormont, preferring instead to enlist the support of de Valera – now returned to power in the south – in their efforts to end partition. This policy, however, did nothing to alleviate the position of the minority and merely entrenched the Northern Ireland government in its lack of generosity to Nationalists. By the 1930s, Stormont had come to symbolise for Unionists as well as Nationalists 'a Protestant Parliament and a Protestant state'. Discrimination became built into the processes of government and the civil service. The minority, on the other hand, equipped with its own social infrastructure of church, schools, hospitals, Gaelic sports and sectarian Ancient Order of Hiberians, virtually opted out of the state, forming a kind of 'state within a state'. Within northern Nationalism there was a constant tension between the constitutional advocates of Irish unity, such as Cahir Healy, and an IRA section which favoured abstentionism and physical force. The partition issue left the small Labour Party with little room for expansion and the brief camaraderie of the 1932 Outdoor Relief riots was not repeated despite the high unemployment and poverty of the interwar years.

Sectarian rioting and sectarian rhetoric were the main hallmarks of the 'hungry thirties'. 1932 saw attacks on Catholic pilgrims travelling to the Eucharistic Congress in Dublin and the rise of the avowedly sectarian Ulster Protestant League. But the worst outbreak of violence since the 1920s occurred in July 1935 when 11 people were killed and over 300 families, mostly Catholic, expelled from their homes in an orgy of rioting, sniping and arson during the Orange marching season. Communal tension was not eased by the gratuitously offensive speeches of politicians and churchmen. In this regard, the public exhortation of Sir Basil Brooke, a future prime minister, to

Protestants not to employ Catholics 'who were really out to cut their throats' was particularly unfortunate. Similarly, Cardinal MacRory's remark in 1931 that the Protestant churches were 'not even a part of the Church of Christ' offended many Protestants.

The British government, of course, retained ultimate responsibility for affairs in Northern Ireland. But while concern was expressed in official circles in the 1930s about minority grievances there, the imperial parliament took the steady view until the 1960s that events in Northern Ireland were 'no business of ours'. The rise of de Valera in the south after 1932, his 1937 constitution with its territorial claim over Northern Ireland and his renewed pressure on London to end partition tended to heighten unionist defensiveness while raising false hopes among northern Nationalists.

When the Second World War erupted in September 1939, the British government prudently decided not to extend conscription to the six counties. However, the north played a vital part in the struggle against Nazism, suffering 850 fatalities in the Belfast blitz of 1941. De Valera's neutrality, however 'benevolent' and sensible from a southern standpoint, widened the gulf between the two parts of Ireland and ensured the north's claim on Britain's gratitude in the post-war years.

The Labour 'revolution of 1945' in Britain had a catalytic effect on politics in Northern Ireland. For the Nationalists, the Labour resurgence was the signal for a major upsurge of anti-partitionist activity spearheaded by a new mass movement, the Anti-Partition League (APL). Supported by all the major parties in Dublin and the 'Friends of Ireland' group in the British Labour Party, the APL waged a worldwide campaign against 'the evil of partition' in the late 1940s and early 1950s. But the single focus of the movement on the constitutional issue, rather than on well-founded grievances, drew no encouragement from the Attlee government whose Ireland Act of 1949, copper-fastening partition in the wake of the south's declaration of a Republic, outraged Irish opinion.

But if the old issues were rekindled after 1945, the immediate post-war years witnessed a veritable revolution as the modern welfare state and major educational reform were extended to the north. These changes were to bind Northern Ireland even more closely to Britain and to give Unionists a 'bread and butter' incentive for opposing Irish unity. A Health Services Act of 1948 followed the British Act in establishing a national health service in Northern Ireland while effective steps were taken to eradicate tuberculosis. In education, the Stormont Act of 1947 provided for free post-primary education for all children while generous university grants put real equality of opportunity within the grasp of all, regardless of social background. Grant aid to voluntary (mainly Catholic) schools was increased from 50 to 65 per cent (a figure raised to 80 per cent in 1968).

The dramatic expansion of third-level education was fraught with great significance for the future since it was to throw open the univerities and the professions to a whole generation of Catholics, previously excluded from such opportunities for socio-economic reasons. In a real sense the dragon's teeth of the future Civil Rights movement were sown by the 1947 Act.

These strides were not taken without friction, however, and sectarian controversy obtruded itself both in educational reform and in the health services where the Catholic-controlled Mater Hospital remained for conscientious reasons outside the national health service. This issue festered until 1972 when, in a rather altered political climate, the Mater finally came in as 'a bright star in a bright constellation'. Another controversial measure of these years was a politically-loaded Safeguarding of Employment Act (1947), passed by Stormont to prevent large-scale immigration of workers from the south. Also in the same year, the regional government sowed the seeds of much future discord by its blatant refusal to follow the British example in adopting 'one man, one vote' for Stormont and local government elections.

From 1943 until 1963, the unionist Prime Minister was Sir Basil Brooke (later Lord Brookeborough), a Fermanagh landlord whose long tenure of office merely confirmed his narrow sectarianism and limited intelligence. Brookeborough's policy was to ignore the minority. His programme of industrial expansion tended to neglect the depressed nationalist areas of the south and west, thus compounding Catholic resentment.

In the 1955 Westminster election, the Nationalist Party stood aside, enabling Sinn Fein, with its emphasis on armed force, to win a massive 152,000 votes and two seats. This was largely a protest vote by a frustrated community, but it was seen by the IRA leadership as providing necessary moral sanction for its futile border campaign of 1956-62. By far the major factor in the ending of the campaign was the lack of any sizeable support from the minority population.

This was partly related to the impact of the 1947 Education Act on middle-class Catholics. A new group of graduates and professionals, articulate and unwilling to settle for a position of second-class citizenship, now preferred to seek 'a tolerable present rather than wait behind the barricades for a heavenly nationalist hereafter'. Encouraged by the more conciliatory northern policy of the new Taoiseach, Sean Lemass, the National Democratic Party had emerged by the early 1960s, pledged to work for Irish unity by the consent of the northern majority – a considerable shift in traditional nationalist policy.

Brookeborough was succeeded in 1963 by his Minister of Finance, Captain Terence O'Neill, a former Irish Guards officer and a scion of an Ulster landed family. While sharing many traditional Protestant assumptions about Catholics, the new premier broke virgin soil by setting out to reduce sectarian bigotry and end the 40 years' 'cold war' with the south. His new 'era of good feeling' was marked by symbolic visits, notably to Catholic schools. The new policy of detente with the Republic found dramatic expression in Sean Lemass's historic visit to Stormont in January 1965.

O'Neill's policy at first earned the goodwill of the Nationalists, led by Eddie McAteer (in 1965, they accepted the role of official Opposition for the first time). However, it provoked the undying hostility of the unionist right-

British soldiers during Falls curfew, Belfast, July 1970
Irish News

wing and, outside Parliament, of Rev. Ian Paisley, 'a stoker of anti-popery fires' and magnetic demagogue. To Paisley and others well-placed in the government and Unionist Party, O'Neill was 'betraying Ulster's British and Protestant heritage'.

In fact, O'Neill gave nothing away to the south while little practical was done in the early sixties to improve the position of the minority. In all major respects, Northern Ireland remained 'a Protestant state'. To the longstanding nationalist resentment at such practices as discrimination and gerrymandering was added uncontrolled anger at the decision to site the region's new university not in predominantly Catholic Derry city, with its long tradition of learning, but in the Protestant market town of Coleraine. Outside Stormont, the Catholic 'eleven-plus generation', epitomised by the young Derry schoolmaster, John Hume, were demanding equality of citizenship. It was their impatience with O'Neillism and mobilisation in the Northern Ireland Civil Rights Association (NICRA), formed in 1967, which proved the most potent threat ever mounted to the system of unionist ascendancy.

A broad-based, mainly Catholic pressure group, the CRA programme may be reduced to a single objective: 'British rights for British subjects'. As a result, it quickly secured British, especially Labour Party, support. In October 1968, a civil rights march in Derry – chosen as 'the citadel of discrimination' – resulted in a police baton-charge in support of a government-imposed ban. The resulting bloody scenes, relayed throughout the world by the electronic media, marked a major turning-point in the north's history. The 'Troubles' had begun.

No longer could Westminster stand idly by. Under British pressure, O'Neill announced a reform package. This conceded most of the protesters' demands including a 'points system' for housing and the reform of local government though it fell short of the basic demand for 'one man, one vote'. But it was too late to prevent the slide into violence. A brutal ambush on a People's Democracy student march at Burntollet, a UVF bombing campaign and O'Neill's failure to secure a convincing mandate in the 'Crossroads' Election of February 1969 forced his resignation and paved the way for the eruption of naked sectarian warfare in Derry and Belfast that summer. Belfast that August became 'a city convulsed', to quote the *Irish News*. Six died and 150 Catholic homes were burned by loyalist mobs, the worst upsurge in sectarian violence since 1922. With the RUC exhausted and discredited in Catholic eyes, and the Irish government of Jack Lynch hovering on the brink of a risky military intervention, the British cabinet took the drastic step of sending in British troops to keep the peace.

Events moved rapidly over the next three years. The initial nationalist welcome for British troops was to evaporate within six months, while the rise of the Provisional IRA at the end of 1969 transformed the entire situation. The disbandment of the hated B Specials and proposals to disarm the RUC made no difference to the militant republicans, now bent on 'a war of liberation'. By 1971, the forces of loyalist paramilitarism had been galvanised into the Ulster Defence Association (UDA) which now launched a 'backlash' against ordinary Catholics. On the constitutional front, two new parties, the Social Democratic and Labour Party (SDLP) led by Gerry Fitt, and the moderate pro-union Alliance Party, emerged to challenge the tottering unionist government, now in its death throes.

The decision of the new hardline Prime Minister, Brian Faulkner, to reintroduce internment in August 1971 to combat the mounting IRA campaign, was seen as an act of war by the entire Catholic population. It required only the horror of 'Bloody Sunday' in January 1972, when 13 unarmed civilians were shot dead by troops during an anti-internment march in Derry, to convince the Conservative government of Edward Heath to suspend the Northern Ireland parliament and impose direct rule. Over 400 people had been killed in the six counties since 1969, 173 in 1971 alone. As the last session of the prorogued Stormont closed on that March day in 1972, it was clear to nationalists and unionists alike that the old system of virtually untrammelled one-party ascendancy had gone forever. Indeed, given the north's bitter history and chronic difficulties posed by a divided society, a decaying economy and an irredentist neighbour, the real wonder is not that the 1920 settlement dissolved in violence but that it lasted so long.

The fall of Stormont did not halt the ongoing political and sectarian violence. However, the next four years were to witness a succession of failed initiatives, aimed at providing a 'power-sharing' system of government which would command broad consent. Following Assembly elections, held on the basis of PR in 1973, Faulkner emerged as the leader of a moderate Unionist *bloc* which joined with the SDLP and the two sovereign governments in initialling the Sunningdale Agreement. This provided for a power-sharing executive and a Council of Ireland. But the Executive was to have only five months in office before it was overturned by a combination of

Brian Faulkner, last PM of NI, with his successor, Sec. of State, William Whitelaw, 1972
Irish News

loyalist intimidation in the form of the Ulster Workers' Council (U.W.C) strike, and the inertia of a weak Labour government. While Paisley and the Unionist right-wing had bitterly attacked the 'Irish dimension' of the agreement, Faulkner remained convinced in his memoirs that 'the outcry against the Council of Ireland was only a useful red herring — the real opposition was to the sharing of power.' Direct rule resumed and, as political progress stymied and violence continued, many observers came to the conclusion that only an arrangement which transcended the 'narrow ground' of the north could offer a long-term solution.

Meanwhile in 1976, the government established the Fair Employment Agency (later the Fair Employment Commission) in an effort to combat sectarian discrimination in employment. The impact of the European Economic Community also became apparent in these years. The first direct elections to the European Parliament in 1979, which gave the region three MEPs, confirmed the stature of Paisley, leader of the Democratic Unionist Party, and Hume, now leader of the SDLP, as the major figures on the political stage. By the end of the 1970s, some 2,000 people, mainly civilians, had died in the Northern Ireland Troubles which showed no sign of abating.

6

The Northern Ireland
Civil Rights Movement

BOB PURDIE

The Civil Rights movement began as a new way of tackling an old problem. Complaints about discrimination against Catholics were older than Northern Ireland itself, but the term, civil rights, was never used to define the aspirations of the minority community in Northern Ireland before the 1960s. Their inspiration was the black civil rights movement in the United States, led by Martin Luther King. It was militant, but its demands were moderate; simply that the United States apply the letter of its constitution. The Northern Ireland Civil Rights movement was based on the same principle: that the standards of civil rights should be the same throughout the United Kingdom. This did not imply a desire to be British, simply a willingness to unite around a basic democratic principle.

O'Neill and Change

To understand where this movement came from you have to look back to the 1960s. There was a widespread belief that change was coming, and that the old divisions of the past would be overcome. These ideas were closely associated with the premiership of Terence O'Neill who, when he came to office in 1963, adopted a liberal image. His best known gestures were the meetings with the Taoiseach Sean Lemass in 1965 and his visits to Catholic schools. But his intentions were less generous than the gestures appeared.

In the 1962 Stormont general election large numbers of Protestant workers had voted for the Northern Ireland Labour Party in protest at unemployment and economic stagnation. And many middle-class voters, particularly in Belfast, had voted for the NILP and the Liberal Party as a protest against the sectarian attitudes of the Unionist Party. O'Neill needed to turn the economy round and win back these disaffected voters. His economic strategy required collaboration with the British government, and incorporation of the trade unions into systems of economic planning. This meant gestures which were substantial enough to create an impression of change, but not enough real change to alienate his existing supporters. He was not prepared, for example, to try to reform the Unionist Party so that Catholics could join it.

Discrimination

There were basic reforms which O'Neill could have brought in and did not. The local government electoral system was outdated and unfair. Many small local authorities could not provide adequate services and had become cockpits of sectarian conflict. Housing was too scarce and some local authorities discriminated in allocating it. There was hidden discrimination in employment in the public sector and often blatant discrimination in the private sector. People in both communities were guilty of discriminating, but Catholics suffered most, and they also had their hands on fewer levers of power. Power confers responsibility, and the Unionist Party seriously failed to ensure fair treatment of all citizens.

Paisleyism

O'Neill, by giving hope of change and at the same time refusing to bring it about, must be blamed for much that followed. There were serious warnings

of trouble ahead in 1964, with the Divis Street riots. In 1966 there was tension around the fiftieth anniversary of the Easter Rising and the emergence of the UVF. These events showed that there was a section of the Protestant community which, although small, was large enough to cause a problem when given political leadership by Ian Paisley.

Paisleyism had two effects. It limited the room for manoeuvre of O'Neill and his supporters, but it also undermined trust in the prime minister amongst those who were to become civil rights supporters. By 1968, O'Neill had succeeded in alienating most Catholics, and many liberal Protestants. This was an important part of the process whereby opposition to the government took to the streets — no other effective means of pressurising the unionist administration had been found, and O'Neill had done nothing to deal with the mounting frustration.

Rev. Ian Paisley, a vigorous opponent of civil rights demands in the 1960s, in characteristic pose
Irish News

The stagnation of the O'Neill years was particularly tragic for the new opposition forces which had emerged in the earlier atmosphere of optimism. There were the constructive Nationalists of the National Democratic Party, the Republican Labour Party of Gerry Fitt and individual nationalist politicians like the Gormley brothers and Austin Currie. The republican movement had given up its guerrilla war and was trying to engage in grass-roots agitation on issues like housing. The Northern Ireland Labour Party broadened its support to include some Catholics and some talented middle-class intellectuals. The Ulster Liberal Party began to revive.

This growing opposition, and the electoral reverses for the Unionists gave hope that Unionism could be ousted at the ballot box by a coalition of opposition groups. But by the 1965 Stormont general election, O'Neill's strategy had prevented this, by winning back Protestant voters. The failure of opposition at the ballot box explains the emergence of the Civil Rights movement.

N.I.C.R.A.

Between 1962 and 1968 there were several attempts to create a Civil Rights movement. The Republicans set up a Northern Ireland Council for Civil Liberties in 1962. In January 1964 a group of Catholic professional people set up the Campaign for Social Justice in Northern Ireland. The same year, students in Queen's University Belfast set up the Working Committee on Civil Rights. In 1965, a group of London Irish people in the British Labour Party launched the Campaign for Democracy in Ulster. But none of these organisations achieved any significant results.

In January 1967, the Northern Ireland Civil Rights Association was formed as a result of an initiative from a republican discussion forum, the Wolfe Tone Societies. It was the association's decision to organise a march between Coalisland and Dungannon in August 1968 which opened a breach in the wall of indifference. The apparent success of the march encouraged the NICRA to agree to proposals from a group of militants in Derry that a march should be arranged for their city.

The Derry March and its Consequences

There were those within the association who counselled caution, but for the majority it was the only way to break out of isolation and frustration. The Derry march, on 5 October 1968, was banned from following its proposed route by the Minister of Home Affairs, William Craig, and an attempt to defy him brought a brutal police attack which was seen right across the world on television news bulletins. In its wake there emerged a mass civil rights movement, with groups organised throughout Northern Ireland. But it also led to a spiral of increasing tension.

In January 1969 the students of the People's Democracy were brutally ambushed at Burntollet, while marching from Belfast to Derry, and in August 1969 serious violence spread from Derry to Belfast and the British army was sent in to take control from the exhausted and demoralised RUC.

The decision of the NICRA to turn to street demonstrations was significant. Street marches in Northern Ireland had a very definite historical and sectarian meaning. The Civil Rights movement was sincere in viewing its marches as non-sectarian, but this view was not widely shared. Many Protestants were upset and angered, and some less politically sophisticated Catholics became more aggressive towards the police and the Protestant community. By August

A civil rights march in Derry, on 'Bloody Sunday', 30 January 1972
Irish News

1969 the tensions had exploded in a massive outbreak of violence and it was no longer possible to find a solution in purely civil rights terms.

Direct Rule

The early civil rights activists wanted to get Britain involved because they believed that Westminster would impose British standards of impartiality and fairness. This was a somewhat naive view but, in any case, when Britain did intervene, it was not mainly to bring about equality of rights, but to contain civil unrest and in a situation poisoned by violence and suspicion. By the time Westminster took over full control of Northern Ireland in March 1972, the British presence itself had become a problem, and the Provisional IRA had changed the terms of the debate. Discrimination shrank back in importance when compared with the problem of political violence.

The Civil Rights movement had a vision which was broader and more generous than any seen in Northern Ireland before. It inspired people who had lost faith in the possibilities of change, although it did not succeed in finding a way to bring change about. The Civil Rights movement died. It was torn apart by violence and sectarian conflict. It cannot be revived, but it can be learned from. Most of the problems now coming to the fore in Europe concern precisely the issues of civil liberties and of relations between ethnic

The *Irish News* records the arrival of British troops on the streets of Northern Ireland, August 1969

and religious communities which Northern Ireland has been trying to solve in the last twenty years. The fundamental decency of the Northern Ireland people and their great common sense will enable them to learn from the new Europe — and also to help that new Europe to learn from their experiences.

7

Margaret Thatcher's Irish Legacy
The Background and Significance of
the Anglo-Irish Agreement

MARTIN O'BRIEN

By any standard Margaret Thatcher was a remarkable Prime Minister. For good or ill she imposed her psychology on Great Britain in a manner and with an efficacy unmatched by any of her predecessors. The legacy of her ll-year long reign will be a subject of constant inquiry and analysis by countless PhD students in seats of learning around the world for many years to come.

In the interests of truth, and in the interests of the intrinsic value of learning — a notion not accorded much importance by Mrs Thatcher herself, it might be noted — it is to be hoped that those students of the Thatcher era do not overlook the profound implications of her Northern Ireland policy for the people of the north and indeed for people of the island generally.

For, as we shall see, Mrs Thatcher instigated a historic shift in British policy towards Northern Ireland when she signed the Anglo-Irish Agreement at Hillsborough Castle on 15 November l985. For that Agreement — whose true significance was publicly recognised only by Unionists at the time — gave another sovereign government an official role in the running of part of the United Kingdom. It powerfully symbolised the British government's commitment — in so far as Britain felt she could go at that time — to recognise and respect the Irishness of the Northern Ireland Nationalists and to place their Nationalist identity on an equal footing with the Unionist identity. It was from a Nationalist perspective the most important advance since l921. It represented a remarkable *volte face* by a Prime Minister who was by conviction a Unionist and who had proclaimed on one occasion in the House of Commons — in reply to a question from the late Harold McCusker MP on 10 November 1981: 'Northern Ireland is part of the United Kingdom as much as my constituency is.' (Mrs Thatcher never did, as far as I can ascertain, utter the actual phrase 'Northern Ireland is as British as Finchley' which has often been attributed to her.)

Just eight months later on and less than three and a half years before the signing of the Anglo-Irish Agreement, on 29 July 1982, Mrs Thatcher again in the House of Commons declared: 'No commitment exists for Her Majesty's Government to consult the Irish Government on matters affecting Northern Ireland.'

The Anglo-Irish Agreement turned all that on its head. It amounted to a British admission that the 1920-21 partition 'settlement' had failed and that the way forward lay in British-Irish partnership in tackling a common intractable problem that had stubbornly defied internal resolution within Northern Ireland itself. The Republic's interest in the north had not only been legitimised but had been given concrete expression in the creation of new Anglo-Irish structures. And notwithstanding the Republic's affirmation in Article One of the Agreement that 'any change in the status of Northern

The Taoiseach, Dr. Garret FitzGerald and the British Prime Minister, Mrs Margaret Thatcher, pictured signing the Anglo-Irish Agreement at Hillsborough, Co Down on 15 November 1985
Irish News

Ireland would only come about with the consent of a majority of the people of Northern Ireland', the Accord diluted the Union. It did not even define what the status of Northern Ireland was, for that was a matter on which both governments agreed to disagree. As Padraig O'Malley reminds us in his appropriately entitled book *Northern Ireland:Questions of Nuance* to ensure compliance with their respective constitutional practices, two differently worded agreements were drawn up. The 'Irish' version put before Dail Eireann was 'an Agreement between the Government of Ireland and the Government of the United Kingdom'; the 'British' version put before the Westminster parliament was an 'Agreement between the Government of the United Kingdom of Great Britain and Northern Ireland and the Government of the Republic of Ireland'. Accordingly, when one talks of the status of Northern Ireland in the context of Article One, the word 'status' can mean exactly what one wishes it to mean. To the Irish it means one thing; to the British another.

So any appraisal of the Thatcher years in Northern Ireland is perforce dominated by the Anglo-Irish Agreement. It has been said of Mrs Thatcher's tenure at the top of the Tory party that she changed everything. In a real sense the Anglo-Irish Agreement did change everything in Northern Ireland. It fundamentally changed the balance of power: it empowered Dublin at the expense of local representatives who were either unwilling or unable to work out an acceptable accommodation among themselves. Formally and theoretically it equalised the Unionist and Nationalist identities here but, because Northern Ireland politics is essentially a zero-sum game, Unionists felt they had lost out even more than they had and because Unionists felt that way Nationalists felt they had been given a greater advantage than was actually the case.

But more important than that, the Anglo-Irish Agreement fundamentally changed Northern Ireland's relationship with the rest of the United Kingdom prompting, Harold McCusker to declare in the House of Commons that it 'betrayed everything that I had ever stood for.' In another sense, of course, the Anglo-Irish Agreement changed nothing. The murders continued with wearying inexorability, underlining the truism that the Agreement — whatever its historic import — was itself no solution. In time, however it may be seen as a seminal event in modern Irish history, a landmark which opened the door to a process leading to a *modus vivendi* respecting the legitimate rights of Nationalists and Unionists alike. So the story of the Thatcher years in Northern Ireland is mainly the story of how the Anglo-Irish Agreement came about and how Mrs Thatcher — described by her finest biographer, Hugo Young, as 'Britain's most Orange Prime Minister'

— stuck to that Agreement in the teeth of a fierce onslaught by Unionists whose political representatives were not even consulted about its contents.

But before we dwell on the political legacy of Mrs Thatcher here let us briefly survey the economic impact of her time in Number 10 as far as we in the north were concerned. I suppose the crucial question is how did Mrs Thatcher's monetarist medicine affect the local economy and, more particularly, the livelihoods of the people who reside here. The answer is that the record is mixed. Northern Ireland's isolated geographical position, the underlying political instability and continuing violence, and its traditional reliance on declining industries like farming, textiles and shipbuilding has ensured that economic progress will always be difficult to sustain — to put it mildly. As a result the manufacturing base has shrunk dramatically over the past two decades and the region has a disproportionate and unhealthy reliance on the public sector. During Mrs Thatcher's time the public sector took a hammering as public spending was cut in real terms across the board.

The most potent economic indicator is the rate of unemployment which more than doubled from 9.4 per cent to 20 per cent in the 10 years up to 1988. Indeed unemployment has been one of the scourges of Northern Ireland life and the traditional unemployment blackspots have tended to be in Catholic strongholds like Derry, Strabane, Newry and west Belfast. But in the Thatcher decade the misery was felt in all sections of the community, as evidenced by a litany of factory closures and lay-offs in places like Carrickfergus, Newtownabbey and Coleraine. But the late eighties saw a recovery with the creation of an estimated 36,000 new jobs in a four-year period, resulting in unemployment falling to a low point of 13.7 per cent in October 1990 — low that is in terms of recent Northern Ireland economic history, but by most other standards still a horrifying level of human idleness. Then the UK recession, which had been accelerated if not actually set off by the Lawson boom, finally began to bite. Unemployment was soon approaching 15 per cent.

However it must be said that Northern Ireland was spared what might be called undiluted Thatcherism. The local direct rule ministers might not be accountable to the Northern Ireland electorate but under Mrs Thatcher they enjoyed an autonomy in economic matters which has certainly made a difference for the better. Harland and Wolff was an ailing state-owned shipbuilder which was privatised on extremely favourable terms. It might easily have gone to the wall. Now under John Parker's inspired leadership it secured orders which have made its world competitors green with envy. Northern Ireland's other industrial giant, the plane-makers Shorts was also privatised and sold to Bombardier of Canada on generous terms and has a brighter future now than seemed likely only a few years ago. The Molins factory in Derry was saved by the resilience of its trade unions and, perhaps surprisingly, by the interventionism of that high priest of Thatcherism, Dr Rhodes Boyson, the industry minister at the time. His successor with responsibility for the north's economy and the environment, Richard Needham, the longest serving and arguably the most energetic of all the NIO ministers since 1972, did a first-class job promoting the rejuvenation of Belfast in very difficult circumstances and made a start on action programmes for places like Derry, Armagh and Newry. He would never have been given such scope were he a junior minister in the Department of Trade and Industry in London.

But now let us return to the central theme of this chapter, Mrs Thatcher's Irish U-turn. When Mrs Thatcher came to power in May 1979 it seemed the Unionists — many of whom had helped her defeat Prime Minister Callaghan in the no-confidence vote that had precipitated the election — had a strong ally right at the very top. Mrs Thatcher's closest adviser on Northern Ireland — indeed one of her closest friends and confidants — had been the Colditz escapee, Airey Neave, who prior to his murder by the INLA a few weeks before that election had displayed integrationist leanings by opposing power-sharing as being impractical and supporting the setting up of regional councils in Northern Ireland. Mr Neave was the man Mrs Thatcher had intended to send to Stormont Castle and his murder made her even more determined that security measures must take precedence over any political initiative to resolve the northern crisis.

But Mrs Thatcher also had a 'can-do' spirit and she relished the challenge of tackling problems head-on and perhaps nowhere was that 'can-do' approach more badly needed than in tackling the appalling tragedy of Northern Ireland, where 1,908 people had died in political violence in the 10 years prior to her election as Prime Minister and where a further 917 people were to die by the bomb and the bullet in the 11 years, 6 months and 19 days of her premiership. And when on a single day at the end of August 1979 the IRA murdered Lord Mountbatten and three members of his party at Mullaghmore in Co. Sligo and 18 soldiers at Warrenpoint, the temptation to mount a political initiative became irresistible. That initiative became known as the Atkins Conference, after Humphrey Atkins, Mrs Thatcher's first Secretary of State. It was doomed from the start, boycotted by the Ulster Unionists who thought it was a waste of time. The SDLP did go along, found nothing to engage them and the conference was wound up in the spring of 1980.

But Mrs Thatcher was not to be dismayed by this setback and having been questioned on what she was doing about Northern Ireland by President Carter at a summit of the leading industrial nations in Ottawa, she succumbed to the charms of a new Taoiseach, Charles J. Haughey, who came to Downing Street with a silver Georgian teapot and forged with her a new if short-lived alliance, based as much as anything on what Hugo Young has colourfully described as 'a certain roguish mutual admiration.' This resulted in Mrs Thatcher travelling to Dublin Castle in December 1980 with her then Chancellor of the Exchequer Sir Geoffrey Howe and Foreign Secretary Lord Carrington and, of course, Mr Atkins for the most high-powered Anglo-Irish summit since the twenties.

The communique pledged both governments to give 'special consideration to the totality of relations between these islands' and announced the setting up of joint studies into a number of subjects including 'possible new institutional structures'. Mr Haughey claimed a historic breakthrough but angered his new ally by permitting his Foreign Minister Brian Lenihan to exaggerate what had been still a significant advance from an Irish point of view, for it sowed the seeds of the Hillsborough Accord five years later.

Events, however, were already unfolding in the H-Blocks of the Maze Prison which plunged the whole island into crisis, gravely polarised the community in the north and created a tidal wave of anti-British feeling within the entire psyche of nationalist Ireland that had not been experienced since the execution of the 1916 leaders. Ten republican prisoners were to die on hunger strike during 1981 in pursuit of five demands including the right to wear their own clothes, demands which Mrs Thatcher rigidly interpreted as a demand by criminals for political status to which she would not accede. The Irish nation was in trauma. A huge cloud of tension appeared to hang over the island. The late Cardinal O Fiaich — who along with Bishop Edward Daly of Derry had grounds for believing he had experienced Northern Ireland Office duplicity in his efforts to break the deadlock — begged Mrs Thatcher to show a spirit of compromise. So did the leader of constitutional nationalism in the north, John Hume. And so did Taoiseach Charles Haughey (more privately). But she would not budge, showing the same sort of principle, determination, intransigence or callous indifference she was to display five years later when she rejected out of hand Unionist demands to suspend the Anglo-Irish Agreement. The election of two hunger strike TDs in the Republic's general election of June 1981 and a strong showing by several others in the Fianna Fail heartlands cost Charles Haughey his majority, but the new Taoiseach, Garret FitzGerald, was just as unsuccessful in persuading the British Prime Minister to soften her line.

Dr FitzGerald's first administration was short-lived and when Mr Haughey succeeded him in early 1982 he was in no mood to support Mrs Thatcher's Falklands campaign. Relations between both leaders, already strained, went into deep freeze and prospects of any Anglo-Irish meeting of minds on the northern tragedy seemed remote. But Mr Haughey's new GUBU-plagued minority administration itself did not last long and the return of a new secure Fine Gael-Labour government led by Garret FitzGerald in November 1982 promised the Republic a stability the country was crying out for by that time. It was this Irish government, more accurately this Taoiseach, Garret FitzGerald, who was to persuade Mrs Thatcher that it was in her interests to sign the Anglo-Irish Agreement exactly three years later.

By this time the situation in the north had deteriorated sharply. The incessant terrorism of the IRA and INLA and the more intermittent but no less deadly terrorism of the loyalist killer gangs continued to inflict enormous suffering on the entire community. And Mrs Thatcher's handling of the hunger strikes plus a series of highly questionable decisions in the courts, allegations of a 'shoot to kill' policy by sections of the security forces, a number of deaths caused by the deployment of plastic bullets, the use of 'super-grasses' by the police to obtain convictions, and persistent allegations of misconduct involving the security forces, especially the Ulster Defence Regiment — and the failure of those in authority to end such abuses and to be seen to be bringing those guilty to justice — contributed to a profound sense of alienation among large sections of the nationalist community, particularly among the young.

This feeling of alienation was heightened by a growing feeling among many Catholics and Nationalists that, nearly a decade and a half after the birth of the civil rights movement, they were still not getting a fair deal. As evidence of this they cited Fair Employment Agency reports like the one into the then Northern Ireland Electricity Service that showed serious Catholic under-representation in the workforce, the failure of a new Secretary of State, Jim Prior, to appoint a distinguished and pre-eminently qualified Catholic public servant, Malachy McGrady, to be chairman of the Eastern Health Board (he had been vice-chairman) and Mr Prior's failure also to remove the ban on the deputy leader of the SDLP, Seamus Mallon, becoming a member of the Northern Ireland Assembly by virtue of his membership of the Republic's Senate.

This sense of alienation found expression in the sudden arrival of Sinn Fein, the political wing of the IRA, as a substantial political force in elections to a Northern Ireland Assembly in October 1982 and in the Westminster election of June 1983. Indeed there can be little doubt that the rise of Sinn Fein at this time can be attributed largely to what many Irish nationalists saw as Mrs Thatcher's brutal intransigence and ignorance of the lessons of Irish history throughout the agony of the hunger strikes.

Those election results which showed Sinn Fein secure, first, 10.1 per cent and then 13.4 per cent (to the SDLP's 18.8 per cent and 17.9 per cent respectively) of the total vote caused consternation in government circles in Dublin where there were real fears that Sinn Fein, already enjoying almost 43 per cent of the Nationalist vote, might actually draw level with or even overtake the SDLP as the party representing most Nationalists. By now, too, there was a new Secretary of State at Stormont, the avuncular Suffolk farmer, Jim Prior, easily the ablest Secretary of State since William Whitelaw. He brought with him to Stormont as his number two the Earl of Gowrie, a colourful member of a southern Irish Protestant family who had spent his childhood holidays in Donegal, who once told me that he reckoned it would take 30 years for an acceptable settlement to emerge in Northern Ireland. Another of Jim Prior's lieutenants was Nicholas Scott, like Prior a One Nation Tory who tried hard to understand Nationalist grievances and whose accessibility made him popular with the Belfast press corps.

But if Jim Prior had a free hand in choosing his ministers he had nothing like a free hand in formulating policy. Mrs Thatcher had sidelined him to Belfast out of the mainstream of Westminster politics and had vetoed his plans for a stronger Irish dimension by reportedly telling him: 'Go away Jim and take the green tinges off it'. Although he was in a hurry to make a name for himself because he still hankered after the Tory leadership, he had little option but to oblige and his proposals for 'rolling devolution' which now barely mentioned the Irish dimension foundered on the rock of an SDLP boycott of his Assembly but not, as we have seen, of the Assembly elections.

But by now the SDLP, particularly their increasingly influential leader John Hume had — to the exasperation of those Unionists who were trying hard to make a go of the Assembly — their eyes elsewhere. Hume persuaded FitzGerald to set up what became known as the Forum for a New Ireland in which the constitutional Nationalist parties of the whole island, Fianna Fail, Fine Gael, the Labour Party, and the SDLP got together to try and formulate a blueprint for a durable settlement to the Irish conflict. It was dismissed by Sinn Fein as 'a lifeline for the SDLP', but after a year's deliberation published a report in May 1984 which said that any settlement must transcend the narrow ground of Northern Ireland, declared its preference for an independent unitary Irish state, listed a Federal/Confederal State and Joint (British-Irish) Authority as other options and, at Garret FitzGerald's insistence, pledged to 'remain open to discuss other views which may contribute to political development'.

Realising that those three models described in the Forum report were, realistically, all non-starters at least in the foreseeable future, the Taoiseach set about persuading Mrs Thatcher to take action on the 'present realities and future requirements' spelt out in Chapter 5. He ran the gauntlet of Mr Haughey who accused him of 'running away from the Forum Report' and when Mrs Thatcher stridently rejected outright 'Out, Out, Out' the Forum's three constitutional models at a news conference after the next Anglo-Irish summit in November 1984, Dr FitzGerald suffered almost a national humiliation. Yet he stuck patiently to his task and mounted an unprecedented lobby in the British and international media in support of a radical British response to the challenge thrown down by the Forum Report.

Almost a year to the day after her 'Out, out, out' statement, and a year after the most intensive Anglo-Irish negotiations since 1921, Mrs Thatcher and Dr FitzGerald travelled to Hillsborough Castle, the former residence of Northern Ireland Governors, to sign the Anglo-Irish Agreement. The most unionist of British prime ministers, who had never really understood the *gravamen* and outlook of Nationalists, had nevertheless been persuaded, after all, to accept the argument that Northern Ireland was a place apart from the rest of the United Kingdom and that its problems were such that they required an Irish as well as a British answer. A number of factors contributed to this about-turn. First and foremost, Mrs Thatcher felt that the Anglo-Irish Agreement would significantly improve security. Secondly, it would enable the British government to deflect embarrassing international criticism by pointing out that they had worked out with the Irish government a common framework for tackling the problem. Thirdly, and crucially, in Garret FitzGerald she had found a man she could trust, or as she might have put it herself, another man she could do business with.

Once Mrs Thatcher put her signature to the Agreement it was inevitable that she would support it through thick and thin. She was that kind of woman. The Unionists tried everything to convey to her their sense of betrayal: monster public meetings, parliamentary resignations, the boycott of ministers, 'days of action', the paralysis of local

---

The Irish News

Pro Fide et Patria

Telex 747170   DONEGALL STREET BELFAST   Phone 222226

Saturday, November 16, 1985   Ferial Day

Now it begins

AMIDST the welter of conflicting reaction to the Agreement signed yesterday by Dr. FitzGerald and Mrs. Thatcher, there was concensus on one point at least—that the new Treaty marks an historic step in the involvement of Britain in the affairs of this country.

For the first time since December 6, 1921, the representatives of the Irish and British governments have entered into a binding international agreement designed, as its preamble states, "to reconcile and to acknowledge the rights of the two major traditions that exist in Ireland."

No one would claim that the document is in itself a solution, but it is a brave and commendable attempt to begin the healing process. Its historic significance can be gauged by the fact that from the establishment of the Northern State in 1921 until the late 1960s, it was not even possible for British MPs to raise discussion of Northern Ireland matters at Westminster. And as recently as 1971 the then British Prime Minister, Edward Heath, delivered a stern rebuff to the Irish government for daring to interfere in "the internal affairs of the United Kingdom."

A number of articles in the Agreement are of immediate interest to Northern nationalists. Article 1, it is true, reiterates the British "guarantee" to unionism but in an important rider, the British government makes a written commitment to implement Irish unity ON ITS OWN INITIATIVE in the event of a majority emerging in favour of that proposal. This is significant for two reasons: firstly, it legitimises for the first time in a solemn international agreement the objective of Irish unity; and secondly, it removes any possi-

government, a Royal Petition, court hearings, rate strikes, but she would not budge. Loyalist thugs mounted a hideous campaign of intimidation against policemen and their families and against Catholic families to no avail. The lady was not for turning.

But although the unionist protests finally died down, ten years after the signing of the Agreement there is little evidence to suggest that Unionists find it any less unacceptable although it is clear many Unionists are acquiescing in it.

Ironically, Mr Haughey as Taoiseach enthusiastically implemented the Agreement he described in Opposition as 'an abandonment of Irish unity and a copper-fastening of the partition of our country...We will certainly not be prepared to accept it in its present form.' But the Anglo-Irish Agreement, Margaret Thatcher's most important Irish legacy, will remain in place until all the parties concerned agree to replace it with something different and something better and after the failure of Secretary of State Peter Brooke's initiative to get off the ground the Agreement, and more significantly perhaps, its underlying philosophy seems more and not less secure.

Since the departures of Thatcher, FitzGerald and Haughey from the political stage the situation in Northern Ireland, for so long set in wearisome and apparently hopeless, deadly deep-freeze, has been transformed. The killing on both sides has stopped. The relevant parties to the conflict appear to be inching their way towards the kind of comprehensive negotiations which must precede a settlement based on compromise and mutual respect. More and more people are believing that the killing has actually stopped for good, as suspicion and cynicism slowly give way to confidence and optismism. Since the IRA and loyalist ceasefires of September 1 and October 13 1994 many things have happened that would have been simply unthinkable a short time earlier. The withdrawal of troops to barracks, a meeting between the President of the United States and the President of Sinn Fein, a toast to the President of Ireland in the presence of the Taoiseach at a Confederation of British Industry dinner in Cultra, County Down, the first official visit by a member of the British Royal family — the heir to the throne at that — to the Republic of Ireland are just some examples that spring to mind.

We are still much too close to such landmark events as the Anglo-Irish Agreement of 15 November 1985, the Joint Declaration of 15 December 1993, the IRA and loyalist ceasefires of 1994 and the Framework Document of 22 February 1995 to assess their true significance. It will be left to future historians to weigh all the available evidence and offer definitive conclusions. That said, some tentative conclusions can be drawn. Enough time has elapsed since the Anglo-Irish Agreement of 1985 to see that it may have been indeed a watershed in modern Irish history. It signalled a new departure by the

British government in its attitude to the problem of Northern Ireland which may have been an important factor in eventually persuading the IRA that the aims and objectives of Irish republicanism can be more efficaciously advanced by purely political means. Instead of the simple ritual guarantee about the consitutional position and an undertaking to devolve power on a power-sharing basis to an administration at Stormont, Britain had now signed up to an Anglo-Irish process that had no pre-determined outcome. The intransigence of the Northern Ireland parties was to be by-passed by the two sovereign governments. The Anglo-Irish Agreement laid the foundations for the Joint Declaration and the Framework Document which, while stressing the doctrine of consent, made it clear that Britain now saw Northern Ireland more and more as a part of the island of Ireland, whose problem was apparently to be solved in the context of an agreed Ireland, as long espoused by John Hume. So much so that Britain's 'primary interest is to see peace, stability and reconciliation established by agreement among all the people who inhabit the island...'

The Anglo-Irish process is much greater than the legalistic text which Margaret Thatcher and Garret FitzGerald put their signatures to at Hillsborough on that historic day in 1985. The Anglo-Irish Agreement which they signed gave birth to a framework in which a peace process could later develop around such key figures as John Hume and Gerry Adams, initially, and later Albert Reynolds and John Major. While future historians may point to the original Hume-Adams meetings of 1988 as having sown the seeds of the peace process of today, the seeds of the Anglo-Irish process which enabled it to be set in motion were probably sown by Margaret Thatcher and Charles Haughey at Dublin Castle in December 1980 and harvested by Mrs Thatcher and Garret FitzGerald at Hillsborough in 1985. Both processes have converged. What their outcome will be cannot be predicted though it seems likely that any political settlement will take many years to negotiate, will involve new thinking and compromise on all sides and will entail the evolution of new and unique structures and institutions which reflect the complexity of all the relationships within and between these islands. What cannot be disputed though is that Mrs Thatcher, an instinctive Unionist, perhaps unwittingly, significantly moved Britain's Northern Ireland policy in a nationalist direction and in so doing left her mark, for good or ill, on late twentieth century Irish history.

8

Southern Policy Towards 'The Six' since 1921
Myth and Reality

TIM PAT COOGAN

Regretfully I must begin by conceding that since the coming of independence, southern Ireland, which has traditionally professed as an article of political faith an ardent desire for unity, has done less for unity than it has to illustrate the wisdom of the biblical reminder that 'Faith Without Good Works is Dead'. The biblical allusion is chosen for reasons other than to demonstrate that that celebrated Book was not created exclusively to repair the obvious deficiencies in unionism's intellectual armoury. To paraphrase Pearse: I feel that it is almost as futile to attempt to understand a Paisleyite with a Bible as it is a Dublin government without one.

Firstly, let us remind ourselves that when the great wounding convulsion of the Treaty debate and the subsequent civil war took place just seventy years ago, Partition was not, repeat not, an issue. The civil war claimed the life of the one nationalist leader who might have gone on to make it one, Michael Collins. It also created conditions which made any practical steps towards ending partition quite impossible.

The first Cumann na nGaedheal government had one overriding priority — survival. It jettisoned Collins's support for a 'forward' policy on partition and tried desperately to balance the books while keeping the almost foundering ship of state afloat in waters made treacherous by unemployment, civil war destruction, political and sometimes military attrition within its boundaries and, without, at best condescension, at worst hostility from London and Belfast.

Political vision had to refocus to a point well below that of the high heroic a point heavily underscored by the *realpolitik* Cumann na nGaedheal were faced with over the Boundary Commission. The boundary settlement of 1925 gave the south not the nationalist areas of the six counties which Collins tried to wrest from a horrified James Craig during their abortive meetings in the spring of 1922, but confirmed the boundary between north and south as it exists today. The development of southern Irish political policies made it inevitable that unionists would be confirmed in their desire to see it stay that way.

Michael Collins (front row, fourth from left) pictured during a visit to Armagh, 4 September 1921
Mr P Hamill

For example, the Statute of Westminster of 1931, which de Valera was later able to use to get rid of some of the imperial trappings of the new state, was a major achievement on the part of southern Irish diplomacy. But southern efforts to loosen the bonds of empire which the Unionists were so anxious to maintain were evidences of a fundamentally different type of mind-set to that which prevailed either at Stormont or in UVF homes bereft and ennobled by the carnage of the Somme.

A more serious impediment to convincing Unionism that the Dublin parliament was not an ante-chamber to the Vatican arose throughout the Cosgrave years (1922-32) as a result of domestic policy. The Free State Constitution of 1922, though emasculated by the British insofar as Republican aspirations were concerned, was not by any means a sectarian document. But, almost unconsciously, the administration allowed a kind of legislation-creep to develop in the direction of what could be perceived, and certainly represented, as sectarianism. The laws which had governed all-Ireland, and which continued to govern the six counties, were altered so as to publicly reflect Catholic teaching on divorce, contraception, and censorship. Less publicly, the government agreed with the Hierarchy that the Church's virtual monopoly on education would not be interfered with.

A process was put in hand of creating a Catholic state for a Catholic people. It was a fundamentally more democratic, tolerant state than the one which took root in the north, but nonetheless it was a democratic, tolerant, Catholic state. The poet Yeats was one of the few influential voices raised in the south against the intrusion of Rome rule into home rule. Speaking in the Senate on the Divorce Bill in 1925, he said:

> If the profound desire of the Irish people for unity between north and south is ever fulfilled, if north and south ever enter the same political association, the north will certainly not abandon any right which it already possesses and it seems clear that if southern Ireland is to be governed by Catholic ideas alone, if you pass laws that the Protestant majority consider oppressive you must give up all thought of unity... .

But in an Ireland which had but lately witnessed the activities of death-squads operating against Catholics with impunity from the ranks of certain sections of the RUC and the B Specials, such sentiments had little impact. Nationalist Ireland was still resentful of the tactics employed by the Unionist/ Conservative alliance to frustrate democratic attempts to introduce Home Rule to Ireland. Had the message of the ballot box been accepted there would have been no 1916, no partition, no six county parliament to accommodate.

They felt every reason to be grateful to the role played by the Church in the independence movement, very little to be mindful of the concerns of the unionist element who had lorded it over their race for so long and helped to bring such misery upon the country. They felt they had gone a long way towards accommodating Unionists by calling off the Belfast boycott and by restraining the IRA. Anything else would be a work of superrogation.

Accordingly, Yeats did not remain a Senator for long. But the laws whose introduction he railed against are with us still, augmented by subsequent developments such as de Valera's 1937 Constitution. In preparing his speech, Yeats showed himself fully aware of the influences shaping Irish legislation. He invoked the memory of his republican mentor, John O'Leary, who had opposed Irish republicans fighting on the side of the Pope against Italian unity. But the papacy of Yeats' day was as little inclined to give ear to the claims of Irish unity compared to those of Mother Church as it was in the days of Garibaldi's Italy.

Less than a month after the Treaty was accepted by the Dail, the Rector of the Irish College, Msgr. Hagan was warning the Irish Hierarchy that they would have to fight 'tooth and nail' to ensure that recognition of the Irish Free State would not mean the coming of a nuncio to Dublin to keep an eye on the bishops and to see that Rome's writ ran. Hagan was an accurate prophet. A nuncio, Pascal Robinson, did come to Dublin in 1929. And a veritable cascade of purple broke over Dublin in 1932. Within a few weeks of de Valera's taking power, the Eucharistic Congress was held and tremendous tableaux of Catholic piety were enacted. These were of enormous benefit to de Valera in his efforts to reassure those worried about his Irregular past that he was on good terms with cardinals, bishops — and nuncios.

His Constitution of 1937 was designed to ensure that he stayed on good terms with them, being vetted by the Vatican before the Irish public got a chance to do so. It was 'worthy of a Catholic country', in the words of Sean T. O'Ceallaigh, a de Valera true believer and, like him, a future president. Its Catholicity did become an object of some controversy in north-south dealings, notably in the early seventies when, for a time, the Unionist M.P. Desmond Boal drew some national attention as a theoretician of Paisleyism. But the famous Articles two and three, which made an explicit claim on Craig's 'loved soil of Ulster', were the principal bones of contention.

Some of de Valera's more daring advisers warned him not to introduce these but, with customary adamantine stubbornness, he disregarded them — thereby creating a classical 'Faith Without Good Works' situation. By putting in the clauses he angered the Unionists, while at the same time creating a situation in which any subsequent attempt at removal would inevitably generate widespread accusations of betrayal within the nationalist community. Worse, by raising a claim, and then going on to do nothing substantive to validate it by being seen to address the fears of either section of the northern community, de Valera's constitution helped to make a bad situation worse insofar as Fianna Fail policy-making on partition was, and is, concerned. One can point to speeches aplenty. Actions are considerably scarcer.

Under de Valera there were sporadic bursts of propaganda about discrimination and gerrymandering, occasional suggestions to the effect that if the Orangemen did not like the prospect of a united Ireland, they could return to mother England and an odd imaginative gesture like the sending of the fire brigades briefly to Belfast during the German bombing in World War II. But this was counter-balanced by an unimaginative negativism which the public was not made aware of. For example, Bord Failte was prevented from cooperating properly with its six-county counterpart and Radio Eireann was reined in also where cross-border cooperation was concerned.

De Valera's most hailed policy, neutrality, copper-fastened partition as the Unionists, who characteristically provided far fewer volunteers or medal winners to Britain's war effort than did the island's nationalists, were able to cynically trumpet their 'loyalty' thereafter, even though they knew that it was de Valera's protests which kept conscription out of the north. There was only one aspect of de Valera's policy which the Unionists did admire. He dealt with the IRA in a ruthless fashion which Amnesty International would never have allowed to go unquestioned.

However, for all the political capital he made out of the issue, de Valera in office could do no more about shifting the border than his predecessors. Like them he came up against the ineluctable reality of an entrenched unionist presence of not inconsiderable economic and military strength, backed up by the immeasurably stronger force of the alliances of old blood and old money between the ruling dynasties of the Six Counties and decision-taking England. His own electorate were preoccupied not with partition, but by economic issues, emigration and unemployment, problems for which he speedily ran out of answers.

The immorality of discrimination and gerrymandering did sometimes move him to privately tell British politicians that were he a northern Nationalist these injustices would have made him resort to physical force. But private morality plays are not public policy. Nor did more public playing of another sort bring any more tangible results. The 'sore thumb' policy of the MacBride-inspired coalition, which dethroned de Valera after World War II, got nowhere. The partition issue was raised at every international gathering attended by Irish representatives to a point where it became synonymous with boredom. The major impact on partition of the declaration of the Republic in 1949 was to produce a consolation prize of vital importance to the unionists in the shape of the much-hyped 'veto' in the shape of the British Labour government's Ireland Act.

We do not know what tangible results might have been achieved by a domestic policy which did not abandon the international forum, but equally concentrated on making southern society acceptable to northerners, while at the same time being seen to be sincerely concerned with civil rights. But we can see the results of the vacuum which resulted from the absence of such concern, either in Belfast, Dublin or London.

We can also see, unfortunately, what happened to the hand of friendship which Sean Lemass held out to Terence O'Neill. Ian Paisley, amongst others, tried to gnaw it off at the elbow. The blood and horrors which have flowed since those historic summits of 1965 place as much moral guilt on the shoulders of those who connived at the batoning of the civil rights marchers off the streets as rests on those of IRA planners.

The historic meeting between the Taoiseach, Sean Lemass and the Northern Ireland Prime Minister, Captain Terence O'Neill at Stormont in January 1965
Irish News

Against such sins of commission, southern sins of omission scale downwards. Yet, it must be admitted that the 1969 eruption in Northern Ireland caught the allegedly unity-keen southern decision-takers sadly bereft of policy. Some looked to the United Nations. Some opted for gun-running. Others preached the gospel according to John Hume. Some prayed that a divine providence would part the land along the border so that the whole place could be towed out to sea and sunk!

Obviously, given the fact that Britain holds the economic, military and political purse strings, the south's options have been limited. How limited could be seen in the wake of the rejection of the Forum report in Mrs Thatcher's 'Out! Out! Out!' speech. But what persistence can achieve, when it is forthcoming, was shown in the subsequent Anglo-Irish Agreement of 1985. It can be fairly claimed that Dublin has taken a constructive part in every major development from Sunningdale to the Brooke Initiative and the historic ceasefires of 1994. And it has contributed three times as much *per capita* to security costs as has Britain.

But, like London, Dublin does stand before the bar of history charged with having moved on the north, not out of any sort of deep-rooted sense of historical and moral obligation, but in direct response to the level of violence. To this day it is impossible to point to anything like a detailed Dublin blueprint for Irish unity, guaranteeing the Protestant liberty of conscience and spelling out the sort of relationships envisaged with Brussels, London, Washington and the UN which it envisages as being necessary to maintain economic and political stability in the wake of a British withdrawal. Many in Northern Ireland might deride such a document. Few could, however, avoid discussing it. Especially if its authors had been shown to have had the conviction to lodge such a charter with the U.N.

Dublin reacted to the hunger strikes, the Birmingham Six, and allied cases, and to pressures to uphold the SDLP against the inroads of Sinn Fein. However, 'Oh lord make me good, but not yet' seemed to be the spirit in which the Dublin decision-takers looked north.

But by 1993, the strength of the American connection, represented by Bill Clinton, Senator Ted Kennedy and the new Ambassador to Ireland, Jean Kennedy-Smith, coupled with Albert Reynold's emergence on the political scene, had added a new dimension to the Irish Question.

A moment of history: An historic hand clasp between Gerry Adams, the Sinn Fein president, Taoiseach Albert Reynolds and SDLP leader, John Hume marks the announcement of the IRA ceasefire, September 1994
Pacemaker Press International

Reynold's 'dynamic approach' on the northern situation surprised many. He had seemed the archetypal Fianna Fail businessman-turned-politician. He had built up a fortune operating dance halls and manufacturing dog food. However, his Longford base and business contacts had given him both an interest and an insight into the northern problem.

Accordingly, on taking office he surprised his aides by declaring: 'Gentlemen, my priority as Taoiseach will be Northern Ireland. If this means my taoiseachship will be of short duration, well so be it.' His taoiseachship was to be of short duration, but not because of Northern Ireland. However, before he vacated his office, Albert Reynolds was to go a good way towards achieving his priority. His contacts with clerical intermediaries and a long talk with John Hume in his first few days in the taoiseach's chair confirmed him in his view that the current northern scene offered what he termed 'possibilites'. Hume's assessment of the situation was an essential factor in Reynolds' thinking. He decided that the time had come to recognise that the way to stop the violence was to bring both sets of paramilitaries into the mainstream of political life.

An important consideration in the overall situation was Reynolds' relationship with John Major. The two had become friendly on the European circuit, in their respective capacities as finance ministers. Both were self-made men, streetwise politicians with an innate sense of decency. One of the ironies of their situation was that, uniquely in the Anglo-Irish relationship, the English Prime Minister was not in the same position of strength as his Irish counterpart. Throughout the peace process, and indeed up to the time of his re-election as Tory leader, the London leader was in a weaker position than the Dublin one domestically. However, the upshot of their efforts was the Downing Street declaration of 15 December 1993 which was to smooth the way for the IRA and Loyalist ceasefires of 1994.

Thanks to Albert Reynolds' vision and persistence, the Irish government is now facing up to its historic responsibilities to all the people of Northern Ireland.

9

From National Schools to National Curriculum
Popular Education in Ulster from 1831 to the 1990s

JOHN MAGEE

In Ireland as in the rest of Europe, the closing decades of the eighteenth century was a period of instability: French revolutionary ideas, agrarian and sectarian tensions culminating in outright rebellion, the danger of invasion by an enemy – all these had combined to persuade the Prime Minister, William Pitt, of the necessity for a legislative union of Great Britain and Ireland. But if the Act of Union (1800) was to provide the security he sought, an effort would have to be made not only to unite the parliaments of the adjacent islands but the bitterly divided communities in Ireland as well.

Almost instinctivly men turned to education for this purpose, and that is the explanation for the flurry of commissions and enquiries in the early years of the nineteenth century. The report of the commissioners of Irish education enquiry, 1825, recommended the establishment of schools 'for the education of the lower classes', but warned that there was little hope of reconciling the communities 'unless it be explicitly avowed and clearly understood that no attempt shall be made to influence or disturb the peculiar religious tenets of any sect or description of Christians'.

Hedge Schools and Chapel Schools

The adoption of such a plan would entail the abandonment of the traditional government policy of entrusting the education of the Irish poor to agencies of the established church (the Church of Ireland). However, Catholics had never attended church schools in any numbers, but depended upon the so-called 'hedge' or 'pay' schools which proliferated on the relaxation of the penal laws in the late eighteenth century. The authorities were concerned about the influence of these schools, as were some of the Catholic bishops, and for some time they had been encouraging parish priests to establish 'chapel' schools, under their own control and financed from parochial funds. In the larger towns education was provided by religious orders of nuns and brothers, but these were insufficient to meet the needs of a rapidly growing population, and the bishops were prepared to cooperate with the government in the creation of a school system which would meet both their aspirations. For a time it seemed that the Kildare Place Society might suffice, but eventually the bishops withdrew their approval when they discovered that the society was extending its aid to schools whose aims were more evangelical than educational. While doing so, they assured the government that they were not rejecting the principle of mixed schools 'provided sufficient care was taken to protect the religion of the Roman Catholic children, and to furnish them with adequate means of religious education.'

The System of National Education

It is against this background that the establishment of the national school system must be considered. The first official intimation of the scheme was given by the chief secretary, Edward Stanley, to the House of Commons on the 9 September 1831. He said that the £32,000 hitherto paid annually from public funds to the Kildare Place Society would henceforth be placed at the disposal of the Lord Lieutenant, for the creation of an educational system in which 'the most scrupulous care should be taken not to interfere with the peculiar tenets of any description of Christian pupils.' The system was to be managed by a board of commissioners appointed by the government. The schools – to be called national schools – were to be open four or five days a week when pupils were to receive moral and literary education in classes together, and on one or two days for the separate religious instruction of the different denominations by clergymen or teachers of their own faith. In the spirit of the time central government was to be seen aiding local initiative, and one-third of the building cost of the schools and of teachers' salaries should be raised by parents and supporters. The commissioners were also required to give priority to applications for aid made jointly by Protestant and Catholic residents of an area.

Opposition to the National Schools

If the government's objectives were to be achieved the cooperation of the three main churches would be required. It was not forthcomming. The board of commissioners had scarcely begun to function when the Presbyterian Synod of Ulster rejected the system: it objected to the ban on reading the Bible during the period set aside for secular instruction and to the proposal to allow Catholic clergy free access to national schools. An extremely emotional campaign was launched in the Presbyterian areas of Antrim and Down, during which schools were burned and their teachers intimidated. At the same time a group of Presbyterian ministers launched a campaign to have the regulations of the national board changed to suit them. In 1840 they made an application for aid for a school at Correen, near Broughshane, County Antrim. This school had already been built with Presbyterian money and the managers requested a grant for books and a small annual contribution towards the salary of the teacher. On the application form it stated that 'no persons except members of committee and officers of the board are permitted ex officio to interfere in the business or management of the school'.

This was a vital change of principle, for it accepted that clergy of denominations other than that of the manager did not have the right of access to a school for the purpose of giving religious instruction. The board no longer insisted that priority be given to joint applications for aid, and, in practice, as the Presbyterians had now got denominational schools, with a rather vague conscience clause, there was a flood of applications from their ministers.

Opposition also came from the clergy and laity of the Church of Ireland, who, when they failed to persuade the government to amend the scheme, created their own network of independent schools and at one stage had over 100,000 pupils in attendance. Some of the clergy, however, supported the national system and one of them, Archdeacon Stopford of Meath, organised

Staff and pupils of Tullywest National School, Co Down at the turn of the century
Ulster Museum

a campaign to have some of the original safeguards removed. After three years sustained pressure the commissioners agreed in 1847 that managers and teachers were not obliged to ensure that pupils were excluded from religious instruction given by persons not of their faith, unless they were asked to do so by the parents of the children.

At the outset the Catholic bishops welcomed the national schools and Bishop Denvir of Down and Connor accepted an invitation to become a commissioner in 1853. The first application in the diocese came from Bernard McAuley, P.P. of Ballymena and had the signatures of both Catholic and Protestant supporters. With episcopal approval, applications for aid from the diocese of Down and Connor and the Archdiocese of Armagh (where Archbishop Crolly was known to support mixed education on principle) increased over the next few years. It would have been surprising, however, if the alteration of the rules of the national board under pressure from the Protestant churches had not caused some anxiety, and Bishop Denvir himself had to complain that Catholics attending the Lancastrian Girls School in Frederick Street, Belfast were compelled to attend scripture readings given by a Protestant mistress.

Apart from the concessions to Protestant pressure that, to Catholic eyes, radically altered the system, other factors were at work as well. The controversies over the model schools and the Queen's Colleges generated a good deal of sectarian feeling, while the famine and the political agitation of subsequent years led the people to put the worst possible interpretation on every action of the government. The bishops changed also: the moderate and compliant Murray of Dublin and Crolly of Armagh were replaced by the more energetic and purposeful Paul Cullen, first of Armagh and then at Dublin. One of Cullen's first acts was to convoke the Synod of Thurles (1850), at which the Irish bishops came out unambiguously in favour of separate clerically controlled but state financed education for Catholics. But they had no intention of abandoning the national schools, which by that date were, in very many cases, denominational in everything but name.

Training Of National Teachers

Chief Secretary Stanley told parliament on the 9 September 1831 that national teachers would be appointed by the managers of schools, but that their training and subsequent inspection for efficiency would be a responsibility of the board of commissioners. But initially they had to make do with untrained teachers and for these they organised a short course in some stables at the rear of the board's headquarters in Merrion Street, Dublin. In 1837 a training college for men was opened in Marlborough Street and in 1844 a college for women was added. The following year a system of 'paid monitors' was devised, and a two-year course of training was introduced for a small number of teachers. For the main body of candidate teachers the course was of five months' duration and consisted of a thorough grounding in the contents of the board's lesson books, and of the regulations which governed the national teachers' work and behaviour in the community. Teachers were forbidden to attend markets, fairs or political meetings, and were expected to inculcate in their pupils a spirit of peace and respect for lawful authority.

The Model Schools

As feeders of the training colleges the commissioners planned to establish 32 model schools throughout the country, and the first of these was opened at Newry in 1849. Other early examples in Ulster were Ballymena, Coleraine, Ballymoney and Newtownards. Belfast Model was built in Divis Street, between Dover Street and Ardmoulin street, in 1857, and must have been one of the most impressive buildings in what was a rapidly expanding industrial area. In design it was quadrangular, with a courtyard in the centre, with ample space for recreation and playgrounds and, in addition to the normal classrooms, had dormitories for pupil teachers, a library, laboratory and other specialist facilities. In the beginning the school attracted pupils of every religious denomination, and in 1857 there were 16 pupil teachers in residence, some from as far away as Galway, Limerick and Waterford. An indication of the importance which the commissioners attached to the Model schools is the fact that they spent £10,394. 16s. 3d. in building the one at Newtownards, and paid Dicksons of Hawlmark £57. 14s. 1d. for landscaping the grounds and laying out the rose gardens.

Condition of the National Schools

By contrast, many of the ordinary national schools were dark, cold, inhospitable places that had little attraction for children. In 1857 the Board of Works was given responsibility for design of the buildings, but managers, on the whole, were more interested in control than in maintenance, and frequently the teacher had to fund the school-house and pay the rent. Repairs and decoration were undertaken by the master and pupils, sometimes by a philanthropist like Vere Foster, who floored classrooms, built outside lavatories, and provided the only pictures that Irish country children had ever seen. Things did improve, but as late as 1878 Inspector Hynes, writing from Enniskillen, reported that in one parish in his district ten of the twelve school-houses were still the property of the respective teachers. Part of the explanation was that there were too many schools: apart from the Catholics, every Protestant denomination wanted to educate its own children and frequently pupils were separated by sex as well as religion. The result was a dilution of resources, so that by the end of the nineteenth century sixty per cent of the national schools were miserably equipped one-teacher affairs. In 1903 the commissioners asked William Starkie, their chief executive officer, to rationalise this situation but the managers were obdurate and to the end of the national system rural Ireland was dotted with one- and two- teacher schools.

The Problem of Teacher Supply

The Catholic bishops placed great emphasis on the role of the teacher in creating the right spiritual ethos in the school, and from 1850 onwards they demanded the right to establish their own training colleges, with government financial support, as all religious denominations already did in England and Wales. When this was refused, Catholic parents were ordered to withdraw their children from model schools and parish priests were forbidden to appoint teachers who had been trained in Marlborough Street, Dublin. There was never a hundred per cent response to these demands from either priests or

Squalor and overcrowding were the hallmarks of Springfield National School, Belfast, 1902
Ulster Museum

people, but it was sufficiently large to put Catholic children at a severe disadvantage. One statistic will illustrate this. In 1874 the Chief Secretary, Sir Michael Hicks-Beach, elicited from the commissioners that of the 9960 national teachers in the country, 6118 had no training of any sort, and of the untrained, five sixths were in schools with Catholic managers. Many of the untrained teachers were young boys and girls, who spent a few years teaching while studying for a post in the civil service or the R.I.C. Inefficient or not, the board's inspectors had to recognise them as no others were available.

The Powis Commission

Before long the Treasury became worried about the national system on a value for money basis. Costs mounted steadily: £125,000 in 1850; £294,000 in 1860; £394,000 in 1870; but this money was largely swallowed up in providing small schools and there was little available for general improvement. As well, school attendances were very poor, and the great majority of pupils never got beyond the Third Book. Because of this combination of circumstances the British government decided in 1868 to establish a Royal Commission under the Earl of Powys, 'to examine the practical working of the Board of National Education in Ireland, and to enquire how far the said Board fulfilled the objects for which it was established.'

The commission was thorough in its investigation, and concluded from its investigation of schools that the progress of pupils was very much less than it ought to be. Other aspects of the system which aroused their concern were the poor attendance rates, quality of management, unsatisfactory teacher training and lack of local participation either in financing or controlling the individual schools.

Understandably the report paid special attention to the quality of the teaching staff. It was critical of the model schools, since their management, staffing, equipment and facilities were quite unlike those of an ordinary school and suggested that able young men and women should be appointed as 'monitors' in good but typical national schools and that training colleges should recruit directly from them. As it was clearly impossible for the college in Marlborough Street to train sufficient teachers to meet the needs of the schools, the report recommended that the government should give financial assistance towards the additional denominational colleges. After some delay, in 1883 St Patrick's College, Drumcondra and Our Lady of Mercy College, Baggot Street, Dublin, were recognised for the training of Catholic teachers and Kildare Place College for Anglicans. Presbyterians continued to be trained in Marlborough Street and at the same time the course of training for all except serving teachers was extended to two years.

In its annual report for 1897 the national board admitted that the five colleges now recognised (De La Salle, Waterford had been opened in 1891) were failing to meet the needs of the schools and that two more colleges for women were to be built, one in Limerick for 75 students and one in Belfast for 80; but when St Mary's College opened on the Falls Road in 1900 there were places for 100 students. For the first time it was possible to envisage and plan for a trained teaching profession.

Payment by Results

The national board was expected to control what went on in the schools by means of a prescribed curriculum that was limited in scope and closely linked to the books which the commissioners themselves published. In the beginning the emphasis was on 'the three Rs' – reading, writing and arithmetic – but gradually geography, needlework for girls and agriculture for boys were added. Levels of attainment were low, for many children attended school irregularly or not at all. The Powys commission considered the introduction of compulsory attendance, but eventually decided on a system of payment by results that resembled fairly closely some of the recommendations that are being made today. Under the results system, introduced in 1872, an additional sum was paid to the teacher for each pupil who made 100 attendances during the year and reached a prescribed standard for his class in compulsory and optional subjects. Results fees, as they were called, were paid annually in one lump sum and added considerably to a sucessful teacher's income; but their effect was to turn teaching into a dull routine, and the school inspector into an adversary to be outwitted on the day of decision.

Because of the almost universal unpopularity which it encountered the results system was abolished in 1900 and replaced by an intricate salary scale, which ranged from £56 a year at the bottom of Grade 3 to £175 a year to a 'first of first' teacher in his last years of service. Promotion from grade to grade was made to depend on the inspectors' reports but strained relations developed between teachers and the boardmen when it was learned that the numbers admitted into each grade was determined by the Treasury and not on educational grounds. Another source of grievance were the notorious 'paper promotions', whereby a teacher was conditionally awarded a grade, but had to await a vacancy from death or retirement before he got the salary for which he had qualified. Because of the acrimony that developed at this time between inspectors and teachers a Vice-Regal Committee of Inquiry, under Sir Samuel Dill, was appointed in 1913 and as a result of their recommendations a new and more acceptable salary scale was introduced in 1917.

A New Approach 1900-1922

The achievements of the national board were impressive. The number of its schools increased from 789 in 1833 to 4547 in 1850, to 6806 in 1870 and 8684 in 1900. Although the population had declined from 8,175,124 in 1841 to 4,704,750 in 1891 school attendance had increased six-fold. There was a corresponding increase in literacy, especially among Catholics. According to the census of 1861 the percentage of Catholics who could neither read nor write in Belfast was 30.2, in Antrim 34.1 and in Down 38.3. By 1891 there had been a remarkable improvement and percentages then read for Belfast 14.4, for Antrim 18.1 and for Down 21.6. All this was achieved by concentration on a narrow range of subjects and a methodology in the classroom that was rigorous and mechanical. Because of this, as the nineteenth century drew to a close, dissatisfaction was expressed at the bookish nature of the education provided and at the schools' failure to provide adolescents with many of the skills required in the outside world. The child-centred movement, inspired by the writings of Pestalozzi and Froebel, was also a persistent lobby and insisted that the needs and interests of the pupils should provide the central focus around which school programmes should be framed.

The Belmore Commission, appointed in 1897, investigated contemporary educational trends in Britain, Europe and America and appointed Dr. William Starkie as Resident Commissioner to implement its main proposals. The results system was abolished and in 1900 a Revised Programme for National Schools was introduced which added drawing, elementary science, physical education and manual instruction to the curriculum in addition to the three Rs. The school was to be made more attractive to pupils, and teachers were expected to adapt the general programme to local conditions. But the scope and nature of the changes were disconcerting for teachers of settled habits and they needed encouragement (in some cases retraining) if they were to respond to the challange. The Treasury was unwilling to provide the funds required and in these circumstances exciting new ideas on the design and equipment of national schools stood no chance of success. Nevertheless some teachers, liberated from the bureaucratic form of inspection, were tempted out of their classrooms with their pupils to visit sites of local geographical and historical interest.

Problems of Finance and Control

The British Treasury had never been happy at the way in which national education was financed in Ireland. Up to 1849 the money available to the board came from a fund placed annually at the disposal of the Lord Lieutenant, to whom the commissioners furnished their estimates and accounts. After 1849 their expenses were met from a parliamentary vote and, as this increased during the nineteenth century, the Treasury concerned itself with the elimination of unnecessary expenditure. But what annoyed the Treasury most was the lack of local financial support for schools and the lack of community involvement in their management. The Chief Secretaries George Wyndham and Augustine Birrell would have liked to restructure the system, but were frustrated by the Home Rule controversy and the outbreak of the First World War. Then in 1919 their successor, Ian MacPherson, introduced a radical measure which proposed to abolish the nominated boards which administered primary, secondary and technical education, and to replace them by a single department with himself as head, assisted by an advisory committee on which all interested parties would be represented. Each county and county borough was to have an education committee, which would raise a local rate and take responsibility for the heating, lighting and cleaning of the schools. Immediately the Catholic bishops sprang to the defence of the existing system and, outside Ulster, MacPherson's proposals did not prove any more acceptable to county and district councils. In these circumstances the government withdrew the Bill and the national system remained intact until the Union came to an end.

Reform and Controversy in Northern Ireland

The Government Of Ireland Act, 1920, provided for the setting up of two governments in Ireland, one for the six Ulster counties which were to form Northern Ireland, and the other for the rest of the country. The Northern Ireland parliament was opened by King George V on the 22 June 1921, and Sir James Craig became Prime Minister. Responsibility for education was transferred from Dublin to a new Ministry of Education for Northern Ireland, under Lord Londonderry, and a period of rapid reform began.

The Ulster Unionist MPs at Westminster had welcomed MacPherson's bill of 1919, with its proposals for the establishment of local education authorities, with powers of rating and with responsibility for the building and maintenance of schools, the organisation of medical and dental services, the provision of school meals and a schools book scheme. This was understandable for Belfast had suffered terribly under the national system which left the initiative to local patrons and it was calculated that 12,000 children were without school accommodation of any kind. On his appointment as Minister of Education, Lord Londonderry brought all branches of education under the control of a single department, and appointed the Lynn

Committee to advise him on how these services could be coordinated and improved. The committee recommended that borough and county councils be made the responsible education authorities for their areas and that, at district level, popular involvement should be obtained by the appointment of school management committees. Thus after nearly a century the national system was dismantled and replaced by one more in line with that introduced in England and Wales by the Balfour Act of 1902. From now on England was to provide the model for Northern Ireland and, within a decade, the educational systems in the two parts of Ireland had significantly diverged.

The Education Act Of 1923

The Education Act of 1923 gave legislative form to the Lynn Committee's recommendations. The new LEAs were empowered to provide schools, to accept schools transferred to them and to give limited assistance to voluntary school authorities who were prepared to cooperate with them; they were also empowered to employ teachers and to oblige parents to send their children to school between the ages of six and fourteen. The Act was drafted fairly quickly, but its implementation was hampered by a lack of experienced administrators, either at the centre or in the regions. Not a great deal of work has been done on the administrative history of these years, but it is clear that the decision of Andrew Napoleon Bonaparte Wyse to move north from Dublin was crucial to the success of Lord Londonderry's new department and to the fact that he concerned himself with elementary education where the need was greatest. The Ministry's priorities were: (1) to remedy the Belfast situation as quickly as possible; (2) to create the new structures in the regions and to have them efficiently staffed; (3) to amalgamate small schools; and (4) to revise the curriculum to take account of Northern Ireland's position as an integral part of the United Kingdom. These were formidable objectives to undertake in a period of turmoil. At the top the government came under relentless clerical and political pressure but at a local level the foundations of the new system were sucessfully laid: sites were found, schools were amalgamated, greatly improved attendances were achieved and a new curriculum was introduced in 1932 which lasted almost to our own day. To their credit, administrators, school inspectors, managers and teachers ignored the fierce battles about principle being waged around them and cooperated to provide for the children the best education possible.

Clerical and Political Pressure

Like Stanley in 1831, Lord Londonderry was determined that every public elementary school in Northern Ireland (the term national school was abandoned) should, if possible, attract children of all religious denominations and the Education Act of 1923 decreed that schools that were financed from central government funds should not provide religious instruction within the hours of compulsory attendance or take religious affiliation into account when appointing teachers. Londonderry argued that this was the only course open to him, as the Government of Ireland Act, 1920, forbade him to 'make a law so as either directly or indirectly to establish or endow any religion'. It was naive of Lord Londonderry to expect that the churches would surrender the privileges they had won from the national board during the nineteenth century. But whereas the Catholic bishops had made the running in the days of the national board, in Northern Ireland the main Protestant denominations, because of the political leverage they could exercise as Unionists, had the school system altered to meet their demands regarding Bible instruction and the appointment of teachers by the amending Acts of 1925 and 1930. The Protestant churches now began to transfer their schools, and by the end of 1932 66 per cent of Protestant pupils were attending provided or transferred schools.

The Catholic authorities could have little bargaining power in the conditions prevailing in Northern Ireland in the early 1920s and what they had was weakened by their refusal to serve on the Lynn Committee. There were 50 parish priests who were prepared to accept four-and-two committees – Bangor, Ballymena and one or two parishes in the diocese of Clogher – but the great majority did not, and apart from the teachers' salaries, received no aid from public funds. It was not until 1930 that a rapprochment was attempted, when doubts having been raised with the British Home Secretary about the legality of certain provisions of the Education Act of that year, the Craigavon government made their first concession to voluntary schools of a 50 per cent grant on approved capital expenditure.

There was little further progress until after the second world war, when Northern Ireland, following the example of Britain, raised the school-leaving age to 15, and decided to provide free secondary education for all children from 12 to 15. This caused fundamental change and almost all Protestant schools transferred to the LEAs. It was clear that the Catholic school authorities had not the resources to upgrade or replace existing schools or to provide the facilities and apparatus that post-war education required. In 1968 an amendment act came to their aid by providing that the church authorities would recieve 80 per cent towards capital expenditure and 100 per cent for maintenence, if they were agreeable to one third of schools' management committees to be nominated by the Government or the LEAs. By the late 1970s almost all Catholic schools had achieved what was known as 'maintained' status. Considering how well the system has worked out in practice and the benefits that have flowed from it, one cannot but regret that trust, on both sides, took such a long time to achieve. Nevertheless, it was disconcerting to learn from recent research that Catholics voluntary schools were still disadvantaged not only in capital expenditure but in grants towards revenue expenditure as well.

The Way Forward and EMU

In the 1980s the British government, concerned about what were alleged to be falling standards in all sectors of education, proposed a number of major reforms which altered the financing and management of schools and provided a national curriculum and a common means of assessing the progress of all pupils in grant-aided schools. Comparable measures were introduced here by the Education Reform (Northern Ireland) Order 1989. A discussion paper which preceded the drafting of the Order acknowledged the high standards which generally prevailed in Northern Ireland schools but expressed concern that at primary level there was undue attention to a narrow range of skills, so that many pupils had no experience of activities involving science, creative work and physical education. The Education Order sought to redress that imbalance and a Northern Ireland Curriculum Council was appointed to advise the Department of Education on a balanced and broadly based curriculum and to work in close liaison with the Northern Ireland Schools Examinations and Assessment Council in establishing the assessment criteria for pupils at the ages of 7, 11, 14 and 16.

There is little new in education and some of the reasoning in the Order resembles that in the Report of the Commission on Practical and Manual Instruction 1897 (the Belmore Commission) and the Vice-Regal Commission on Primary Schools in 1913, while the prescribed programmes of study for each subject, attainment targets and statements of attainment evoke for some a return to the rigidity of the 'payment by results' era. Teachers have accepted the challenge of the new order but there are some fears that the administration and frequent testing involved may reduce the time they can spend on essential classroom teaching.

Protestant and Catholic children in Northern Ireland are, for the most part, educated in separate schools and it is often claimed that this separation contributes to the perpetuation of the bitter sectarian divisions for which the province is notorious. Controlled and voluntary schools are superficially similar, but there are inevitably different emphases within the syllabuses and difference also in events commemorated and in the games played. As long ago as 1962, Barritt and Carter in their book *The Northern Ireland Problem* commented on this fact and observed: 'The first change needed here is that both Protestants and Catholics should be willing to learn more of the other's heritage and beliefs.' Twenty-five years later the Department of Education attempts to facilitate that process by including the cross-curricular themes of *Education for Mutual Understanding* and *Cultural Heritage* in the national curriculum. In his book *The Price of Peace*, Cardinal Daly wrote:

> I welcome the commitment of the present Minister of Education, Dr Brian Mawhinney, to the promotion and facilitation of Education for Mutual Understanding, and I am glad to say that this movement is being strongly supported throughout the Catholic school system. I welcome also the inclusion of cross-curricular themes in education programmes, including mutual understanding and heritage. I support the government commitment to the belief that 'the curriculum of every child should include elements of Education for Mutual Understanding which has already helped to foster valuable cross-community contacts among many of our schools'.

Schools are rightly regarded as indispensable vehicles for acculturation but the changing of deep-seated suspicions and prejudices is a mammoth task and schools certainly cannot achieve it on their own.

10

Health and Welfare in Ulster since 1891

E. MARGARET CRAWFORD

'There is no doubt that the vitality of the Irish people has seriously diminished... When one looks at an Irish crowd one could almost tell the diet of most of them. These anaemic girls have tea running in their veins instead of blood. Those weedy-looking boys have been fed on white bread. The new diet is more expensive than the old. We not only pay more for it in cash, but we pay more for it in sickness, in loss of vitality and of pleasure in life, and capacity.'

AE (George Russell) *Irish Homestead*, 1913.

Notwithstanding the rise in living standards following the Famine, late-nineteenth century Ireland was an unhealthy place. Tuberculosis plagued the nation, killing more people than any other disease. Dr Henry O'Neill, editor of the *Belfast Health Journal*, wrote in 1891, 'one person out of every six dies of consumption ... (and though) we hear much of the ravages of typhoid fever, ... where typhoid slays one, consumption slays six or seven.' Unlike Britain, where tuberculosis was on the decline, tuberculosis remained rife well into the twentieth century.

Many believed that tuberculosis was hereditary and a stigma on victims and family alike; sympathetic doctors, therefore, recorded tuberculosis deaths as 'pneumonia or respiratory disease'. In fact, the disease was an infection spread by droplets carried through the air, or by contaminated cooking utensils or infected dairy products. It was no respecter of class or creed. What differentiated the classes was the intensity of its ravages. Tuberculosis was severe among the poor; the better-off suffered less because of lower frequency of exposure, superior nutrition and better living conditions.

The appalling death rate in Belfast at the turn of the century was brought to public notice by Sir John Byers, of Queen's College, Belfast in 1906. High mortality, especially among young working-class females, pointed a suspicious finger at the poor factory conditions, particularly in the linen industry. A moist atmosphere was required and the clothes of workers became soaked with water. In wet garments, they made their way home to ill-ventilated houses and meals of bread and tea. When one member of the family was stricken tuberculosis spread rapidly among the others.

Numerous statutory and voluntary organisations tried to combat the 'white plague'. In 1878 Drs Purdon and Simpson opened a dispensary in Donegall Pass, Belfast exclusively for the treatment of chest diseases which became the Hospital for Consumption and Diseases of the Chest. By 1881 it had moved to Joy Street, and moved again to College Square North. In 1896 it was amalgamated with the recently- built Forster Green hospital, established with funds given by the prominent Belfast tea merchant, Forster Green.

In 1908 the Tuberculosis Prevention Act pioneered legislation to control the disease. It allowed county councils to provide hospitals and dispensaries specially for the treatment of tuberculosis. A year before, the Countess of Aberdeen founded the Women's National Health Association, one of its aims being to fight the ravages of tuberculosis. A key feature of its campaign was the travelling caravan containing exhibits to educate the community about the disease, and a team to lecture on, and demonstrate healthful cookery. By the outbreak of the First World War, three hospitals were accepting

Christmas Day in the Workhouse: a children's ward in Belfast Union Infirmary about 1906
Ulster Museum

tuberculosis patients from Belfast and surrounding districts. They were the Throne hospital, the Abbey Sanatorium at Whiteabbey and Forster Green Hospital. In 1946 the Northern Ireland Tuberculosis Authority was created. By then, successful treatment was close at hand in the form of streptomycin. The scourge of tuberculosis soon became a shadow of the past.

During the first half of the nineteenth century cholera had paid several unwelcome visits to Ireland with devastating consequences. Early in 1892 the press warned of a fresh epidemic spreading from Afghanistan. Initially, medical opinion was confident that the disease would be halted in Europe, but in July 1892 cholera reached London. The following month the *Irish News* warned that 'Belfast people have no reason to feel much assurance as to their safety, for cholera is no respecter of persons'. The Belfast Board of Guardians did prepare a small unit with six beds, and appointed a doctor and two nurses to attend the victims. Their judgment proved right, for no widespread epidemic materialised. Although cholera reached Ireland in 1893, Belfast suffered only 112 cases, a fraction of earlier visitations and half the measles mortality for that year.

A quarter of a century after the spectre of cholera was finally laid Ireland, like much of Europe, was afflicted by a lethal epidemic of influenza, described by an editorial in the *Irish News* of October 1918 as 'the new plague (which) bids fair to become one of the most formidable enemies of the human race... since the days of the Black Death'. Influenza spread rapidly and by, October, the country was in its grip.

Despite great public concern, the City Corporation was accused of fuelling the spread of the disease by its intransigence in settling a strike of binmen. As influenza raged, admissions to hospitals soared, medical staff were hard pressed to cope and the military authorities offered help. Doctors, nurses and the clergy, by the nature of their occupations, were very vulnerable. The Rev. Thomas Murray, the chaplain to the Mater hospital, was an early victim. In its tribute, *Irish News* revealed his fortitude, 'working to the last hour of his young life's strength, ministering with noble zeal to the influenza-strickened patients in the Mater'. The nursing profession suffered too. So critical was the shortage that Londonderry Guardians granted nurses an additional five shillings per week during the epidemic. In addition, volunteers were recruited.

The Belfast Corporation eventually engaged in a flurry of activity. Factories, workshops and other public places were disinfected with Jeyes fluid. Quinine tablets were recommended as a preventative. During November 1918 the epidemic was reported to be on the increase, and fear was expressed that large crowds on the streets to celebrate the signing of the Armistice would fuel the spread of infection. School attendance sharply declined and

many closed. Picture houses were asked to shut, though many did not comply. In Ulster over 7,500 died of influenza during 1918/19 and in Belfast almost 2,000 succumbed.

Tuberculosis and influenza raged against a background of endemic infections. Deaths from infectious diseases remained stubbornly high in the late nineteenth century. Typhoid, typhus, diphtheria, scarlet fever, measles, whooping cough and cholera together contributed to over 10 per cent of total deaths annually during the 1890s, compared with fewer than 0.5 per cent today. In 1891 Belfast was the unhealthiest city in Ireland, apart from Dublin. The Corporation was sufficiently concerned to set up a special committee to consider public health. This concluded that while overall mortality was not excessive for an industrial centre, the death rate from infectious diseases was unusually high.

One disease particularly prevalent in Belfast was typhoid fever. Its incidence was nearly six times greater than in Manchester, and more than twice that of Dublin. Typhoid was transmitted by contaminated water or food. Shellfish gathered along the polluted shores of Belfast Lough and sold by hawkers in working- class areas was identified as a major agent for spreading the disease.

Infant mortality too was very high. The first year of life was particularly hazardous. Deaths of infants under one year old constituted one-eighth of the entire country's deaths. The northern counties had a particularly bad record. In Belfast in 1915 the infant mortality rate was 137 per 1000, as compared with only 7 per 1000 for 1989.

Poor housing, poverty, lack of hygiene, and inadequate hospital accommodation all played a part in keeping Belfast unhealthy. The poor, aged and infirm without relatives to care for them had no alternative but to enter the much-hated workhouse. Irish poor law administration provided medical relief, and every workhouse had an infirmary with an appointed medical officer. In 1862 workhouse infirmaries were opened to the sick who were not destitute. Facilities were meagre and the 'nursing staff' largely consisted of able-bodied female inmates. There was prejudice against these hospitals and so they were the ports of last resort.

In addition, there were numerous hospitals supported by voluntary subscriptions including the Belfast Royal Hospital in Frederick Street, later to become the Royal Victoria Hospital (Grosvenor Road), the Belfast Hospital for Sick Children and the Mater Infirmorium Hospital, founded by Bishop Dorrian in 1883 at Bedeque House on the Crumlin Road. Notwithstanding this clutch of institutions, the Medical Superintendent Officer of Health, Dr Whitaker, lamented in 1896 'that in no large city in the three kingdoms is there so little accommodation for the sick'. Ten years later a fever hospital

Insanitary housing at Mitchell's Court, off the Shankill Road, 1912
Ulster Museum

was built near Purdysburn and opened by Lord Aberdeen, the Lord Lieutenant of Ireland.

In 1851, an Irish dispensary service had been established under the control of the Poor Law Commission. It was available to all who could not afford to pay for medical attention. Initially Ireland was divided into 723 dispensary districts, each with one or more medical officers. Because doctors wishing to enter the dispensary service had to hold certificates in medicine, surgery and midwifery, a new breed within the medical profession emerged, the 'general practitioner'.

Treatment for the mentally ill was very primitive. Some lived in the workhouses, but others were housed in lunatic asylums. The Belfast District Hospital for the Insane Poor had been established in 1829 and was located on the present site of the Royal Victoria Hospital. It was replaced by Purdysburn Demesne in 1894.

July 5 1948 marked a major turning-point in the provision of health care in the form of the National Health Service. 'From the cradle to the grave' general medical, dental, eye and pharmaceutical services became available to the entire community. Initially there was opposition to the scheme from many quarters, not least the medical profession. The *Irish News*, too, was not impressed, venting its scepticism in the editorial under the title 'Dependence Day', and remarking that 'those opposing the social measures that begin today may be denounced as cranks and faddists. But time will show which side is right.' Opposition eroded, however, and the NHS was used by virtually the whole population, diminishing death rates reflecting its success.

Improvements in health care, combined with major medical discoveries, changed morbidity and mortality patterns. Cholera, smallpox, diphtheria, typhoid, typhus fever and tuberculosis no longer plague our society, and rarely do measles, whooping cough and scarlet fever threaten our lives. Affluence, however, has brought a crop of new diseases to the fore. Heart disease, to name but one, is now a major killer, being particularly prevalent in Northern Ireland. Nevertheless, there are few Irishmen who would wish to return to the disease-ridden environment of their forefathers.

11

The Land Question in Ulster

1845-1950

FRANK THOMPSON

In 1886, Paschal Grousset, a French journalist travelling in Ireland, observed that the land in Ulster was better cultivated and agriculture more prosperous than in the south and west of Ireland. Yet, he continued, 'even in Ulster...the tenant bears chafingly the yoke of landlordism'. In other words, the land question — that is, the question of landlord-tenant relations — was no less an issue in the north than it was in the rest of the country.

Ulster in the second half of the nineteenth century was still a predominantly rural society. Although the province was less seriously affected by the Great Famine than the south and west, it did not escape entirely unscathed. Labourers and cottiers, as one might expect, were hit hardest by the catastrophe, but all classes of rural society suffered to some degree, even the landed classes, a number of whose members were forced to sell out.

Landlordism, however, remained in the post-famine years as powerful an institution as ever. In a society in which over eighty per cent of the population depended on agriculture for a living, three quarters of all the land was in the possession of only five hundred individuals with the forty largest proprietors owning between them no less than a quarter of the entire province. Prominent among these were great landed aristocrats such as the Duke of Abercorn with 68,000 acres in Tyrone and Donegal and the Marquis of Downshire with 75,000 acres in Down. The average estate, of course, was a good deal smaller than this, but it was aristocrats such as Abercorn and Downshire and the larger landed gentry who, on the basis of their interest in land, dominated the economic, social and political life of the province.

If nineteenth-century Ulster was a province of large estates, it was also one of small farms. Although tenant numbers had been seriously depleted by the Famine, there were still in 1871 nearly 200,000 tenants, the great majority of them holding land on a yearly basis, liable in theory to be evicted at the whim of the landlord or to have their rents raised without notice or reason. Tenant grievances in the north, however, were never as acute and landlord-tenant hostility never as palpable as in the south and west. Practically half of the Ulster tenants were Protestants, mainly Presbyterians, who generally held the better land and whose fear of Catholicism encouraged them to identify more closely with the landed ascendancy than they might otherwise have done.

The landlord-tenant relationship, in fact, was complex and reciprocal. In return for social and political deference, landlords were expected not to press to the limit their rights under a legal system which, up to 1870, allowed the tenant virtually no rights at all. It was unusual, for example, for a tenant to be evicted for arrears of less than three or four years' rent. And landlords were expected to contribute to local charities, support schools, infirmaries, orphanages and generally take an interest in the well-being of their communities (though it should be said that these social donations rarely amounted to more than a fraction of their income from rents).

Tenants in the north also had the protection of the so-called Ulster custom of tenant-right. Under this custom — and it was only a custom — a tenant was allowed, firstly, to remain in undisturbed possession of his farm as long as he paid his rent and, secondly, to sell his interest in the holding — his tenant-right — at the end of his tenancy. Because of this custom, tenants were believed to have a greater incentive to invest and this, it was maintained, explained the greater prosperity and relative tranquillity of the northern province.

Yet tenant-right was not the panacea for agrarian ills that it has sometimes been made out to be. Indeed, it was not even confined to Ulster. Similar customs were to be found on many of the larger estates in the south. And there were estates in the north where tenant-right was not recognised at all. Moreover, the agricultural statistics of the period lend little support to the view that agriculture in Ulster was more efficient than elsewhere in the country. Donegal, for example, where the custom was well established, was one of the most critically impoverished counties in Ireland. Flax, linen-weaving and industrialisation had perhaps more to do with the relative prosperity of the north than tenant-right.

Nor was tenant-right any guarantee against eviction. Admittedly evictions in Ulster after the immediate post-famine years were uncommon and farms frequently remained in the same families for generations. But evictions did happen. The years of the Famine period — with over 5,000 evictions in Ulster between 1849 and 1852 — and events such as the notorious Derryveagh clearances of 1861, in which 47 families were put out of their holdings so that the landowner could create a sheeprun, were not easily forgotten. Small tenants, of course, were always more likely to get into difficulties and therefore always more at risk. But no tenant could forget that at the end of the day, whether he paid his rent or not, he was totally dependent on the goodwill of the landlord. The tenants' complaint was less against what landlords did than what they had the power to do.

It was the same with rents. It was generally accepted that rents in Ulster were, on average, moderately set and on most estates it was unusual for revaluations to be made at intervals of less than twenty or thirty years. However, there were properties where rent-raising was arbitrary and excessive, and there were examples — many examples — of rack-rents. Modern research has shown that the majority of landlords did not maximise their rents, preferring rather a guaranteed regular income and a quiet life. But it was not the majority of landlords that the tenants complained about; it was the minority who abused their position and, more particularly, a system which allowed them to do so.

Agriculture actually prospered in Ireland in the decades after the Famine with farmers taking advantage of an expanding market for meat and dairy products in Belfast and Britain. Bank deposits, housing, diet, education and every other aspect of economic and social well-being improved during these years. Of course, not all farmers benefited to the same extent, or in some cases at all, from this new rural prosperity. There were still areas — west

'The Most Unpleasant Duty': Members of the Royal Irish Constabulary escorting a bailiff to a rural eviction at the turn of the century
Irish News

Donegal, south Armagh, the mountain areas of Monaghan, Tyrone, Derry and other counties — where inadequate housing, poor diet, and the absence of virtually all the material comforts continued to be the norm; and there were still tens of thousands of tenants who never enjoyed, even in good times, more than a frugal level of subsistence. In 1871 some fifty per cent of Ulster farms were under 15 acres in size, and tenants on these farms, especially with the decline in handloom-weaving in the post-famine decades, never found it easy to make ends meet.

However, while many tenants in different parts of the province remained poor and dependent, there had clearly emerged in Ulster by the 1860s a tenant class which was rapidly acquiring all the trappings of middle-class life. The paradox was that the more prosperous they became, the more insecure they felt because the more they had to lose; and in Ulster this meant not only their tenure and their standard of living, but also a tenant-right investment in the soil which was variously estimated in the 1870s at between £20-£40 million.

It was the uncertainty surrounding tenant-right and fear for its value which more than any other single factor caused tenant unrest and disquiet in Ulster. Poor harvests, a higher rate of eviction and attacks on tenant-right encouraged northern tenants to join in the agitation for land reform in the immediate post-famine years. This campaign died out with the rise in prosperity during the 1850s, but towards the end of the following decade, in the face of landlord threats to tenant-right, there was renewed agitation for protective legislation. Gladstone's Land Act of 1870 was more successful than most historians have allowed, giving at least a measure of legal protection to tenant-right which had not been there in the past. But it did not fully settle the question. Continuing doubts about tenant-right and especially the failure of the act to control rents created demands during the 1870s for amending legislation.

These demands were taken up by the Ulster Liberal Party which, because of its support for tenant-right, was able to enjoy unprecedented growth in the province. For the Presbyterian middle-class leaders of this party and for many Presbyterian ministers, land was an issue on which they could challenge the Tory government and landed ascendancy in the province. But the tenants themselves rarely looked beyond their own immediate interests. Their main objective was land reform and most of them supported the Liberal Party only because it suited them to do so.

Indeed, with the depression in agriculture at the end of the 1870s, many of them were equally prepared to support the Land League. For a brief period it looked as though the land question might bring the Protestant tenants of the north into the nationalist movement. In reality, however, there was little danger of this happening. It was the potential of the League for securing land reform and reducing rents that attracted Protestant support, not any sympathy with the political objectives of the League leaders. Once Gladstone conceded their demands, Protestant tenant support for the League — and, indeed, for the Liberal party – quickly fell off. And with the emergence of Home Rule as the paramount issue in the 1880s, Ulster divided along hard sectarian lines.

Gladstone's Land Act of 1881 gave the tenants what they had been campaigning for during the previous decade — security of tenure, fair rents to be settled by arbitration and the legal right to sell their interest in their holdings. No longer was landlord power unbridled. But the land question did not cease to be important. More and more tenants wanted to buy their farms and, with many landlords reluctant to sell, the demand developed during the 1890s — under the leadership of the maverick Liberal Unionist MP for South Tyrone, T.W. Russell — for the compulsory sale of estates.

A series of acts from the mid-1880s provided facilities for tenant purchase. However, the major breakthrough came in 1903 when the Wyndham Land Act introduced terms which were generous to landlords and tenants alike. This act, in conjunction with amending legislation in 1909, brought about a social revolution in the countryside. By 1914 nearly seventy per cent of Ulster farmers owned their farms. A further Act in 1925 introduced the principle of compulsory sale so that the landed estates which had dominated rural life in the nineteenth century finally disappeared. The landed classes, it is true, continued to play an important part in public life, but land purchase had fundamentally changed the structure of rural society.

The land question from the mid-nineteenth century had been perceived as a question of land tenure and landlord-tenant relations. That problem was effectively solved by government legislation. But other more intractable economic problems remained. Land purchase, in itself, did little to ensure greater agricultural efficiency or greater productivity. Indeed, it can be argued that it had the reverse effect, that it tended to fossilise fields and holdings that were in many parts of the province too small for efficient commercial farming. Agriculture, after a temporary boom during the first world war, was depressed for much of the inter-war period. The introduction of protection, subsidies and quotas from the 1930s and, in particular, the second world war stimulated recovery but, as always, it was to unevenly distributed. Small farmers still found it difficult make farming profitable and migration from the rural areas continued.

The single most important development during the whole of this period was the break-up of the landed estates and the transfer of land ownership. But for the small farmer, the fundamental struggle for survival continued. In this respect, at least, things remained the same.

12

Industry in the North of Ireland
since the 1890s

PETER COLLINS

The industrial and agricultural history of the north of Ireland, over the last hundred years, has been one of uneven development. As the economy of the region has largely been export-orientated it has been inordinately affected by the vagaries of the world trading and financial systems. Thus the effects of financial and trading depressions such as 1908, the twenties and thirties and latterly the seventies and eighties have been most marked here. In addition, having been intimately bound up economically with Britain and the empire, during a period of decline for the former and a loosening of the links with the latter, the economic fortunes of the north have consequently declined. This however was emphatically not the case in the earlier period in that, as that fortunes of the empire were riding high, so also prospered Belfast and its hinterland. After World War One, there was a short boom followed by a wider slump. The north, in common with other regions in Britain still depending on traditional industries such as textiles, shipbuilding and engineering, went into a downward spiral. The new electronic, chemical and motor industries did not take a hold in Northern Ireland between the wars.

There has not been a total inexorable decline during this century, however. For example, both world wars have ushered in economic booms particularly in and around Belfast. In the 1960s there was a moderate boom led by the world trading upturn and in some measure also through government encouragement of incoming multinationals. This was slowed down in the seventies by the economic slump in the west, resulting from the sharp rise in oil prices, and virtually killed off by the dismal effects of twenty-five years of conflict. More recently there are again grounds for optimism generated by the 1994 ceasefires and the pledge of international financial aid and investment as well as a significant increase in tourism.

The north was at its economic zenith at the turn of the century. In Belfast, the scale and variety of industries was breaktaking. Linen, the prime industry, had set in motion the growth of Belfast as an industrial centre. That industry was also widespread in the Lagan Valley and elsewhere in mill villages such as Bessbrook and Sion Mills. The linen industry employed about 70,000, mainly women. Of these some 65,000 were in factory employment, a figure which rose to 75,000 by 1913. In addition 18,000, mainly women, were employed in factories and many more as outworkers, in the off-shoot shirt-making industry around Derry. The shipbuilding industry largely grew up to serve linen by bringing over Scottish coal and carry the finished products for export from the port of Belfast. By the turn of the century, there were two yards in Belfast, Harland and Wolff employing in 1914, 14,000 and the so-called 'wee yard' of Workman Clark, which had 7,000 employees by 1902. In the years 1909-1912, Harland and Wolff's gross tonnage output was 342,000, while that of Workman Clark reached 290,000 tons, making Belfast arguably the largest centre of shipbuilding in the world.

Workers emerging from the Belfast shipyards in 1911
Irish News

Another spin-off industry was ropemaking which grew up to supply the maritime industry. Belfast Ropeworks also supplied the needs of many other industries and pursuits, so much so that by 1900, with 3,000 employees, it was the largest such enterprise in the world. Engineering was closely linked to both linen and shpbuilding. Textile machinery, produced at first for the local industry, was soon being exported to textile areas as far away as Catalonia, the Indian subcontinent and South America. Belfast foundries such as the Albert Foundry of James Mackie and James Combe's Falls Foundry, later Combe Barbour, and about eighteen foundries beyond Belfast supplied the textile industry. Coates made steam engines, water turbines and electricity generators. Musgrave Brothers made stoves which were widely exported and, indeed, reconditioned versions of their Belfast Stove are much sought after in Europe today. The Sirocco Works of Samuel Davidson, a Comber man, who patented tea-drying machinery while working in the Assam plantations, was one of the world's leaders in ventilating equipment. Indeed both the British and German fleets had Sirocco ventilation equipment at the Battle of Jutland. There was a continuous interchange of employees and engineering skills between these enterprises and the shipyards.

Diversification, particularly in Belfast, gave a multiplicity of employment opportunities for both men and women. The largest tobacco factory in the world was that of Thomas Gallaher in York Street, Belfast which employed at one time 3,000, mainly women. Murray Brothers of Sandy Row exported pipe tobacco all over the world. Belfast was also a centre of printing. The leading firm of Marcus Ward were pioneers of the Christmas card and manufacturers of Vere Foster school stationery. McCaw, Stevenson and Orr produced labels for packaging which were also used in the linen mail order business from warehouses such as Robinson Cleavers. David Allen became such a big supplier of colour posters for theatre and advertising billboards that the firm eventually moved its headquarters to London. Whiskey distilling was important to Belfast, Derry, Coleraine and Bushmills. Belfast, in fact, accounted for well over half the Irish whiskey exports, at a time when it was still almost as popular as Scotch. Mineral water was a Belfast speciality due to the very pure artesian springs at Cromac. Names known throughout the world were Corry, Grattan, Cantrell and Cochrane and Ross while Belfast manufacturers laid claim to the origination of tonic water and ginger ale. There were many other smaller scale industries, usually family firms. In the second half of the nineteenth century, the rapid expansion of Belfast had led to a boom in the construction industry providing houses, factories, offices and warehouses and many impressive city-centre buildings such as the City Hall which was under construction from 1898 to 1906.

So great was the volume of imports and exports being handled by the port of Belfast that it went from third biggest in Ireland in 1800 to third in the United Kingdom, behind only London and Liverpool, by 1900. There was consequently a large number of men employed in the docks and carting. They felt that they were not sharing in the wealth of their city and so in

1907, led by Jim Larkin, the dockers and carters became locked for months in an epic strike against an employers' combine led by the tobacco magnate Thomas Gallaher who was also chairman of the Belfast Steamship Company. The strike's length and ultimate failure caused great hardship for the poorest of Belfast's citizens. The following year, Belfast was badly hit in the international trade slump which followed the 1907 American financial crash. There was great distress in the city and soup kitchens were set up in the poorer districts. However, the city soon put these disasters behind and resumed its 'business as usual' stance.

With the outbreak of war in 1914, Belfast, in particular, experienced a boom created by wartime demands. Many foundries switched to munitions production. Linen was in great demand for uniforms, tents, hospital supplies, threads and aircraft fuselages and the workforce reached 90,000. Thirty thousand were employed in the shipyards in building, refitting or replacing battleships, hospital ships and merchantmen. Harland's tonnage in the war years amounted to approximately 400,000, while that of the Workman Clark reached some 260,000 tons. The Belfast Ropeworks provided half the Admiralty and War Office rope and cordage requirement. By the end of the war, aircraft production had begun in Belfast. For farmers, war meant increased demand and higher prices, particularly in the British market. The area of land under the plough, in what became the six counties of Northern Ireland, increased from 637,681 acres in 1910 to 856, 719 in 1918.

After the war there was a short boom while the backlog in demand for consumer goods and housing was made up. In 1919 the demand for linen goods and replacement merchant ships reached its peak. This was not to last and the boom of the last decade now gave way to a pernicious period of depression that would only be mitigated by another world conflict. From 1921 on, the worldwide slump hit Belfast hard, especially as the demand for new ships was now sated. The southern boycott of Belfast goods, during the 'troubles' which attended partition, temporarily made matters worse. However trading links between the north and the rest of Ireland had never been strong. Only border towns like Newry and Derry City, with hinterlands now in the Free State, were hit economically by partition. The traditional basic industries of shipbuilding and linen were in decline and no attempt was made to replace them with the newer type of electronic, chemical and automobile industries that were being introduced in the midlands and south-east of England. Northern Ireland was no different in this than other regions like the north-east and north-west of England or the Clyde. The new Northern Ireland government showed itself largely unable or unwilling to deal with macroeconomic problems. It was not inclined towards bringing in new enterprises, being very much politically wedded to the linen and engineering manufacturers, while its financial powers were severely restricted by the 1920 Act.

Nevertheless Belfast shipbuilding fared better than that of the British yards in these years. Indeed in 1929, Harlands launched both the greatest overall tonnage and the largest single ship, the *Britannic*. However, even from this position of comparative strength, there was no resisting the whirlwind set in motion by the Wall Street crash. By 1932, employment in shipbuilding stood at a tenth of its pre-1930 level. Unemployment in the industry peaked at 80 per cent. In 1932 only two ships were launched and it was said that grass was growing on the shipyard slipways. In 1935, Workman Clark closed its gates but prospects were improving at Harland and Wolff, partly because it was diversifying into projects such as locomotive building. However, there would not be a full recovery till war came, not least because Belfast appeared not to be getting a fair share of Admiralty contracts. One bright spot in the thirties' tale of industrial woe was the coming to Belfast in 1936 of the aircraft manufacturers Short Brothers which would eventually equal shipbuilding in importance. The linen industry entered a spiral of permanent decline after the immediate post-war boom. This was due to a marked fall in demand for linen due to changing fashions in clothing and household items. There was also competition from foreign dumping and the new man-made textiles. Linen also suffered from the overall inter-war depression with consequent unemployment. By the 1930s, only about 40 per cent of the pre-war level of flax was being processed. However, the Irish industry managed to hold on to its overall share of the shrinking world market.

The other principal industry, agriculture, in which a quarter of the overall workforce was involved, compared to only 7 per cent in Britain, was not shielded from the consequences of world-wide economic difficulties in the inter-war period. Due to a fall in world demand and increased competition from non-belligerent food-producing countries, which had emerged during the Great War, there was a dramatic fall in prices at the beginning of the thirties. Farms were in many cases too small-scale, with 70 per cent under 30 acres and 86 per cent under 50 acres. This resulted not surprisingly in a *per capita* output of less than half of the British figure, though it rose slightly in the thirties. Consolidation of holdings was politically unacceptable to either Unionists or Nationalists. One source of strength was that northern agriculture was much more heavily based on dairying and livestock husbandry than that in Britain. Cereals accounted for only 1.5 per cent of gross agricultural output compared to 10.3 per cent in England and Wales. Pastoral products were more profitable and so, while still far behind in overall output, Northern Ireland improved its relative position in comparision to Britain in the inter-war years. In addition, the Anglo-Irish economic war of 1932-38 temporarily removed southern agricultural competition in the British market. While real incomes rose in farming in this period, it remained the case that farmers, with holdings of less than 30 acres, generally earned less than industrial workers and that farm labourers, with an average weekly wage of 25 to the 30 shillings, had less than the 30 shillings unemployment benefit due to a married man. Government intervention in agriculture did have some effect. The compulsory marketing schemes and subsidies for milk, cattle and bacon which came directly from the Treasury in London, all resulted in increased output. Most spectacularly, the work of the Pigs' Marketing Board resulted in production tripling between 1930 and 1938.

As in 1914-18, the coming of the war in 1939 proved an economic blessing to the north. There was no conscription and as well as the 40,000 who joined up, the industrial expansion during the war led to a massive increase in employment. The shipyard of Harland and Wolff built 170 warships and converted another 3,000 to war purposes. Its workforce peaked at over 30,000 in 1944. Short Brothers, who employed a record 23,000, produced 125 Sunderland flying boats and almost 1,200 Stirling bombers. Mackies worked on aircraft subcontracts for Shorts, but was mainly involved in munitions, producing over seventy-five million shells and sixty-five million bomb components. The linen industry was fully occupied despite the dislocation of traditional flax sources from Russia, Belgium and France. The industry

Linen workers at work in the weaving shop of Brookfield Factory, Belfast, about 1900
Ulster Museum

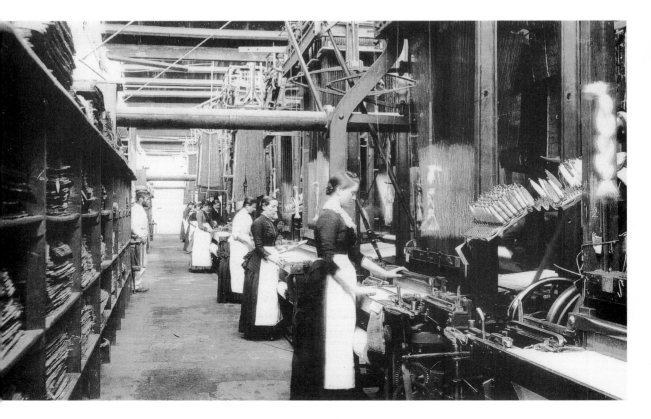

made millions of parachutes, tent covers, machine-gun belts, uniforms and much else for the war effort. The linen mills and factories of provincial towns were commandeered on a much larger scale than in the previous conflict. The number of women employed in traditional male preserves rose dramatically. In engineering the figure rose from 250 in 1939 to 12,300 by 1943. The Belfast Ropeworks supplied a third of the needs of the War Office. Sirocco made grenades, gunmountings and radar parts. Agriculture saw a switch to cereal production with tillage rising by a third. Cattle numbers went up by a fifth, sheep by a quarter and eggs by nearly three-quarters. Pigs declined in numbers due to the lack of the imported feedstuffs required by them.

The ending of war naturally resulted in cut-backs. By 1950, Shorts had reduced its staff by half to 6,000. The shipbuilding industry was filling orders to satisfy the high demand for replacement of war losses. The workforce stabilised at around 20,000. By the end of the fifties, foreign competition and a fall in demand had hit all British yards, not least Harland's. In 1960, it launched its last great liner the *Canberra*, in effect the end of a proud era. Linen, fortunately, still had to catch up on demand stifled by the war. The food processing and clothing industries increased production to keep pace with rising living standards. Ths building industry was involved in rebuilding blitzed dwellings and factories and the new schools and hospitals required in the new post-war Welfare State dispensation.

This mild post-war boom ended with the recession caused in 1951 by the outbreak of the Korean War. Linen was badly hit by this and the competition from cheap imports and man-made fibres. Employment in the industry fell from 76,000 in 1951 to 58,000 in 1958. There was comparatively little local investment in industry, reflecting a loss of confidence in the traditional sectors of the economy. Although Stormont development grant aid was available, it was not much taken up by indigenous enterprises. Rather, it would take outside initiative and investment to create new industrial growth. The Ministry of Commerce, under Brian Faulkner, encouraged inward investment, by British and overseas companies, by tax incentives and advanced factories. The result was the virtual replacement of linen by man-made fibre companies like the British ICI and Courtaulds in East Antrim, the American Dupont in Derry and Dutch Enkalon in Antrim. Tyre manufacturers, American Goodyear in Craigavon and French Michelin at Mallusk, America Ford subsidiary, Autolite at Dunmurry, the American Hughes Tool and British ICL computers at Castlereagh, British Carreras Tobacco in Carrickfergus, German Grundig tape recorders and televisions in Dunmurry and British BSR record players in Derry were all examples of the incoming electronic and light engineering industries that were making up for the decline of the traditional base. Shorts were pursuing the development of new missile technology and planes like the Skyvan. It now employed as many as the shipyard.

In the Belfast area, where some 100,000 were engaged in manufacturing industry, mainly due to the 20,000 new jobs created by the largely multinational incoming firms, unemployment figures sat at only 3 per cent. Naturally this engendered a mood of economic optimism. However, as most of this new industry was sited, largely on government direction, in Counties Antrim and Down, there was criticism, particularly from west of the Bann, of political bias. Certainly towns with high unemployment like Strabane and Newry felt themselves excluded from this industrial renaissance. The building industry was stimulated by the new factories, slum clearance replacement and the creation of satellite towns and dormitory suburbs around Belfast. Gallahers were still in business in Belfast and Ballymena. The Ropeworks had closed down by the end of the seventies, however.

The end of the sixties boom came when the western economy was hit hard by the oil price rise imposed by the Arabs in 1973-4. Northern Ireland, as a peripheral region, was badly affected by the increased transport costs resulting from the oil price rise. The oil crisis was disastrous for Harland and Wolff as it had recently modernised itself to produce supertankers which were no longer needed. In 1974 the Government took over the yard and there followed a decade of huge subsidies and attempts were made at further diversification. Despite this, the yard went from a profit of £2.5 million in 1976 to losses of £25 million, £43 million and £32 million in the three following years. Not surprisingly, the workforce was cut from 9,300 in 1976 to 5,500 in 1985. By the 1970s, most of the linen industry had disappeared. In 1948 the number of workers was 58,000, a figure which by 1978 had contracted to 13,000. Perhaps worse still, many of the new man-made textiles firms that had replaced linen were themselves being wiped out by the recession. The same applied to many other foreign subsidiaries which withdrew to their home bases. The campaign of economic bombing, begun in the early seventies by the Provisional IRA, contributed, of course, to the general rundown of industrial capacity. By 1982, unemployment had reached 17.8 per cent in Belfast and was worse in most provincial centres.

Northern Ireland has not fared badly from the 'Thatcher Revolution', which created a 'leaner and fitter' industrial sector in Britain, resulting in the closure of many firms. For a start, there was not the same high level of industrialisation as in Britain. Also, because of the troubles, the region was treated differently and a higher level of Government investment and subsidy was maintained here. In addition, a large number of civilians have been employed in security-related jobs. So the economic wasteland created in many parts of Britain did not materalise, certainly not as a result of government policy. European funding has helped with infrastructure projects though northern nationalists and particularly farmers have complained that the government has not fully represented the region's case at Brussels. It is easy to contrast favourably the benefits gained by the Republic from Europe, particularly in relation to agriculture. Government bodies like the Industrial Development Board (IDB) and the Local Enterprise Development Unit (LEDU) have been set up to encourage local and incoming industry, with varying degrees of success and some notable blunders such as the Delorean scandal. Other firms from abroad have been accused of cynically milking government incentive schemes and then pulling out.

More recently, an encouraging trickle of investment has begun to come in, from the 'tiger economies' of the Pacific Rim, such as the South Korean Daewoo Electronics, which set up a factory in Antrim. Development bodies such as Laganside Corporation in Belfast and the Londonderry Development Office have set in motion urban regeneration and encouraged enterprise. Schemes like Making Belfast Work and Belfast Action Teams targeted areas of deprivation and poured in money and expert advice to help local private and community enterprises. Enterprise Zones helped give small businesses good accommodation at favourable rates. 'Small is good' is the motto in encouraging local initiative. Building has been stimulated by the Urban Development Grants which has encouraged city shopping developments like Castle Court in Belfast and the building of new office blocks. The cross-harbour road and rail bridge and the continuing programme of the Housing Executive has continued to keep many building firms in business. Local entrepeneurs have scored outstanding success as exemplified by firms like Antrim's Mivan Overseas in construction and Newry's Norbrook Laboratories in pharmaceuticals which have become export leaders.

The 1990s, which began as the third decade of violence, have been transformed by the ceasefire of 31 August 1994. As the peace process develops, one can report optimism tinged with uncertainty. Is there a peace dividend? On the bright side, there is the promise of investment and subventions from Europe and America, in addition to that of the existing International and Ireland Funds. The tourist industry is booming, with plans for at least six new hotels. Yet, with little tangible political *détente*, crises can blow up during the marching season or other significant anniversaries, which threaten the new-found peace. Without a political settlement, the industrialists of the north cannot yet contemplate the forthcoming millennium with optimism. However, if a settlement can be reached, the twenty-first century should be an improvement economically on the present one.

13
Shorts
An Industrial Success Story

EDDIE O'GORMAN

Shorts was set up in November 1908 by three of the four sons of Samuel Short, a colliery manager from the north-east of England. The eldest was 36 year-old Horace — a brilliant engineer who was to live only another eight years after the founding of the company. A childhood accident led to a bout of meningitis and left him with an abnormally large head, which gave him a somewhat intimidating aspect. But his fearsome appearance disguised a sharp intellect and a fierce energy.

But while Horace was to be the driving force behind the development of Short Brothers, it was the enthusiasm of his younger brothers Eustace and Oswald for the increasingly popular pastime of ballooning which led indirectly to the formation of the company. However, it was the younger brother, Oswald, who was the first to realise that the future lay not in balloons, but in powered flight. But he and Eustace soon realised that if they were to move into the business of aircraft manufacturing, they would need the creative genius of their elder brother. The new partnership was registered at Battersea in November 1908, as Short Brothers. It had a capital of £600, with each brother contributing £200.

The company's first aircraft factory was established the following year at Leysdown, on the Isle of Sheppey, where work soon began on a contract for six aircraft for the American aviators Orville and Wilbur Wright. The Wright brothers paid £1,000 for each aircraft, with a down-payment of £200. The engines cost around £400 apiece, and were provided by the customer. That early order has allowed Short Brothers to lay claim ever since to the title of the world's first aircraft manufacturer.

During the First World War, the company concentrated mainly on seaplane development and production, and although Horace's death in April 1917 deprived it of its main driving force, the surviving brothers were determined to carry on the business. But after the company's rapid expansion during the war years, the priority in the immediate post-war period was one of survival. That the company survived at all was a tribute to the outstanding business ability of the youngest brother, Oswald — 'the Kid', as Horace used rather dismissively to refer to him. While securing what orders he could from the RAF and the Admiralty, he also used the Rochester factory on the River Medway in Kent (where production had been transferred early in the war) to make barges, motor boats, and even bus bodies, which were produced in their thousands until well into the 1930s.

Meanwhile, however, the main aeronautical activity at Shorts during the inter-war years was in the development of the all-metal flying boat. But the real breakthrough into civil aircraft manufacture came with the S-8 Calcutta, a three-engined flying boat which made its maiden flight in 1928. It had a maximum cruising speed of 97 mph, and a range of just 650 miles. This meant that there had to be frequent stops for refuelling, so that a journey to the Arabian Gulf could take as long as 12 days.

In 1939, Shorts was also involved in the construction of the four-engined Sunderland flying-boat for the RAF. By that time the factory at Rochester was clearly inadequate for the increasing volume of production, and after long deliberation, the decision was taken to set up the firm's second manufacturing operation in Belfast. In June 1936, a joint company was set up with Harland and Wolff, called Short and Harland, which started turning out twin-engined bombers.

Shorts' main contribution to the war effort was the Stirling bomber, the first four-engined bomber of the war, and an aircraft which bore the brunt of Bomber Command's workload until the emergence of the Halifax and the Lancaster. Meanwhile, the Sunderland continued to reinforce its reputation in its role as a long-range reconnaisance, patrol and anti-submarine aircraft. Around 750 of these famous aircrafts were built, at Rochester and Queen's Island, and it was subsequently said that without them the Battle of the Atlantic could never have been won.

But in its relations with the Ministry of Aircraft Production, Shorts was not so fortunate. Wrangles over production rates and over the Ministry's high-handed attitude in forcing the resignation of Oswald Short as chairman of the company led to much acrimony, which reached its peak when in March 1943 the ministry, without prior warning, took over the company, expropriating all its assets, and beginning 46 years of state ownership.

The end of the war brought a slump in orders as had occurred after 1918, and even though it was now a state-owned company, very little work came Shorts way. In an attempt to stay afloat, it took whatever was available, resorting to the manufacture of milk churns, wringers, and carpet sweepers in its efforts to remain in business. In an attempt to cut costs, the decision was made to close the Rochester factory, the company's main production unit for more than 30 years, and to concentrate its activity on its Belfast plant.

However, Shorts' position improved when, as a result of the outbreak of the Korean War, the government introduced a major rearmament programme, and Shorts became one of the sub-contractors in the production of the twin-engined Canberra bomber. In the ten years between 1952 and 1962, the Belfast company built more than 130 of these aircraft, work which did much to restore morale and maintain employment during a difficult time. At the same time, the company was developing a new line of business — the Precision Engineering Division (PED) — which was located in a separate factory in Castlereagh, and which soon began development work on an optically-guided missile for the Royal Aircraft Establishment at Farnborough.

Although the programme was later cancelled, the setting up of the PED was the first step in what was eventually to become the Shorts Missile Division, and the start of a long-term involvement in the development and construction of missile systems for the Ministry of Defence such as the Blowpipe and Seacat, and more recently, the £225 million contract for the Starstreak system.

During the 1960s the company returned to the design and manufacture of its own aircraft, and the result was the SC-7 Skyvan, which made its maiden

The Shorts Sherpa which has been developed to meet a wide range of short haul and military duties
Shorts

flight in 1963. In 1965, Shorts set up its aerostructures division, and soon won a contract for the design and manufacture of complete sets of wings for the Dutch aircraft manufacturer Fokker's Fellowship F-28. The company also landed a £6 million contract to manufacture engine pods for the Rolls-Royce RB-211 engines. This gave Shorts the chance to develop a specialist niche in which it has become one of the world's leading manufacturers of engine pods for turbo-fan engines, and a major supplier to the Boeing factory in Seattle.

In 1974, it unveiled what was to become one of its best selling aircraft. The SD3-30 — generally known as the 330 — was designed as a short-range regional aircraft. Along with its freight-carrying derivative, the Sherpa, it was in continuous production for the next ten years, during which time around 130 were sold to customers throughout the world. The larger version was even more successful. It was introduced in 1981, and was in production until 1992; a total of 160 were sold over the ten-year period. By the late 1970s, Shorts was making landing-gear doors for the Boeing 747 jumbo jets, and this led in 1979 to the most valuable contract in the company's history, supplying wing components for the Boeing 757.

Despite the deep recession of the early 1980s, Shorts continued to develop its three divisions. In the missile division, it brought out the Javelin, a new and updated version of the Blowpipe. In aerostructures, it became a risk-sharing partner in the development of the Fokker F-100, with a contract to supply the wings of the new airliner. It also won contracts to supply the nose cowls for the Rolls-Royce RB211 engines used on the Boeing 747 and 757, and is responsible for the design and production of complete nacelles on the BAE 146, as well as supplying complete nacelle systems of the A320 Airbus in collaboration with the US company Rohr Industries.

In aircraft manufacture, it returned for the first time to the production of military aircraft, when it linked up with the Brazilian company Embraer to win a contract to supply the RAF with 130 Tucano jet trainers, worth in the region of £125 million, and in the process generating around 1,000 jobs at Shorts' Belfast factory.

Then, in 1988 the government suddenly announced plans to take the company back into the private sector, but it was clear that before this could happen, one major problem had to be overcome. Managing director Roy McNulty, who took over from Sir Philip Foreman in 1988, made it clear to the government that the company would need a massive injection of funds to clear an accumulated deficit of around £270 million. This deficit was not the results of years of unprofitable trading. It was largely the consequence of the increasing burden of interest charges incurred as a result of borrowings which Shorts had been forced to make from the private sector at commercial rates.

Privatisation of the company finally took place in 1989, the government putting in more than £750 million to put the finances back on an even keel. In June of that year it was announced that the new owners were to be the Montreal-based company Bombardier, a relatively recent entrant to the aircraft manufacturing industry, and until its acquisition of Canadair, better known as a manufacturer of snowmobiles and carriages for the New York subway.

The return to the private sector after 46 years in the ownership of the state has transformed the Belfast company's prospects. Just a few years ago, for all its apparent success, Shorts faced an uncertain future, weighed down by a mountain of accumulated debt. Now privatisation has given it a sound capital base, raised morale within the company, and reinforced its position as a major player in the world aerospace industry. It's also benefiting from a continuous programme of investment. Bombardier are putting £200 million into Shorts over four years (investment in the years before privatisation, by contrast, was around £5 million a year).

Although privatisation and a return to a position of comparative financial stability was essential for its long-term survival, equally crucial for Shorts is the experience and ability that exists within the company, and it is this more than anything which will determine the level of its achievements in future years.

Not least among the company's problems over the past few years has been the issue of fair employment. A survey carried out in the engineering industry in the mid-1980s revealed that the proportion of Catholic skilled workers employed by Shorts was under ten per cent. Similarly, less than ten per cent of apprentice recruits were from Catholic schools. Shorts now claims that the percentage of Catholics in its workforce has risen to twelve per cent, and says that twenty per cent of recruits are Catholics. Managing director Roy McNulty says he wants to see that figure increased to twenty-five per cent.

The change has been achieved by advertising in Catholic newspapers, more contact with Catholic schools, and by pressure from the United States. Mr McNulty has admitted that when contracts with American companies like Boeing were being negotiated, the US government has asked for details on just what the company has done to change the balance of the workforce. But he says that the primary incentive for change does not come from outside, but from the determination which exists within the company to eradicate any suggestion of discrimination by increasing the representation of the Catholic community at all levels of the workforce.

14

The Labour Movement in the North
from the 1890s to Recent Times

PETER COLLINS

The Belfast Trades Council was set up in 1881 and soon became the forum of the organised workers of the city, most of whom were Protestant. The *Irish News*, soon after its foundation, came into conflict with the unions when printers complained that the paper was being printed in a non-union 'black house' in Dublin. However, after representation from the Trades Council the paper's management relented.

The relationship between the paper and labour generally reflected the nationalist community at large. They saw the movement essentially as a further stick to beat their unionist opponents, and in no way their true political home. This was despite the fact that the vast majority of the Catholic population in the city were working class — a large proportion of them unskilled labourers or in low status linen mill jobs. On the other hand, the appeal of Joe Devlin, Nationalist MP for West Belfast, was enhanced for these people as he was often styled a 'Labour' representative maintaining good relations with the Trades Council and working especially hard for the women linen workers.

These 'linen slaves', as James Connolly called them, endured deplorable conditions both at work and in their poor housing, much of it owned by the linen barons. Mill girls worked long hours, for mostly uncaring employers, in dank, fetid rooms, often up to their ankles in water. Dust from the flax contributed to diseases of the lungs. TB in females between the ages of fifteen and thirty-five was rampant. This was compounded by unsanitary housing with privies and open cess pits giving rise to regular and virulent outbreaks of typhoid. Indeed the *Irish News* of 24 October 1896 reported that at a city council inquiry it was stated that Belfast had an average death rate, in the previous twenty years, nearly 20 per cent higher than that of the 23 largest English towns. That situation was to take many years to improve.

The most pitiable workers in Belfast were the outworkers — known colloquially as 'spriggers' — engaged in the finishing process on fine linen items. They were paid scandalously low piece rates, with mother and daughters working long hours in ill-lit homes for a few pence an hour. This was known as 'sweated' labour and the Labour movement fought long and hard to eradicate the practice. Joe Devlin joined with William Walker and Mary Galway, the linen union organisers and the Trades Council in a campaign which finally persuaded the government to set up a Trade Board in 1913 which prescribed minimum wages and better conditions in the industry.

In 1894 the trade union movement in Ireland came of age with the establishment of the Irish Trade Union Congress (ITUC) to which most Belfast unions affiliated. In Belfast in the 1890s two developments had an important effect on the movement. The first was the setting up of unions for previously unorganised unskilled workers. The second was the establishment of an Independent Labour Party branch, the leader of which was William Walker, an active trade unionist and member of the Trades Council. Both developments radicalised the movement, previously dominated by more conservative craft unions. Walker was a Labour Unionist who believed in maintaining the link with Britain. He wished to confront the political domination of the Conservative Party, the Orange Order and the Nationalist Party by organising British Labour branches in Ireland.

Walker became a city councillor and President of the ITUC in 1904. He was by then the most important Labour leader in Ireland. In 1905 the Westminster seat in North Belfast fell vacant. The Conservatives and Orange Order were divided at the time. Walker, standing against an unpopular Conservative opponent, looked set to become the country's first Labour MP. However, he felt the need to establish his unionist credentials and answered positively to a virulent anti-Catholic questionnaire put to the candidates by the Belfast Protestant Association. His opponent not only refused to sign but had Walker's affirmation circulated at chapel doors and published in the *Irish News*. This lost Walker most of the thousand or so Catholic votes in the constituency and, arguably, the election in which he was defeated by only a few hundred votes. This was an illustration of the difficulty of Labour to appeal to a working class divided on sectarian lines which has bedevilled the movement to the present day. Walker's influence has remained strong in the local Labour movement.

In 1907 James Larkin, a Liverpool Irishman, arrived in Belfast to revive the branch of the National Union of Dockworkers (NUDL) which had collapsed in an earlier strike. The dockers were poorly paid and worked in terrible conditions. In many cases they were from the same families as the mill girls. However, Larkin faced hostile employers led by Thomas Gallaher, the tobacco and shipping magnate, who were determined to smash the union before it could get a foothold. A strike soon followed and though Larkin tried to get discussions going, the employers refused to deal with him. Larkin's energy and fiery oratory galvanised the dockers and carters into action. The strike was attended by violence as pickets attacked 'blacklegs' who had to have police protection.

The police, themselves overworked and underpaid, resented this hazardous duty. Indeed many sympathised with the strikers and letters to the *Irish News* at the time reflect this. Over 300 police led by Constable William Barrett gave notice to their officers that they would refuse to police the strike. The *Irish News*, unsympathetic to the strike thus far, could relate more easily to these dissident police. An editorial on July 25, 1907 noted: 'The English Government has used the "Irish Police" to keep hold of their mastery over Ireland: perhaps we may soon see the "police" fighting as acknowledged masters of the English Government. Anything is possible in a country like ours.' The authorities, fearing a mutiny, acted quickly, dismissing Barrett and other ringleaders and transferring most of the rest out of the city. Troops were brought in and soon were involved with rioters on the Falls Road. Two young innocent bystanders were shot dead when troops opened fire on rioters. The strike had already begun to crumble as strikers and their families endured near-starvation.

Opponents of Larkin used the events on the Falls Road to drive a sectarian wedge between the strikers. Control was taken from Larkin's hands by the English union leadership who, fearful that the strike was bankrupting the union, settled it over his head. The strike had lasted over four months. The employers had won and only took back workers on their terms. Nevertheless, the events of 1907 have passed into the folk memory of Belfast people as the year the underdog stood up to the oppressor. Larkin, feeling betrayed by the English union leadership, set up the Irish Transport Workers' Union in 1909. It became the strongest union in Ireland within a short space of time.

In 1910 Larkin appointed James Connolly as Belfast organiser of the Transport Union. He soon became a prominent, and to some notorious, figure in the trade union and political life of the city. Connolly, a Republican Socialist, tried to wean the movement from the influence of Walker's Labour unionism. It was a time of political turmoil, with the UVF organising against Home Rule and the expulsion of Catholics from the shipyards showed how dangerously polarised the working class was becoming on sectarian lines.

Nevertheless, Connolly threw himself into the fray organising a campaign against the exclusion of Ulster from Home Rule. He was drawing increasing hostility from the unionist workers who identified the Labour movement as a whole with his activities. The movement was split by Connolly's intervention and even his closest supporters were taken aback by his activities in opposing the war when it began in 1914. He held Friday evening meetings at Upper

Library Street surrounded by hostile crowds incensed by what they regarded as Connolly's pro-German stance. He was glad to be transferred to Dublin from what he referred to as an 'Orange hole'. From then on he was on the road to Easter Week 1916.

The Great War, which saw prosperity for industrial Belfast, ended with the victory of Sinn Fein in the south and Unionism in the north in the 1918 general election. Nevertheless, Labour was a comparatively strong force. The candidates of the Belfast Labour Party gained a respectable poll average of twenty-five per cent in the election. In 1919 engineering workers in Belfast brought the city to a halt during a national strike for a 44-hour week. These skilled, mainly loyalist, workers were flexing their considerable industrial muscle. The national strike leadership, however, capitulated leaving the Belfast workers isolated. Without strike pay, they had to return to work.

However, Labour gained considerable support through the strike and this was turned into electoral advantage when the Belfast Labour Party won thirteen Corporation seats out of a total of 60 in 1920. Labour's political expectations were soon dashed by developments in the Anglo-Irish war. The increase of IRA activity elsewhere in the country and sectarian conflict in the city led to a further round of expulsions of Catholics from workplaces in 1920. This was extended to Protestant Labour and trade union activists known to loyalists as 'rotten Prods'.

In the May 1921 elections to the new Northern Ireland parliament, in the face of intimidation and pogrom, the four Labour candidates were routed, averaging only two per cent of the poll. In the birth pangs of the northern statelet there was no place for an independent force like Labour. James Craig, the first prime minister, was later to say of the new parliament — 'What I want to get in this House...are men who are for the Union on the one hand, or who are against it and want to go into a Dublin Parliament on the other.' The political mould of Northern Ireland was already beginning to set.

After partition, the movement, north and south, began to move into separate if parallel directions. The Irish Labour Party was led in the Dail by Tom Johnson, a Liverpool man who had lived in Belfast for twenty years. The Belfast Labour Party became the Northern Ireland Labour Party. Northern delegates nevertheless still attended the ITUC. There was some electoral success for the NILP in the twenties and thirties with Harry Midgley emerging as the leading light. His career is interesting in reflecting the frustration of many talented Labour activists with the lack of progress by the movement and, as a result, their careers. He started off as an anti-partitionist, set up his own unionist- orientated Commonwealth Labour Party during World War Two, finally joining the Unionist Party, to become Minister of Education and a director of Linfield Football Club to boot.

The thirties were years of depression and hardest hit were the unemployed, of whom there were over 100,000 in Northern Ireland. The system of Poor Law and the notorious Belfast workhouse were incapable of humanely dealing with this. The demand for an alternative comprehensive system of outdoor relief led to an impressive protest movement encompassing both Protestant and Catholic working class in 1932. The Labour Movement and the Marxist Revolutionary Workers Group played a role in organising and to an extent politicising the discontented masses. Demonstrations, with marchers converging from all districts of Belfast, escalated into riots with the police, the difference this time being that the poor of both religions were on the same side. This threat to the government was mitigated by some improvement to the outdoor relief provisions and a carefully engineered outbreak of sectarian violence around the 'Twelfth' to divide the protest movement.

People for Peace: thousands of workers attend a peace rally organised by the Irish Congress of Trade Unions at Belfast City Hall, 18 November 1993
Irish News

The years after the Second World War saw increasing polarisation, within the Labour Movement, over the border question. The majority within the

NILP were moving towards a generally unionist position. Those who remained anti-partitionist either left active politics or joined the northern branches of the Irish Labour Party. Jack Beattie, a Protestant Socialist-Republican, elected MP for West Belfast in 1945, was a leading example of the anti-partitionists who had left the NILP. What had been split up was the only body capable at that time of detaching both sections of the working class from their traditional political loyalties. Nevertheless the rump NILP did have some electoral success in the late fifties and early sixties when it became the official opposition at Stormont. However, it was not prepared to take any steps that risked alienating hard core Protestant support. By the time of the Civil Rights struggle in the late sixties the NILP had neither the will nor the support to contribute significantly to the fast changing political situation.

The Irish Congress of Trade Unions (ICTU) had to contend with non-recognition from Stormont on the grounds that it was an all-Ireland body. This seriously hampered its ability to negotiate with government and employers and was an affront to normal democracy that was not unknown in other aspects of Stormont policy. However, due to pressure from industry and the churches, the prime minister, Terence O'Neill, in the face of much opposition from unionist colleagues, granted full recognition in 1964. He was later to describe it as 'probably one of the most difficult hurdles I surmounted during my premiership'.

During the present troubles, ICTU has walked a veritable political tight rope, maintaining that the constitutional position of Northern Ireland is a matter for the electorate. This has not satisfied many of its nationalist members. It identified wholly with the aims of the Civil Rights movement and opposed internment. It is wary of alienating its Protestant membership and has stayed clear of issues identified with the Provisional IRA, such as at the hunger strike campaign. It was involved in an attempt to march to work during the Loyalist Workers' Strike and has organised two major anti-sectarian initiatives, 'The Better Life For All' campaign of the mid 1970s and the Peace, Work and Progress campaign, opposing intimidation, discrimination and sectarianism at work. One of it most spectacular successes was the organisation of a series of public 'peace demonstrations' in November 1993 in the run-up to the IRA and loyalist cease-fires. However, these efforts are of necessity piecemeal in the absence of a political solution. Until that comes about, the Labour movement, in its political and union manifestations, must remain, as throughout its history, unable to realise the potential implicit for it in an industrial city the magnitude of Belfast.

15

The Law

One Hundred Years of Legal Change

JOHN F. LARKIN

Legal systems, except during revolutions, normally resist change. It is not necessary here either to deplore or understand this phenomenon, but to look at how one hundred years have seen alterations in the legal system of the north of Ireland, and how much has remained unchanged.

An obvious starting point might be the perspective of a legal Rip van Winkle who returns after the absence of a century to resume practice. If one assumes that this (say) junior barrister has the fortitude to cope with the architectural and social shocks that confront him on his awakening, he will probably be able to handle most of the legal surprises.

If he wishes to resume his familiarity with the practice of criminal law he will probably, as he would have done in 1891, make his way up the Crumlin Road to the Courthouse. If he enters Court number 2 before a trial begins, he will probably note a few minor changes in layout but be reassured by the Royal Arms behind the judge's seat, and the familiar sight of the petit jury and grand jury boxes. He will soon be prompted to ask, however, what has happened to the grand jury, its criminal law function of presenting or ignoring bills of indictment having been abolished finally in 1969.

Other questions will follow: what is a County Court judge doing sitting at the Assizes? Why are felonies and misdemeanours joined on the same indictment? These questions will long await an answer if he asks any one of the improbably large number of young counsel sitting in court or milling about the main hall. If he asks a more senior member of the profession, he may see a flicker of recollection across the other's face as he informs him that in 1945 misdemeanour and felony could be joined on the same indictment, but that the terms were abolished in 1967. As for assizes and quarter sessions, all previously existing criminal courts were replaced by the crown court in 1978.

Perhaps thinking he has had enough the veteran of 1891 may stagger from the new-fangled but still recognisable jury trial in court number 2 to see what is going on in court number 1. Here he will observe serious offences being tried without a jury. Although he may recollect from the 1880s that a non-jury three-judge court was actually established by a Liberal administration, it never sat nor did anyone expect it to. He will be told that this court is the product of 'emergency' legislation; his feelings on hearing that it has been in existence since 1973 are best left unexamined. Once the shock has begun to recede one can imagine certain features of this court such as the duty to give reasons for a conviction, and the automatic right of appeal, meeting with approval.

The right of appeal will appear particularly attractive given that in 1891 the ability to appeal in criminal cases was strictly circumscribed and largely dependent on the leave of the trial judge. Perhaps trying to fit into the legal world of the 1990s the visitor will talk knowingly about going to Dublin for the Appeal. Here, surely, is the greatest shock of all. To have to explain to someone who was in 1891 probably a rather conservative Irishman that twenty-six counties are now no longer part of what he knew as the United Kingdom of Great Britain and Ireland will require great sensitivity.

Partition affected the internal concerns of the Irish legal profession as much as, if not more than, any other national institution. The creation of new institutions such as the Inn of Court of Northern Ireland in 1926 followed a short and unharmonious period when the Irish bar struggled on united after partition. But for the old northern circuits — the North East and the North West — partition meant immediate disappearance.

It would probably be best not to tell the legal Rip van Winkle anything about the struggle that preceded partition, and especially to be silent about the alternative court structure that came into being during that period. He would perhaps have been horrified with the Dail courts of 1919 — 1922 and their apparent rejection of the common law, and dependence on Brehon and continental authorities.

Still, he might have been reassured (or merely amused) by the unmistakable resemblance the revolutionary courts bore to those they professedly replaced. A visit to Dublin might afford still further reassurance. Apart from frequent and mysterious reference to the constitution, the visitor would understand that law and procedure in the Republic are in some respects closer to those of the late nineteenth century than the Northern Ireland legal system.

If the young barrister of 1891 had been fortunate enough to be acquainted with the work of those talented west Cork ladies, Somerville and Ross, he might enjoy a frisson of anticipation on learning that the office of Resident Magistrate continues to exist in Northern Ireland at least. Alas, any prospect of amusement in the doings of Major Yates's successors would speedily evaporate by contact with the rather staid individuals who currently hold the office. That is not to say that summary justice is not without its comic aspects on occasion (some things never change); it is just that the entertainment is less frequently supplied by the magistrate.

In the Ireland of 1891 divorce was possible. Since the dissolution of a valid marriage required a private act of the imperial parliament, the social impact of divorce on Irish society was negligible. A visit to the Family Division of the High Court of Justice in Northern Ireland any Friday morning during term time where a marriage may be dissolved after an oral hearing of ten minutes might prove astonishing in itself, but is likely to prompt melancholy reflection about the almost bureaucratic manner in which this type of family litigation is processed. The legal protection of marriage in the Republic would not be surprising, although a lawyer trained ln traditions of parliamentary sovereignty might hesitate at the idea of constitutionally enshrined rights and safeguards.

A rare photograph of Belfast Crown Court, 1912
James Kelly

Lawyers, despite apparently inhabiting a world of intense formalism, make human sense of it at times by developing a comprehensive knowledge of and interest in the individuals who occupy major positions in the legal firmament. No doubt the visitor from 1891 will be anxious to see what names from that period are remembered in the 1990s. The greatest surprise would probably be elicited by the fact that someone who was a QC on the Leinster circuit in 1891 is remembered so warmly by one section of the community in Northern

Ireland. To understand why Edward Carson is buried in St Anne's Cathedral would require experience or remembrance which someone who fell asleep in 1891 could not be expected to possess.

Luminaries of 1891 whose reputation has survived to the present legal generation are few. That Christopher Palles, Chief Baron of the Court of Exchequer, should be one of them would surprise no one who knew Palles during his lifetime. One of Palles's pupils at the bar might also be remembered, although in the less flattering context of his soubriquet, 'Peter the packer'. Although he died as Lord O'Brien of Kilfenora, after having served as Lord Chief Justice of Ireland, Peter O'Brien's reputation is probably unfairly reflected in the surviving tradition of his jury-packing career as Irish Attorney General. O'Brien might be better remembered for his genial humour which finds expression in several of his reported cases such as Barrett v Irvine and The Queen v Drury.

Curiosity is bound to arise as to the major figures of Irish legal life since 1891. The early twentieth century does not contain the names of many new 'greats'. There are of course the legal eccentrics like Joyce's contemporary in UCD, Louis J. Walsh, probably best known today for his play *The Auction at Killybuck*. Walsh was a solicitor with offices in Ballycastle and Magherafelt who was forced to go 'on the run' in 1920. After a period of internment in Ballykinlar he surfaced as a member of the Free State Judiciary committee in 1923 and ended his days as District Justice in Donegal. His early enthusiasm for language revival never left him; in later years it merely took the form of marked leniency towards Irish-speaking offenders who appeared before him. Strangely, Walsh's many short stories and plays never deal with post-partition Ireland; they are invariably set in some idealised pre-partition Ulster where sectarianism exists simply as an additional source of comedy.

Two legal figures who have done much to enhance the international reputation of Irish law since 1891 belong to the period after partition and made their contribution to the different jurisdictions into which the island has been divided since 1920. Of the two, one Lord MacDermott, Lord Chief Justice of Northern Ireland was called to the bar just as the legal system was dividing; the practice of the other, Mr Justice Brian Walsh, judge of the Irish Supreme Court, began only after partition had become a fact of legal life. Both men during their respective judicial careers increased the stature of Irish law. Both men, while faithful to the traditions that underlie the states they served, recognised in the search for justice what both legal systems had in common.

Of course, for the lawyer returning from 1891 the spectacle of failure in the search for justice would be a century later a familiar but unwelcome experience. Lawyers are not widely supposed to care greatly about abstract issues of justice, an impression fuelled perhaps by their limited power to influence the legal system at key points. Welcome developments towards the injection of greater justice in the legal system include the increase in access to law afforded by legal aid and the greater protection given to consumers and employees.

Indeed, if a loyal member of his profession, what might alarm the visitor from 1891 most about the 1995 legal scene would be the vulnerable position of the legal profession itself, particularly the bar. Solicitors in the Republic now have rights of audience in all courts — a prospect to horrify a late Victorian barrister — and the calls for the curtailment of restrictive practices seem to become no less insistent with the passage of time. In Northern Ireland the attack on the legal profession at present is financial. The profession there, because of the general economic condition of the community, is largely kept busy through legal aid work. If, as appears likely, the availability of legal aid is narrowed,or if the level of fees is lowered, the profession will enter a very difficult time indeed.

The prospect of economic attack renders futile any attempt to predict the shape of the Irish legal profession one hundred years from now. There is a feeling abroad that the pace of change may well merit the epithet revolutionary — and not in any favourable sense. Certainly while it can be said that the visitor from 1891 will discover much that is familiar in the 1990s, the same cannot be claimed of the legal landscape of 2091.

16
Banking in the North of Ireland since 1891

PHILIP OLLERENSHAW

Over the course of the last century major changes have occurred in the ownership, control, functions, staffing and sometimes even the names of banks operating in Northern Ireland. Almost all these changes would have occurred whether or not Ireland had been partitioned in 1921. Even so, the banks have sometimes been profoundly affected by political developments from the development of the Home Rule movement onwards.

At the end of the nineteenth century banking in the north of Ireland was dominated by seven joint stock institutions which dated mainly from the remarkable period of bank promotion between 1824 and 1836. The major exception was the Bank of Ireland, the country's largest bank, which was established in 1783. The three banks based in Belfast, the 'Northern', 'Belfast' and 'Ulster', had, as their names suggest, primarily a northern focus and they dominated business in the province. The Provincial Bank was London-based but had originally pioneered branch banking in Ulster. Two other banks which have been labelled as broadly Catholic and nationalist were the London-based National Bank, of which Daniel O'Connell had been a founder in the 1830s, and the Dublin-based Hibernian, which had developed an aggressively expansionist policy of branch banking in Ulster in the later nineteenth century.

All of these banks, except the Hibernian, issued their own notes and all, by the mid-1960s, experienced amalgamation so that four of them lost their separate identity altogether. Only the Bank of Ireland, Northern and Ulster retained their original names.

Before 1914, Ulster was promising territory for banks. They had developed into safe, well-managed institutions and were closely involved with the rise of all the major industries, by providing extensive and flexible credit facilities most obviously to linen, shipbuilding, engineering and distilling companies. As the banks' reputation for honesty and stability grew, so more people in the towns and in the countryside were prepared to move their cash from under the mattress or the chimney and deposit it in the bank safe.

Ulster's diversified industrial, commercial and agricultural base enabled the banks to spread their business and protect themselves from overdependence on one sector. The banks deliberately projected an image of stability in several ways, including the payment of a steady dividend and the construction of reassuringly permanent looking offices, especially head offices.

Until the First World War, banking was overwhelmingly a male occupation, and the extent of male domination was scarcely less than in the shipyards. It was an occupation that offered both security of employment and reasonable promotion prospects. Even in 1911, however, there were probably no more than a thousand bank staff in Ulster, a far smaller number than were employed in any of the larger linen companies where, of course, the workforce was largely female.

The richly ornamental facade of the Allied Irish Bank (formerly Provincial Bank), Royal Avenue, Belfast. Built in the 1860s during Ulster's commercial heydey, it contained a magnificant domed banking hall
Irish News

If the economic environment before 1914 was favourable to banking, the banks themselves did face problems from the political uncertainty arising from the campaign for Home Rule during and after the 1880s. Above all, there was the danger of an orchestrated 'run' on the banks' deposits in order to create instability with a view to achieving political aims. This tactic was not new – it had occasionally been employed as part of the Repeal agitation of the 1820s and 1830s, but it was revived sporadically between 1893 and 1922, though it came nowhere near achieving its desired goal.

Of more consequence was the drop in bank share values which accompanied the introduction of the first two Home Rule Bills in 1886 and 1893. Within a month of the introduction of the latter, some £983,000 had been wiped off the market value of seven Irish banks and rather more off the shares of Irish railways.

Whatever the political views of bank officials, there was a firmly-held view in boardrooms that banking and politics simply did not mix. Banks tended to make very few openly political statements while, at the same time, striving to stifle political debate at shareholders' meetings. The determination to keep a low political profile lay behind the Belfast banks' refusal to participate in projected discussions on the formation of a provisional government at the height of the Ulster crisis in 1913.

The volatile political situation after the First World War presented bankers with particularly severe operational problems. There was a strand of nationalist opinion which held that 'southern' money went to finance northern Protestant/unionist businesses and that those engaged in these were prominent in frustrating the formation of an all-Ireland Home Rule government. Threatened withdrawal of deposits, together with armed raids on bank offices to get money or confidential information were features of the violent years 1919-22. The partition of the country and the end of the 'Belfast Boycott' and civil war brought at least some semblance of peace and for that reason alone would have been warmly welcomed by the banking community.

In addition to the political situation, the banks had further problems to contend with after the First World War. These included unprecedented collective action by their own employees and a long spell of industrial depression and unemployment that set in after 1920. These events resulted in the formation of the Irish Bank Officials' Association (IOBA) in 1918. By the early 1930s more than 90 per cent of bank employees were union members, and by the late 1960s the figure had grown to 98 per cent. This figure was exceptional by any standards and means that Irish bank employees can exert very considerable pressure on employers.

Important changes occurred also in the control of banks in the North. In 1917, the London City and Midland Bank announced it was to amalgamate with the Belfast Bank, and another major English bank, the London County and Westminster, declared its intention to take over the Ulster Bank. The London City and Midland provided a Foreign Exchange Department at its newly opened Castle Place branch in Belfast, an important facility that the

Belfast Bank did not have. Unlike most amalgamations in British banking, both the Belfast and the Ulster Banks were allowed to retain their original corporate identities. Both the Northern and the Ulster Banks retained their substantial presence in the Free State after partition.

Over a large number of years the banks slowly lost their Victorian image, but banking between the wars remained a predominantly male occupation. Only during and after the Second World War did the female element in the banking labour force assume significant proportions.

Profound changes occurred in the banking structure and the rate of change accelerated sharply in the mid 1960s. The first move in the post-war amalgamation movement was made by the Bank of Ireland which took over the Hibernian in 1958. Then in 1965 the oldest joint stock bank in Ireland, the Northern, was taken over by Midland. In the following year the Bank of Ireland further consolidated its position by taking over the Irish business of the National Bank while those institutions remaining outside a major banking group, the Munster and Leinster, Provincial and Royal joined together to create Allied Irish Banks. Four years later the Belfast Bank was merged into the Northern. This spate of amalgamations in a short space of time was the most far-reaching structural change ever experienced in Irish banking. The Trustee Savings Banks date from the 1820s and they too experienced an amalgamation movement, being largely merged with the Belfast Savings Bank during the 1930s and 1940s.

Northern Ireland remains one of the small number of areas in which the issue of private currency notes is still allowed. However, the scale of the transformation of the financial sector meant that from the mid-1960s no major private financial institution operating in Northern Ireland (whether bank, building society or insurance company) was locally owned. The disposal by Midland of the Northern Bank to National Australia Bank in 1987 further confirmed this trend.

Looking back, and considering the magnitude of the previous changes, it would be fair to conclude that banking in the 1990s would indeed be a foreign land to the bankers of a century ago.

17

The Protestant Churches
and the Inter-Church Relations
in Ireland since 1891

JOHN M. BARKLEY

T o say that there were no Inter-Church relations in Ireland in 1891 would be true, but it would not be the whole truth and nothing but the truth. All the Churches adopted an attitude of aloofness and superiority to the others. Others, without exception, were rivals over whom it was necessary to gain a victory. In the light of this it is necessary to say something about the churches in Ireland as they were in 1891.

The Church of Ireland had been the Church of England and Ireland up to disestablishment in 1870. It was a minority Church and had gone through a traumatic experience during the previous twenty years. It had been the Church 'by law established' and she had been in a favoured position under the law. Now other Churches were legally on an equal footing. She had had to construct a whole new system of internal government and to adapt to a completely new civil, social and ecclesiastical set-up. It was 'a shattering blow' to those Anglicans who had never questioned the position of their church within the context and implications of national life and witness. Its standards of doctrine and worship remained *The Thirty-nine Articles* and *The Book of Common Prayer*. The foundation of recovery had just been laid.

Methodists were also affected by this Act. They owed their origin to the evangelistic campaigns of John and Charles Wesley. In Irish census returns up to 1871 they were counted as Anglicans. From that date they have been recorded separately. In 1871 Methodism was divided into two groups: the Primitive Wesleyan Methodist Society, who maintained Wesley's original idea of a 'Society' inside the Established Church, and the Wesleyans who held they were an autonomous body. Disestablishment opened the door for their union in 1879. During the next decade all adjectives were dropped and the term 'Methodist' alone was used. Their standards of doctrine and worship were John Wesley's sermons and a revised form of the *Book of Common*

Prayer, with the hymns of Charles Wesley playing a major role. Methodism was starting out on a denominationally united venture.

The Roman Catholic Church also had undergone a considerable change in the previous half-century. In the sixteenth century the majority of the population in Ireland had continued within the mediaeval church. Under the penal laws they were treated as second-class citizens and because of their religious allegiance they suffered many disabilities. Then came Catholic emancipation in 1829. At this period many bishops and priests were Gallican, but in the half-century before 1891 the Church of Rome in Ireland became solidly ultramontane. This meant that friendships like that between Archbishop James Doyle and James Carlile in Dublin, and between Father Hugh O'Donnell and Archbishop William Crolly and the Presbyterian ministers in Belfast, came to an end. Irish Catholicism had become rigidly Tridentine and had adopted the *Syllabus Errorum* of Pius IX. This position may be summed up in the oft-quoted words of Cardinal MacRory, 'The Protestant Church in Ireland – and the same is true of the Protestant Church anywhere else – is not a part of the Church of Christ'. This remained her doctrine up to the promulgation of the Decree on Ecumenism, *Unitatis Redintegratio*, of Vatican II in 1964. Up to that, ecclesiastical separation remained in force, except for a few cases of individual friendship.

The members of the Presbyterian Church in Ireland had been second-class citizens in the eighteenth century, and had the previous year celebrated the golden jubilee of the Union of the Synod of Ulster and the Secession Synod. At its General Assembly the Rev. William Park, donning the mantle of a prophet, had declared, 'We may expect, I think, that the next half century will see a great movement towards union among the Churches...'. Its Moderator in 1891 was the Rev. N. M'Auley Brown, to whom has been attributed Gladstone's slogan of the 'Three F's – fair rents, fixity of tenure, and free sale'. During this period the Presbyterian Church was developing her home and overseas missions, educational, social and benevolent work. Under scripture its standards of doctrine and worship were the Westminster Confession of Faith and Directory for the Public Worship of God.

These were and remain the four largest bodies numerically. Roman Catholics numbered about three quarters of the total population of Ireland; the Anglicans and Presbyterians were about equal in strength, accounting for about four fifths of the remaining quarter but the former were more widely spread over the thirty-two counties and the latter having their greater strength in Ulster; the Methodists were about one fifth of either of these and had their main strength in west Cork and where there had been English settlements (as opposed to Scottish) in Ulster, especially in the west. Some smaller groups existed, for example, Baptist, Brethren, Congregationalists,

Religious Society of Friends, Moravians, Non- Subscribing Presbyterians, and Salvation Army. All are small, but they too have a place in God's grace and are relevant to inter-church relations.

In 1891, each of the churches existed unto itself. Each behaved as if it was infallible. Protestants/Roman Catholics and Anglicans/Presbyterians were often at daggers drawn. The Protestants held that the Church of Rome needed reform. The Church of Rome regarded Protestants as heretics and no part of the Church of Christ, so it remained outside the Ecumenical Movement until 1964. This means that the story of inter-church relations is confined to Protestantism up to that date.

Let us look at this in broad outline. The first official relationship was established in 1904 when in response to an invitation of the Presbyterian General Assembly the Methodist Conference agreed 'to the appointment of a Joint Committee to meet from time to time to consider questions of common interest.'

In 1907 Pope Pius X promulgated the *Ne Temere* decree. One result of this was to unite the Protestant churches in Ireland. Presbyterians were unwilling to have their marriages unrecognised as they had been up to 1845 and Anglicans had no desire to have their marriages placed in the same position as Presbyterian marriages had been during the Ascendancy. For the first time Presbyterians and Anglicans appeared together on the same public platform with Baptists, Congregationalists, Methodists, Non-Subscribers, and others, in Dublin, Belfast and Scottish and English cities.

The situation was further aggravated by the McCann case in Belfast in 1910 which raised the whole issue of 'mixed marriages'. That same year the General Assembly approached the General Synod regarding the appointing of a Joint Committee for 'cultivating friendly relations and co-operating in the things pertaining to the advancement of the Kingdom of God, in regard to which common action might be wisely taken'. This was agreed. So from 1911 there were two sets of bipartite talks, Presbyterian/Methodist and Presbyterian/Anglican. At the latter in 1919 it was proposed that its scope should be extended 'to include co-operation with other Evangelical Churches in Ireland'.

When this proposal was submitted to the General Synod it requested that consideration of it should be postponed until after the Lambeth Conference in 1920. So the United Council of Christian Churches and Religious Communions in Ireland did not come into being until 23 January 1923. Here several things may be said. Firstly, this long name did not point so much to 'unity' as 'disunity'. Secondly, in 1966 its name was changed to the Irish Council of Churches (ICC). The ICC was 'constituted by Christian Communions in Ireland willing to join in united efforts to promote the spiritual, physical, moral and social welfare of the people and the extension of the rule of Christ among all nations and over every region of human life'. The original members were the Church of Ireland, the Presbyterian Church, the Non-subscribing Presbyterian Church, the Methodist Church, the Moravian Church, the Congregational Union and the Religious Society of Friends. The only changes have been the withdrawal of the Congregational Union and the Salvation Army have become members. Since 1978 Roman Catholic observers have attended Council meetings.

During the 1930s there were a number of groups which attempted to foster an ecumenical spirit, for example, 'Gas and Light' in Belfast and its counterpart 'Ham and Eggs' in Dublin. Both were small numerically but made a positive contribution by enabling members to discuss ecumenical issues, increasing understanding, and on occasion easing tensions over baptism, pulpit exchange, and ministerial etiquette. They consisted of private individuals and had no official standing. In the 1950s under the leadership of the Rt Rev. F. J. Mitchell, Bishop of Down, there were the Dundrum meetings. Being episcopally organised they were more formal. At them, learned papers on the Eucharist, Inter-Church relations, and Church-Order were read and discussed. These meetings had no ecclesiastical authority.

More influential were the links with the 'Faith and Order' and 'Life and Work' conferences; and that the Irish Anglican, Methodist, and Presbyterian Churches were founding members of the British and World Councils of Churches (BCC and WCC) in 1942 and 1948 respectively. All these relations brought great enrichment to Irish Protestantism, bringing it into contact with world thinking.

The Decree on Ecumenism of Vatican II, promulgated on 21 November, 1964, led to a change in Protestant/Roman Catholic relations. It declared that 'it is through Christ's Catholic church (that is, the Church of Rome) alone...that the fullness of the means of salvation can be obtained'. This fullness 'subsists' in the Roman Catholic Church alone. All others while 'Christian' have 'defects'. This, as Schillebeeck says, is a completely new ecclesiology. Other churches are no longer referred to as 'sects' and 'heretics', but as 'Christians' and 'separated brethren'. This is more restricted than Scripture (St.Matt.18.20) and Ignatius of Antioch, 'Where Christ Jesus is, there is the Catholic Church'. However, it has enabled the church of Rome to participate in the Ecumenical Movement. Now it is possible to speak of a Protestant/Roman Catholic inter-church relationship in Ireland.

Naturally, after four hundred years of enmity, the first moves were tentative and unofficial. They began with an invitation from the Most Rev. Abbott Joseph Dowdall, O.S.B., to a number of scholars and churchmen in the various churches to a residential Ecumenical Conference in Glenstal Abbey,

County Limerick in 1964. This meets annually to the present day. It consists of individuals and has no ecclesiastical authority. There is full, free, and frank discussion on subjects, such as liturgy, baptism, Eucharist, mariology, education, Holy Spirit and so on. From this in 1966 grew the one-day conference at Greenhills (County Louth). The friendships formed and the trust and integrity experienced at these meetings helped to make the establishment of official relations much easier.

In 1970, the Irish School of Ecumenics was established. It owes its origin to the vision and enthusiasm of the Rev Dr Michael Hurley, S.J. Inter-denominational in character, it has brought the Irish Churches into contact with scholars and students from many lands and enriched our understanding of the Church worldwide.

The first official relations could be said to have begun in 1970 when the Irish Council of Churches and the Roman Catholic hierarchy set up joint-working groups. They have produced many erudite reports on social, educational and personal issues; and have produced a Peace Education programme for schools. The Churches unfortunately have not made the use they should have of this material.

Relations between the Churches have improved markedly since the mid-1960s. Here, Rev. Rodney Sterritt, Rev. Winston Good and Archbishop Robin Eames, the Church of Ireland Primate, join Cardinal Cahal Daly in a visit to Tyrone Crystal in Dungannon, 1992
Irish News

In 1970 the Irish Council of Churches, in the light of civil unrest in the community, approached Cardinal William Conway suggesting a joint meeting. He replied asking for a committee to discuss all aspects of Ecumenism. After some discussion, the Ballymascanlon talks were set up, the first meeting being held in 1973. In recent years its constitution and structure have been revised to achieve greater efficiency. Here topics and problems of mutual importance are discussed. While greater progress was hoped for, it is vital to Ireland's future as a Christian country. No matter what frustrations arise, the Irish Inter-Church Meeting (to give Ballymascanlon its new name) must not be allowed to collapse. It must continue to exist. There was nothing in 1964: we now are not only speaking to each other, but know each other and are able to act together on many issues. It is 'a door of hope'.

In recent years the Ecumenical Movement has been deliberately undermined in Ireland by misrepresentation, falsehood and innuendo. So there is said to be a cooling off so far as ecumenism is concerned. Many, including distinguished Roman Catholic scholars, consider Pope John Paul II 'reactionary'. There has been the silencing of some learned and outstanding theologians. The Presbyterian Church in Ireland was a founding member of the WCC, BCC and ICC, but withdrew from the WCC in 1980 and refused to become a member of the Council of Churches in Britain and Ireland. Both the Anglican and Methodist Churches have been subjected to adverse criticism over their WCC membership.

As I have written elsewhere, 'We appear to be retiring to our polemical trenches so far as ecumenism is concerned....There are sections of Protestantism today which are still preoccupied with fighting old battles. The Papacy is still intent on upholding paternalistic authoritarianism.... We must not let present difficulties and frustrations rob us of the conviction that Christ created one Church and that its unity, under Him, must be made visible to a divided world'.

18
Catholicism in the North of Ireland since 1891

OLIVER RAFFERTY

By the early 1890s Catholicism in the north of Ireland had already assumed many of the features which would ensure its sustained growth over the next hundred years. Although by the middle of the nineteenth century the church in Ulster could be said to have been relatively underdeveloped, it was to respond with great alacrity to the stimulus for growth bequeathed to Irish Catholicism by Paul Cullen.

Cullen returned to Ireland from Rome, having been appointed Archbishop of Armagh, in 1849. He immediately set about imposing an 'ultramontane' stamp on Irish Catholicism. The north, in particular, was ripe for this brand of virulent papal Catholicism. Historically the church in Ulster had been slow to recover from the effects of the Penal Laws and the 'devotional revolution' which marked Irish Catholicism from the 1820s on had almost bypassed the north. Whilst northern Catholicism had a tradition of *rapprochement* with its Protestant neighbours, associated with the likes of Archbishop Curtis, Bishop Denvir and Dr Russell of Maynooth, sectarianism was a marked feature of northern life throughout the nineteenth century – a phenomenon which is only gradually breaking down in our own day.

From 1850 to 1890 there was an enormous expansion of Catholic activity and enterprise in the north. For the most part this was simply a question of arithmetic. The Catholic population of Belfast, for example, rose from 4,000 in 1812 to 100,000 by the end of the century. The Catholic impact on northern society was partly encouraged by the growth of the Catholic middle classes in and around Belfast and, to a lesser extent, in Derry. The educational activity of religious orders of nuns, along with the Irish Christian Brothers and the De La Salle brothers, helped dispel the impression of an ill-educated and raffish Catholic underclass.

The arrival of the Vincentians in Armagh in 1863, and of the Passionists in Belfast in 1868, followed by the Redemptorists in 1896, gave northern Catholics their first introduction to religious orders of men since penal times. The Jesuits had a house in Dromore for four years in the 1880s, but such a brief sojourn in a relatively backward diocese was hardly calculated to make much of an impact.

Of more lasting significance was the mission preached in St Peter's Church, Falls Road, Belfast, by Fr James Cullen S.J. in March 1889. The mission culminated in Cullen administering to 300 men and women the 'heroic offering' whereby they pledged themselves never to drink alcohol again. It was from this and similar experiences that Cullen was led ten years later to found the temperance association, the Pioneers of the Sacred Heart.

As with all new ventures, the work of the religious orders did not always proceed smoothly and disputes between the Christian Brothers and the bishop of Down and Connor over the class of boys whom they would educate, and between the bishop and the Passionists over their exact role and means of finance, did not augur well for the ministries of these groups. Added to this was certain internal pressure that the Christian Brothers, in particular, laboured under, forcing them to withdraw from Strabane in 1878 and Enniskillen in 1880.

The religious life of most northern Catholics has varied little over the last hundred years. Devotion to the Mass and sacraments, attendance at forty hours devotions, perpetual adoration, novenas, stations of the cross, scapulars, devotions to the Sacred Heart and the Blessed Virgin, pilgrimages – especially to Lough Derg – all these formed the backbone of northern Catholic piety. At an organisational level, the Saint Vincent de Paul Society made its appearance on the Belfast scene in 1850 and quickly grew. This was to be parallelled in the 1920s by the foundation in the north of the Apostolic Work Society and the introduction of institutions such as the Legion of Mary and the Catholic Young Men's Society.

Politics in the 1890s in the north, as elsewhere in Ireland, were dominated by the split in the Irish Parliamentary Party over the question of Parnell and the famous O'Shea divorce case. A great deal of the opposition to Parnell was led by Catholic priests and bishops. In Belfast the bishop, Dr Patrick McAlister, went so far as to establish his own newspaper, the *Irish News*, because he disliked the pro-Parnell stance of the *Belfast Morning News*.

In Derry the anti-Parnell Irish National Federation was supported in very large measure by the priests of the city. There was of course a much larger question here concerning the extent of clerical influence and control of Irish political life. This became crystallized around the split in the Irish Parliamentary Party between Tim Healy, who accepted the necessity for clerical interference, and John Dillon who, despite the fact that he opposed Parnell in 1891, wanted politics to be free from clerical domination. Indeed, as late as 1899, the Nationalist candidate in Derry, Count Arthur Moore, was selected to stand by Fr William McMenamin, a close friend and confidant of Bishop O'Doherty. However, the clergy were also divided and it has to be said that when, in 1900, priests in Derry withdrew from political activity the local party machine all but collapsed and allowed the Unionists to hold the Westminster representation uninterrupted for thirteen years.

The healing of the division of the Irish Parliamentary Party in 1900 was presided over by Bishop Patrick O'Donnell of Raphoe, who was to end his days as Archbishop of Armagh. He acted as treasurer of the Parliamentary party finances and exercised considerable influence in Irish nationalist politics. O'Donnell was one of four Catholic bishops to attend the Irish Convention of 1917, chaired by Horace Plunkett, which sought, unsuccessfully, to delineate the shape of the new Ireland in the aftermath of the 1916 Rising and the First World War.

The Belfast political scene of those years was equally complex. Bishop Henry Henry was determined to run an old-style political operation through his Belfast Catholic Association which was firmly anti-Parnellite and pro-clerical in complexion. The theocratic politics of this truculent man were opposed not only by some priests of his own diocese but also by several fellow bishops. Dr Henry's quixotic-like actions in the West Belfast by-election of 1903 helped to ensure the defeat of the Nationalist candidate and the return of the Liberal-Unionist Arnold Forster.

There is evidence to suggest that, in the years before partition, northern Catholics were only too anxious to actively participate in all the functions of the state, when given the opportunity. A former Belfast solicitor, originally from Newry, Lord Russell of Killowen ascended the ranks of the judiciary to become Lord Chief Justice of England. There were three Catholics among the higher echelons of the academic staff at Queen's College, Belfast, including the distinguished professor of medicine, James Cumming. The Catholic authorities were most anxious for civic representation and recognition at the official opening of the Mater Hospital in Belfast on 23 April 1900. The ceremony was performed by the Lord Mayor of Belfast, Alderman R. J. McConnell, a fervent unionist. Among the benefactors present on that occasion was the Marquis of Dufferin.

With the settlement of the university question Catholics felt freer to attend Queen's and whilst their numbers were never very great – as late as 1957 there were only 490 Catholics studying there – they were given official encouragement from Rome to do so as early as 1911. The foundation of a lectureship in Scholastic Philosophy enabled the bishop of Down and Connor to send seminarians to Queen's for the study of the humanities.

Alas, the spectre of sectarianism was never far from the educational administration at Queen's. The College authorities refused finances from the Gaelic League to found a chair in Celtic Studies. When a lectureship was finally set up, the university appointed the Reverend F. W. O'Connell, a Church of Ireland clergyman, as the first holder of that post.

If northern Catholics did not exactly cultivate the British aristocracy, neither were they strangers at their dinner tables. When Queen Victoria visited Ireland in 1900 she entertained Cardinal Logue to a splendid repast at the Vice-Regal Lodge in Dublin. He was given every consideration and the Queen found him 'a very charming' man. Whilst Logue has the reputation of being an avowed nationalist, he was nonetheless able to declare to Lord Denbigh on that occasion that he was really a conservative at heart and wished that Irish Catholics could be free from their dependence on English radicals. He showed more circumspection in subsequent years, refusing to attend the coronation of Edward VII in 1902 because it was 'a Protestant service'.

The partition of the country in 1921 left northern Catholics with a sense of isolation and betrayal. Ironically the civil war which raged in the twenty-six counties over the question of the Republic had little impact on northern Catholics. Of much more immediate concern was the wave of persecution of Catholics which swept the north in the aftermath of the 1920 Government of Ireland Act. At almost every level Catholics were made to feel excluded from the new state.

For their part the northern bishops, while they condemned partition, quickly became reconciled to dealing with the northern political reality, mostly to protect Catholic interests in education in the face of Lord Londonderry's attempt to introduce non-denominational education. They urged as early as 1923 the abandonment of abstentionism as a political weapon.

The defensiveness of the northern Catholic community since 1922 has given rise to strange anomalies. Having, for the most part, been excluded from many facets of northern political and social life, Catholics attempted to create an alternative society within the overall structures of the state. The energies, which in a more normal environment would have been channelled into society at large, were turned inwards and gave to the practice of Catholicism in the north an intensity rarely displayed elsewhere in the country. Although the Church was never formally persecuted, it distrusted the pervasive Protestant ethos of much of northern life. Unspoken hostility at times spilled over into nakedly sectarian violence. Catholic pilgrims to the Dublin Eucharistic Congress in 1932 were stoned by Protestant mobs in several towns throughout the north. However, in time, the Church hierarchy would not only accept the northern state, but would actually defend it. In 1956, the bishops condemned the IRA border campaign and, moreover, declared it a mortal sin for any Catholic to even express verbal support for the IRA.

The change of attitude in the Catholic Church as a result of the Second Vatican Council (1962-1965) was slow to have its effect on northern Catholics. Although there was widespread acceptance of superficial changes, such as the move from Latin to the vernacular in the Mass, on the whole the Council's reforms did not inspire that vital energy which would have transformed the face of northern Catholicism. This was partly because the prevailing political hostility of the state continued to obtain, despite Terence O'Neill's efforts to bring about a more open society. The result was that Catholics still did not feel at home socially or politically in Northern Ireland in the 1960s. As a community, they continued to experience discrimination at all levels and this was coupled with political gerrymandering.

Given these circumstances it is hardly surprising that the northern Catholicism of those years was marked by an adherence to a somewhat archaic and triumphalist view of the Church, holding out as it did an eternal vindication in the face of the ills inflicted by the sectarian state. Often Catholics were encouraged to see themselves as a faithful remnant in a wilderness of Protestantism.

The last thirty years has seen enormous change in the leadership of the Catholic Church in the north. The cautious liberal-conservatism of Cardinal William Conway as Archbishop of Armagh, and the first Belfast man to be made a cardinal, was matched in Down and Connor by the sophisticated conservative theology of William Philbin. Although both highly gifted men – Conway was regarded as *papabali* – neither possessed 'the common touch' and, consequently, gave the impression of being somewhat aloof. It was to be the 1970s before the other northern dioceses had the benefit of younger and more dynamic leadership in the shape of Edward Daly in Derry and Joseph Duffy in Clogher.

The two individuals who have most dominated the Irish Church in the period under discussion were both northerners. Dr Cahal Daly finally returned as bishop to his native diocese in 1982, succeeding to the Primacy in 1990. He had for years provided the serious intellectual reflection in much of the Irish hierarchy's comment on Irish society in general and on the affairs of the north in particular. However, it was the warm personal charm and exuberance of the late Cardinal Tomas O Fiaich which most captured the imagination of northern Catholics in the 1970s and 1980s. A serious scholar, who wore his learning lightly, he was a committed ecumenist and yet passionately concerned with matters of justice and equality. For all that, he inspired distrust in many northern Protestants and sections of the British establishment for his unrepentant nationalism.

Clearly the years of the troubles have been a time of great difficulty for the Church. Widespread social unrest, IRA violence, state repression, internment without trial, sectarian assassinations, the hunger strikes of 1981, all these have posed enormous political, moral and spiritual dilemmas for Catholics and for the Church authorities. This has been coupled with a decrease in the influence and prestige of the Church among working class Catholics whose practice rate has tailed off dramatically. Yet the Church continues to play a vital role in northern life as it has done over the last hundred years. Its endurance is indeed a testament to faith.

Cardinal William Conway
pictured in conversation
with President de Valera
in the 1960s
Irish News

19

Culture and the Arts in the
North of Ireland since 1891

JOHN GRAY

Harry Furniss, writing in the English magazine *Black and White* one hundred years ago, observed that 'people do not go to the theatre in Belfast. There are those who would as soon visit the infernal regions'. Ulster was to prove a hostile environment for pioneers of the arts generally for much of the following century.

In the 1890s the Theatre Royal played host to English touring companies. Irish drama was represented by Dion Boucicault's melodramas, with *The Shagraun* offering particular opportunity for party cries from an audience of 'shipyard workers in their dungarees, men from the linen and rope factories, shawled mill girls, clerks old and young, and stage-struck apothecary apprentices'.

True J. P. Warden, owner of the Theatre Royal, went on to build the Grand Opera House in 1895, but for lavish pantomimes rather than serious theatre. Between 1904 and 1908 the Opera House was renamed the Palace of Varieties. Bland and respectable variety, pioneered at the Empire, opened in 1894, was already eliminating the old bawdy music hall of the Alhambra, where the celebrated W J Ashcroft attempted suicide on the stage in 1895 and went bankrupt in 1900. The Alhambra was to enjoy its revenge. The first films were shown here in 1896, harbinger of an entertainment which was to sweep all before it. In 1916 even the Theatre Royal fell to make way for the Royal Cinema.

Whether high-brow or low-brow, live performance reflected little of Ireland or Ulster. There was a distinct toughness about Ulster audiences – performers said that if you could survive Belfast and Glasgow you could survive anywhere. In the 1890s Sir Henry Benson was jeered off the Theatre Royal stage when he introduced the first uncensored version of Richard III. In 1900 Marie Lloyd suffered a similar fate at the Empire. At the Grand Opera House a net caught rivets and porter bottles hurled from the Gods. At the Alhambra ammunition came from the North Street vegetable stalls. At some venues Protestants and Catholics attended on different nights.

The Ulster Literary Theatre, founded in 1902 and inspired by the Irish Literary Theatre, offered an idealistic response to this environment. Failure with Yeatsian poetic drama soon suggested a 'difference', a realisation 'that our talent is more satiric than poetic'. They wrote their own plays and placed authentic Ulstermen on the stage. An annual season at the Grand Opera House, visits to the Abbey in Dublin and English and American tours followed. The difficulties of the venture were illustrated by their use of pseudonyms rather than their own names on programmes, and by difficulties of programmes themselves – in 1909 a leaflet showing 'King Billy' on a rocking horse for *Suzanne and the Sovereigns* had to be suppressed.

In fiction Shan F. Bullock in his Fermanagh novels pioneered the serious local novel. Donegal man, Patrick MacGill in his *Children of the Dead End* (1914) provided a searing portrait of rural exploitation and emigration and is still read today, while a summer school in his name also flourishes. St John Ervine's *Mrs Martin's Man* (1914) provided an authentic Belfast setting, though his more daring play *Mixed Marriage*, set against the background of the 1907 Belfast dock strike, was not performed locally.

Elsewhere the new century offered a window of opportunity for cultural diversity. The Linen Hall Library, which moved to new premises in 1896, and for long outstripped the public library service, supported an extensive cultural programme including the Belfast Harp Festival of 1903. Limitations were evident in 1907 when the Governors censured the nationalist, Francis Joseph Bigger, for delivering a 'political' lecture. Bigger and others had helped revive the *Ulster Journal of Archaeology* and were to maintain a high standard of local history journalism, even in Unionist newspapers, well into the 1920s.

By then, the Ulster Theatre, had dropped the world 'literary' from its name, suggesting a narrowing of horizons and lost momentum. Rutherford Mayne, and George Shiels remained household names, but hardly for arousing controversy. This was easily done in the 1920s when even a pure comedy such as Louis J. Walsh's *The Pope at Killybuck* had to be renamed *The Auction at Killybuck* to secure performance.

Richard Hayward's Belfast Repertory Company put on an annual season at the Empire from 1929 and was notable for its discovery of Thomas Carnduff whose *Workers, Machinery* and *Traitors* all transferred to the Abbey. Attempts at the Little Theatre (1933-6) and the Playhouse (1937) to provide full time local theatre failed. Refugees from these ventures and strong local amateur companies, were to enjoy greater success at the Group founded in 1940. St John Ervine's '*Boyd's Shop*' was an early triumph for the new theatre, perhaps because it showed 'the Presbyterian Ulsterman as he likes to believe he is'.

St John Ervine, writing in 1937 as a strident supporter of all things Ulster as against 'Eirean', conceded that Ulster's 'artistic activities were sporadic'. Of local authors he could list, only Forrest Reid's reputation stands. Much local writing suffered from what the novelist Michael McLaverty described as 'a preponderant use of dialect degenerating into an arid provincialism'.

The Alhambra Theatre in Belfast's Lower North Street in 1937. Cinema-going was popular with all social classes by the 1930s
Ulster Museum

There was no danger of this at the BBC which came to Belfast in 1924. Here English accents alienated both communities. Fine early documentaries by Denis Johnston and Louis MacNeice were the exception rather than the rule. Celebrating St Patrick's Day proved a politico-cultural minefield, and Second World War minefields found local radio working hand in hand with the Stormont government to eliminate the word 'Ireland' from the airwaves. Catholics and more adventurous northern writers turned to Radio Eireann and writers welcomed Sean O'Faolain's Dublin based *The Bell* founded in 1940.

Ulster's first post-partition literary magazine, *Lagan*, was founded in 1944. Here John Boyd called for a new 'regional literature' and argued that 'an Ulster writer cannot evade his problems by adopting either a superimposed English or a sentimental Gaelic outlook'. John Hewitt entitled an article on the problems of local writing 'The bitter gourd', and David Kennedy attacked a theatre that 'skated over the thin ice of political and sectarian animosities'.

There was post-war hope. The Group flourished and, from 1945 onwards, the Arts Theatre under Hubert Wilmot offered foreign and experimental plays. The BBC opened its doors to local writers and performers and Sam Hanna Bell pioneered outside recording and cultural documentary. A mass audience was finally won with Joe Tomelty's celebrated Belfast back street serial 'The McCooey's'.

The Festival of Britain in 1951 encouraged Unionists to explore regional culture under an acceptable banner. It was a cultural way out of an *impasse* for a Northern Ireland still opposed by nationalists. These included Mary O'Malley, then a Labour councillor and also founder in 1951, with her husband Pearse, of the Lyric Theatre, a venture committed to the tradition of the Irish Literary Theatre.

There were limits, too, to Unionist enthusiasm for regionalism. These did not include accommodation for opponents such as John Hewitt, the most radical Ulster regionalist, who was excluded from appointment as Director of the Belfast Museum and exiled quite literally to Coventry. It did allow for a belated acceptance of local schools broadcasting, for the creation of the Ulster Scot Historical Society in 1957, the Ulster Folk Museum in 1958, and the elevation of the Belfast Museum to 'national' status in 1964. Other institutions stirred in response to the new climate with Queen's University creating a chair of Irish History and, in 1965, the Institute of Irish Studies.

Meanwhile the growth of radio and the introduction of television in 1955, followed by the arrival of Ulster Television in 1959, brought the first wave of cinema closures, and threatened serious theatre. CEMA and later the Arts Council were to fill the gap but with a close eye to political acceptability.

Direct censorship was to find a formidable opponent in Sam Thompson whose *Over the Bridge*, the first Ulster play to confront sectarianism frontally, was censored by the directors of the Group Theatre in 1958, with the full support of the cultural establishment. Thompson and his allies eventually secured a triumphant five week run at the Empire, and thus opened up the boundaries of the Ulster stage.

Novelists too were becoming more daring and Brian Moore and Maurice Leitch both fell foul of southern censors. Sam Hanna Bell's *December Bride* (1951) and Moore's *The Lonely Passion of Judith Hearne* (1955) have both been filmed, a tribute to their enduring qualities.

Growing artistic confidence was reflected in a broad-based campaign for a state-funded Northern Ireland Civic Theatre. This, however, collapsed in acrimony in 1964 when the campaign chairman, Sir Tyrone Guthrie, spoke of the 'wildly artificial' border.

The Lyric Theatre, meanwhile, was winning an enviable reputation for poetic drama and a wider repertoire, all performed at a drawing room base which protected it from cruder cultural storms. When it sought to expand at Ridgeway Street, it faced loyalty tests from potential business supporters and from the Arts Council – both required the playing of the National Anthem. Debilitating though this row was, the onset of the troubles as the new theatre opened posed a greater threat to live theatre.

In 1968 the first issue of a new literary magazine, *The Honest Ulsterman*, edited by James Simmons, had declared 'revolution'. This was a call for the new moral freedoms of the hippy era rather than political revolt.

Queen's University, focal point of political crisis, also spawned a new northern poetry. The group associated with English-born lecturer Philip Hobsbaum, or who saw publication in Queen's Festival pamphlets in 1965 included Michael Longley, James Simmons, Derek Mahon, Seamus Deane, and most celebrated of all, the Nobel winner Seamus Heaney, now perhaps the best known poet in the English language. Paul Muldoon and others were soon to follow. All disclaimed any direct influence on politics. Heaney acknowledges 'a slow, obstinate, papish burn, emanating from the ground I was brought up on', but seeks no more than 'a field of force' allowing full play to 'the perspectives of a humane reason' which 'grants the religious intensity of the violence its deplorable authenticity and complexity'. To find space of this kind has not been easy, and he has been criticised for the 'nationalist' knee jerk of his Open Letter (1983) attacking the *Penguin Book of Contemporary British Poetry* for including him as a 'British' poet.

Fiction has made less impact on cultural debate despite an explosion of thriller literature making essentially exploitative use of our circumstances. Bernard McLaverty's *Cal* (1982) has been filmed, and amongst newcomers

Glenn Patterson with *Burning Your Own* (1988) and Robert McLiam Wilson with *Ripley Bogle* (1989) are ones to watch. Perhaps most successful has been Derry based Jennifer Johnston who since *Captains and the Kings* (1972) has established a major reputation.

The Derry-based Field Day Theatre Company, founded in 1981 by Brian Friel and Stephen Rea, has suggested a more specific cultural agenda. Brian Friel, already one of Ulster's best known playwright, since *Philadelphia Here I Come*, enjoyed critical acclaim for *Translations*, Field Day's first play, which was less evident in Belfast. Here Frank McGuinness's *Observe the Sons of Ulster Marching Towards the Somme* (1985), a play rejected by Field Day, was viewed more sympathetically for its understanding of the roots of the loyalist tradition. In terms of public success, Martin Lynch's *Dockers* and Graham Reid's *Billy* plays have made perhaps the greatest impact.

If even literary critics can separate along traditional lines, the restrictive impact of such tensions has lessened. Attempts to construct a Catholic and national literature, or conversely a Northern Ireland literature, have long since failed. Writers acknowledge their roots but dissent. Preoccupations with 'Borderlines', as in the title of Derry poet Sam Burnside's 1985 collection, or with map- making as in *Translations* or Ciaran Carson's *Belfast Confetti* (1989) remain but, as John Hewitt put it in 1984, 'the whole tarnished map is stained and torn, never to be read as pastoral again'. The John Hewitt Summer School has become a major focus for cultural debate and interaction.

Writers have benefited from the emergence of local publishing, encouraged by the establishment in 1971 of an Arts Council literature programme and pioneered in the same year by Blackstaff Press who remain the leading imprint. These publishers also serve the great increase in interest in local history. A handful of local history societies have grown to 70 in number today. The virtual exclusion of Irish studies from schools, has also been succeeded by rapid syllabus change.

Rapidly increased funding for education and the arts has helped although during the 1970s and 1980s the Arts Council, was criticised for funding safe 'flagship' enterprises such as the Ulster Orchestra and the Grand Opera House, which it re-opened in 1979, rather than more potentially controversial ventures. The Queen's Festival at Queen's, the second largest festival in the United Kingdom, has been criticised for playing safe.

Government itself now sees potential in culture and the arts as social cement. The Cultural Traditions Group has explored the possibilities, but has also identified problems. For writers and artists one is that their history in the first one-hundred years has been one of struggle to emerge from the tyranny of existing traditions. Another is that the new literature and the sophisticated debate that surrounds it may not transmit to the ghetto interfaces.

20
The Irish Language in Ulster
from the 1890s to the Present Day

ROGER BLANEY

The fortunes the Irish language in the north of Ireland have shown great changes in the period from just before the Great Famine up to the present time. Paradoxically, never before in the history of Irish have there been as many readers of the language as there are today. Also new in the history of the language are the many pre-school groups, the Irish language primary schools, Radio na Gaeltachta, Irish being broadcast by the BBC on radio and, more recently, on television, and of course, the regular publication of the daily newspaper, *Lá*. However, we still have one ingredient that has not changed. The voice of gloom is always with us, warning the people that Irish is on its last legs. Frequently, the harbingers' credentials are tarnished in that they have no Irish themselves, casting doubts on their motivation.

Yet, the warnings are often made in a friendly tone, and not all comments on Irish are as dismissive as those made by Lord Craigavon in the Northern Ireland Parliament in March 1936, when he said: 'What use is the Irish language to the people of this progressive and busy part of the British Empire?' It is easy for us today, with hindsight, knowing the subsequent fate of both the empire and Stormont, to dismiss Craigavon's viewpoint as completely unenlightened and intolerant. But it is important to remember that much worse than any comments he could have made was the actual abandonment of the language by the very people who spoke it, as their ancestors had spoken it over a period of two thousand years. After all, Craigavon never had the chance of learning Irish and so was completely unaware of its virtues and advantages. The rest of the world and other members of the European family, most of whom have a facility with two or more languages, might reasonably expect us to have something to offer culturally, and would hardly be pleased to learn that we, the Irish, north or south, had taken on ourselves to reject or discard parts of our heritage, particularly a treasure so important as the language, which happens to be also the rightful property of the whole human family, and which we have no right to suppress.

Over the period covered by this select review the language has been subject to economic, cultural and political forces to varying degrees. Sometimes these have worked for Irish and sometimes against. Politics has been an uneasy and sometimes treacherous ally of the language. It is most unfortunate that politicians and 'professional patriots' have thought it a good idea to use the Irish language to further their own party's narrower ends. Cultural units in society and political entities on the map rarely coincide, and so it is both unrealistic and detrimental to the language to tie it to the nation state.

In the battle of language dominance, the language 'which will get me a job' tends to win the advantage. Yet the Methodist Chapel in Wales has been probably the greatest bulwark of all in protecting the Welsh language against the onslaughts of English. In contrast, the Catholic Church, with very notable exceptions, has been one of the greatest forces for anglicisation in the development of Ireland. The clergy surpassed their congregations in the belief that English alone provided the prospect for improvement. This was because the clergy were largely recruited from the peasantry of Ireland who, in the main, had become so downtrodden that their image of themselves and their sense of identity had become so negative that they rushed in haste to discard as many of their traditions as seemed to them associated with poverty and deprivation.

For whatever reasons, the general trend for the last 150 years has been for the traditional Irish speakers to give up the language. The Gaelic League and similar organisations must be given the credit for stemming this haemorrhage to some extent, but more so for having pressurised the authorities and government to take a responsibility for the conservation of the language, or even better, to make attempts to promote the Irish language. So a counterflow in the Gaeltacht has been successfully created, and thus there is a great growth in the number of parents rearing their children with Irish as the mother tongue. This is decidedly an urban phenomenon and is particularly strong both in Dublin and Belfast. Such Irish speakers have been nurtured by the Gaeltacht.

If Irish is to progress, it can only be by previous English speakers turning over to Irish as their first language. This is already happening, but has created havoc in the traditional thinking of the Gaelic League, which has not come to terms with such a revolution. Official statistics about Irish speakers in Northern Ireland up to 1911 come from the 10 year censuses. In 1851, immediately after the Great Irish Famine, the number of Irish speakers in the six counties which now constitute Northern Ireland was 39,236, coming to 2.7 per cent of the population. These figures must be seen as minimal, because many did not want to admit that they were Irish speakers.

By 1911 the number of officially recorded Irish speakers was 29,423, coming to 2.3 per cent of the population. This was the last census for which the questions on Irish were asked. The 1991 census was the first one to include the question since the formation of the state.

There was probably no time ever when Irish was not spoken in Belfast. The very name is Irish, meaning the mouth (*beal*) of the sandbank (*feirste*), which also gives its name to the Farset River (*Feirste*). The new arrivals made very little attempt to alter the ancient names of places and all townland names are in the Irish language, albeit spelt phonetically.

An Irish motto, 'Erin Go Bragh' ('Ireland Forever') at the Ulster Unionist Convention, held in Belfast in 1892
Ulster Museum

Queen Victoria's one and only visit to Belfast was in 1849. In her diary of Saturday 11 August, the day she was driven in a carriage through the city, she writes:

I have all along forgotten to say that the favourite motto written up on most of the arches, etc, and in every place was: "Cead Míle Failte", which means 'a hundred thousand welcomes' in Irish, which is very like Gaelic; it is in fact THE language, and has existed in books from the earliest period, whereas Gaelic has only been written since half a century, though it was always spoken. They often called out, 'Cead mile failte!' and it appears in every sort of shape.

Victoria, by Gaelic, meant the Gaidhlic of Scotland. There is plenty of confirming evidence that many of the Belfast banners were written in Irish on her visit to Belfast. One of the banners depicted the following greeting:

> Cead mile failte ar mhilliun don Bhanrion.,
> Go Cuige Uladh na hEire;
> Go mba mharthanach slan a n-urraim is a dtain di,
> Le gean is le gra ona geillteain.

– which may be translated:

> A hundred thousand welcomes a million times
> over to the Queen on her visit to the Ulster
> Province of Ireland – May their respect and their
> popular support for her unsullied and
> everlasting, with fondness ard love from her subjects.

Two years after the founding of the national Gaelic League in Dublin, the Belfast Gaelic League held its inaugural meeting on 19 August 1895. It had grown out of the Irish classes run by the Belfast Naturalists' Field Club under the control of P. J. O'Shea who had initiated them in 1892. It has been stated that the Belfast branch was the first in Ulster, but the Glenties branch in Co. Donegal was founded a month earlier. The inaugural meeting took place in the house of P. T. McGinley, 32 Beersbridge Road. Dr St Clair Boyd was elected president, P. T. McGinley elected vice-president and E. Morrissey as temporary honorary secretary. Also present were P. J. O'Shea and Eoin MacNeill, co-founder of the League and a native of Glenarm in the Glens of Antrim.

During December and January, the Irish classes were held at 49 Queen Street, in the Belfast Art Society's Rooms which had become the centre for classes and meetings. Classes continued as a core activity, but the Belfast Branch also took an active interest in the general welfare of the language. They considered it essential to visit the Gaeltacht regularly not only to keep up their own linguistic skills, but also to encourage native speakers to be loyal and support the language at all times. For this end, they visited the Glens of Antrim, Draperstown, and Omeath, in which places Irish was spoken as a living language, and they were happy to find general support.

Even ardent Irish language enthusiasts were surprised to find the extent of spoken Irish in East Ulster. St Clair Boyd referred to this in his address to the Branch at the first annual general meeting. Membership now stood at 120, most of them going to classes. The branch was supported by many influential people and support was coming from every religious and social grouping. By September 1896, there were three Irish classes in progress, graduated according to level of ability, the *Ard-rang* (advanced class) being taken by O'Shea and MacGinley, intermediate by Mr Ward, and the beginners class taken by Hussey and Martin.

The branch members were not afraid of taking an activist stance from time to time and they issued a public statement during 1897 criticising the Resident Magistrate, William Orr, who had sentenced a Patrick Connors of Dungarvan to a week in prison because he had given evidence in Irish. At the 1897 annual general meeting, the Church of Ireland Bishop-elect, to be translated to Ossory, Canon John Baptist Crozier, was presented with a laudatory address expressing appreciation for his acting as a patron of the Belfast Gaelic League and wishing him well, yet expressing sadness that he has leaving them to go to Kilkenny. Canon Crozier made a reply, of which 200 copies were printed by the branch, saying that it was from his teacher that he got a love of Irish and that he hoped that the language would never die. He then distributed the various prizes to the winners.

At the beginning of 1898 Lawrence Clery recommended that the Belfast branch be recognised as the primary Ulster branch and that the president of each other Ulster branch be de facto a member of *Craobh Bheal Feirste*. The Protestant poetess Alice Milligan, who was a member from the beginning, was delegated to approach the Society for the Extension of University Teaching to ask them to provide a course of lectures on the Irish language and its literature.

In these early days, there was some tension between those members who felt that it was most appropriate that the Ulster variety of Irish should have first place, and on the other hand those who believed that such an emphasis was 'provincial'. On one occasion, for example, Eoin MacNeill recommended that the Belfast branch should publish a book in the Ulster dialect. The majority of members agreed and suggestions were made that the publication would be founded on the stories and texts from Neilson's *Grammar* along with other Ulster stories, but a vociferous minority, which included Ward, argued strongly against such 'provincialism'.

On the 26 October 1899, exactly a year later, the Belfast Coiste Ceanntair held its first annual meeting attended by nine registered branches. By November 1904, there were 11 branches registered with the Coiste Ceanntair. A major public meeting was organised for December 1904. Cardinal Logue (himself a native speaker from Donegal) was in the chair and, in his address, was at pains to point out that the Irish language was a force for friendship between Catholic and Protestant. His point was that the Irish language was 'affording a common platform to Catholic and Protestant, Gael, Sean-Ghall, and Nua-Ghall, north and south'. Furthermore, he was of the opinion that 'the League was softening the asperities of Irish life, bringing the people together and giving them a common platform to Catholic and Protestant and giving them a kindly feeling for each other.'

A logical development was an overall Assembly for Ulster, *Dail Uladh*, founded in 1905 to co-ordinate the work of the counties. The Dail ran The Ulster Training College of Irish, called Ardscoil Cholm Cille in the Donegal Gaeltacht of Cloghaneely. It was founded in 1906 with the aim of training teachers in Ulster Irish. It was later known as Colaiste Uladh. A number of other significant developments occurred in these years.

The Feis Ceoil

The first modern *Feis Ceoil* (Musical Festival) was held in Dublin in May 1897. Belfast, the second city of Ireland, was chosen for the second ever Feis for 1898. The Belfast Feis Ceoil was clearly a Protestant, and probably also a unionist, event. The two patrons were Lady Annesley of Castlewellan and Lady Arthur Hill of Gilford. Among the General Committee were Charles H. Brett, John St Clair Boyd, F. J. Bigger, W. G. Churchill, M. Crymble, W. H. Derrick-Lane, Lord Mayor of Belfast James Henderson and Robert Young.

The Belfast College of Irish was founded in 1905 with the Protestant nationalist lawyer, F. J. Bigger, as its patron. It was housed in St Mary's Hall, Bank Street and existed until 1923. It operated under the auspices of the Belfast Coiste Ceanntair and the principal was Sean O Cathain, assisted by Maire Ni Mathuna M.A., Sean O Ciarsaigh, and, sometime afterwards, *Cu Uladh* (P.T. McGinley). The latter was appointed around the time that he had raised a motion at the 1908 meeting of the Dail Uladh requesting Coiste Ceanntair Bheal Feirste to make sure that at least one teacher in Colaiste Chomhghaill had Ulster Irish. For some time after its foundation only Munster Irish was taught in the College. Belfast Irish speakers finally gave up trying to change this situation and instituted the Ard-Scoil Uladh (The Ulster High School), in which only Ulster Irish would be used. So deep was the antagonism against Colaiste Chomhghaill that this organisation is referred to only indirectly in *An Craobh Ruadh*, a journal published by the branch of the same name in 1913. It gets a mention as a school mainly for training teachers but the committee had broken off from the control of the Coiste Ceanntair and had made it virtually their own property.

An Association for Ulster, Comhaltas Uladh, was formed in the year 1926 as a result of a meeting in Armagh City Hall on 3 October. Whereas the old Dail Uladh was simply a co-ordinating body and subordinate to the central Gaelic League in Dublin the new body was virtually independent. The thrust for this move was concern to preserve Ulster Irish. Fr Larry Murray, the chief architect of this development, had already founded in 1924, a journal, *An tUltach* (*The Ulsterman*), which has been published regularly ever since. Comhaltas Uladh has been the main Irish language organisation in Ulster up to the present time. It has sent countless children to the Gaeltacht to learn Irish. Today, few people have not heard of Colaiste Bhride, Ranafast, Co Donegal, the famous Irish summer college.

Another important body was the Gaelic Fellowship founded in the late 1940s by John (Sean) Pasker (1903-1965), a Presbyterian civil servant from Belfast, with the object of 'studying the Gaelic, music, etc, and to provide a means whereby the Protestants who are interested in these subjects many become acquainted'.

The prospectus also stated that the Fellowship was strictly non-political, and 'membership is limited to persons who are in agreement with the ideals of the YMCA and who know, or would like to learn, Gaelic.' The prospectus stressed that the Fellowship was strictly non-political and wedded to the ideals of the Y.M.C.A. Pasker's ambition was to help towards healing ancient wounds and in a more tolerant society his efforts would doubtlessly have been recognised by official honours. His good work was, on the contrary, ignored by the Stormont civil service. The Irish language community, however, were very conscious of his courage and his valuable work.

St Brigid's College, Omeath, County Louth, was founded by Eoin MacNeill and Fr Donal O Tuathail (O'Toal) a Belfast curate, on 22 August 1912. It offered a six-week course in Irish for three standards of ability, elementary, middle and advanced. The teaching staff included Eoin MacNeill and Peadar O Dubhda. In 1914 about a hundred students attended. In 1913 St Malachy's Council was set up in order to keep alive Irish in Counties Down and Antrim and to spread it further. The two most actively Irish speaking areas were Rathlin Island and the Glens of Antrim. Rathlin was chosen for a summer college and was run by the council of which F J Bigger was the president as well as being one of the lecturers. Bigger's summer retreat at 'Castle Sheain', Ardglass, County Down, was a regular focus for Irish language enthusiasts.

The annual Ard-fheis of the Gaelic League for 1915 was held in Dundalk. This is forever remembered as the meeting at which was adopted the change in the constitution making 'an Ireland free and independent' as an objective of the League, which up to now had been clearly non-political and non-sectarian. Later, in the same meeting, the movement's founder, Dr. Douglas Hyde, refused to let his name go forward as president. This division between Hyde and the organisation which he had fostered from the beginning had a great symbolic effect on how the League was subsequently perceived and is said to have had a significant influence on unionist opinion. Among the many friends which the Gaelic League lost was Cardinal Logue, who in a letter testified, 'Since the Gaelic League has become a political machine, I fear that it will be totally sterile in relation to the revival of Irish'.

A landmark in the language revival in Dungannon was the initiation of Irish classes in St Patrick's Academy in 1900. This signalled the beginning of a great swell of activity in the area. Other schools soon followed suit and by 1907, a great number of schools were teaching the language. The language gained an early foothold in a number of northern centres, notably Lurgan where the local branch of the Gaelic League published a monthly journal in the 1940s. Derry and Newry have also been Gaelic strongholds.

Professor Eoin MacNeill, the co-founder of the Gaelic League, Cardinal Logue, and the Belfast Protestant Nationalist, lawyer, F.J. Bigger pictured at Omeath Irish Summer School, 1912
Rev. Prof. F.X. Martin, OSA

Some biographies

Organisations and movements such as those mentioned could not function without the devotion and commitment of dynamic and dedicated individuals. The Irish language has never lacked such supporters.

Robert Shipboy MacAdam (1808-1895) has left a significant and lasting imprint on the story of Irish in East Ulster. He was born in High Street Belfast in 1808. On the formation of the Ulster Gaelic Society in 1830, he was made a co-secretary along with Dr Reuben Bryce. For the rest of his life he continued to implement the objectives of the society, even after it ceased to exist. His most significant contribution was to harvest as much written Irish literature as possible, and the extensive manuscript collection at present housed in the Belfast Public Library, although only a fraction of the total which he originally collected, is a fitting monument to his diligence. In 1835, while he was still a young man, he wrote an Irish grammar for use of the Irish classes in the Royal Belfast Academical Institution, his *alma mater*.

P. J. O'Shea (Conan Maol) (1855-1928) was one of a number of Irish-speaking Customs and Excise Officers who came to Belfast and who were influential in spreading Munster Irish through the city to the extent that they provoked a movement for the rights of Ulster Irish, led later by Fr Larry Murray. Posted to Belfast in 1892, he started an Irish class under the patronage of the Belfast Naturalists' Field Club.

Peter Toner Macginley (Cu Uladh) (1856-1942) a native of Glenswilly, Co Donegal, was educated in Dublin and later joined Customs and Excise with which he was an officer for 47 years. The first meeting of the Belfast Gaelic League took place in his house, 32 Beersbridge Road, on 19 August 1895. Spurred on by the lack of Ulster writers in Irish, he began writing himself, using the pen name of *Cu Uladh* (Hound of Ulster). His play *Eilis agus an Bhean Deirce* (*Alice and the Beggar Woman*) was first performed in Belfast, on 1 November 1900. His later publications include other plays, a handbook of Irish teaching, short stories, folk tales, songs and historical works. He was chairman of a meeting in December 1923 which founded Comhaltas Uladh for the promotion of Irish. This was not, however, Comhaltas Uladh of today founded by Fr Larry Murray. He was president of The Gaelic League from 1922 to 1925.

Dr John St Clair Boyd (1858-1918) While remaining consistently unionist, the Boyd family appear to have inherited a liberal tradition. Only son of John Kane Boyd, St Clair Boyd spent his youth in Holywood, Co Down. Having qualified in medicine at Queen's University, Belfast, he was still engaged in a busy professional life when he began to take an active interest in Irish cultural affairs. This was even before the formation of the Gaelic League. In that year (1893) he was already a member of the Belfast Naturalists' Field Club, an organisation much affected by the Celtic Revival. When the Belfast Gaelic League was formed in 1895 he was made its first president. At the first Oireachtas of the Gaelic League held in the Round Room, Rotunda, Dublin on Monday, 17 May 1897, Dr Boyd was on the platform along with President Dr Douglas Hyde and other persons prominent in the Irish language movement.

Francis Joseph Bigger (1863-1926) Joseph Campbell has described Bigger as follows:

> 'I think I see him now, as in his prime...
> A brown-faced, quiet-mannered human man,
> Whose noble mind was mirrored in his eye;
> Who loved his people and the land that bore him...'

Frank Bigger was a consistently diligent supporter of the Irish language all his life, and his involvement began as early as 1894 when he attended the Irish classes run by the Belfast Naturalists' Field Club and taught by P J O'Shea (Conan Maol). For some years he was a member of the Coiste Gnotha (Executive Committee) of the Central Gaelic League and became President of the Coiste Ceanntair in Belfast. He was well known to the great cultural leaders of the day, including Douglas Hyde, Eoin MacNeill, Shane Leslie and Alice Stopford Green.

Fr Larry Murray (1883-1941) The Irish language movement was most fortunate in having such a diligent worker as Larry Murray of whom it was said that every major endeavour which he undertook ended in success. A native of Carlingford, he was the moving force behind the founding of *An tUltach*, St Brigid's College Ranafast, and Comhaltas Uladh, all of which prospered and all of which still flourish today.

Ernest Blythe (1889-1975) Earnán de Blaghd, as he was called in Irish, was born of a Church of Ireland father and a Presbyterian mother in Magheragall near Lisburn. His lifelong interest in Irish began as a boy when he discovered that the first language of servant girls on their farm was Irish and not English. The home of these girls was in Newry and South Armagh. He also discovered that he had Presbyterian relatives in the Castlewellan area who were native Irish speakers.

He became fluent in Irish after his sojourn in the Kerry Gaeltacht, and later evolved as a significant writer in the language. It was his first love, and his activities as an important politician, including being a cabinet minister in the Cosgrave Government, and as theatre manager, were secondary. Many, especially politicians, find Irish useful for other ends, but for Blythe Irish was an end in itself. Therefore as manager of the Abbey Theatre, always on his agenda was the promotion of plays in Irish. He encouraged Mac Liammóir and Edwards to found Taibhearc na Gaillimhe, the Galway Irish-language theatre.

One of his monumental achievements was the foundation of An Gúm, the government publishing house for the printing of hundreds of books in Irish, many of them translations from English and other languages including German, French, and Russian.

Robert Lynd (1879-1949) Robert Wilson Lynd, the famous essayist, son of a Belfast Presbyterian clergyman, was devoted to the Irish language. Indeed he met his wife to be, Sylvia Dryhurst, when they both were members of the Gaelic League in London. They reared their children. Sighle and Màire, through Irish.

Heinrich Wagner (1923-1988) He belonged to the long tradition of German speakers who became interested in Irish. In fact his enthusiasm was awakened by his grammar school teacher in Switzerland, J.U. Hubschmied, and later Heinrich became a pupil of Julius Pokorny, the famous scholar of old Irish. It was Pokorny who advised him in 1945 to go to Ireland to learn the language. By 1951, when he was only 28 years old, he was Professor of Germanic lingustic studies in Utrecht and became Professor of Celtic in Queen's University in 1958. His great work, the Linguistic Atlas and Survey of Irish Dialects, was published in four volumes in the sixties. The survey work was a vast undertaking and involved asking 1175 questions of each of the Gaelic speakers he visited in 87 towns in Ireland, Isle of Man, and Scotland.

After twenty one years spent in Belfast he took up post as a professor in the Institute of Advanced Studies in Dublin. His death in 1988 was a great blow not only to scholarship in the Irish language but to his innumerable friends everywhere.

The Belfast Gaeltacht

Perhaps the most striking success of the language movement in Northern Ireland has been the creation of the Belfast Gaeltacht, the only city Gaeltacht in Ireland. This can be traced back to a meeting of a group of young Irish-speaking parents in 1960.

Having decided that the way forward was together as an Irish speaking community, they overcame all obstacles and the result is that now there are 11 families with over 60 people, several primary and nursery schools and, just beginning, a secondary grammar school. There are plans for further expansion, and the project shows what can be done with determination, hope and enthusiasm.

21

Sir Samuel Ferguson

1810-1886

GRÉAGÓIR Ó DÚILL

Rugadh Samuel Ferguson sa tSráid Ard i mBéal Feirste in 1810. Fuair sé bas i mBáile Atha Cliath in 1886. Is é an file is tabhachtaí ó oirthear Uladh ó Shéamas Dall Mac Cuarta go Louis MacNeice, nó b'fhéidir an file is fearr sa chúige uilig i gcaitheamh na tréimhse sin. Is tabhachtaí féin ná a chuid filíochta an bealach oibre a bhí aige, an modh smaointe. Ba dhuine é ar cheap dílseoirí Uladh agus náisiúntóirí míleata gur díobh é, ach níor mhair a cháil go maith mar gheall ar a neamhspleáchas aigne agus gnímh, mar nár chloígh sé leis na blocanna móra cumhachta agus smaointeachais.

Sir Samuel Ferguson
(1810-86)

Ba de mhuintir phlandáil Uladh é; síolraíodh é ó Albanach a tháinig le harm agus tine gó hÉirinn sna 1640í, agus bhí traidisiún láidir sa teaghlach gur throid sé fórsaí an rí aimsir an Chúnaint. Bhí Ferguson anbhródúil as an sinsearacht Albanach seo a bhí aige, agus deireadh sé gur dhream amháin iad Gaeil na hÉireann, muintir na hAlban a tháinig de phlandáil Ghael Éireann in Albain míle éigin bliain ó shin agus sliocht a sleachta sin a phlandáil cúige Uladh sa seachtú céad déag. Níorbh é an Béarla caighdeánta a bhí á labhairt thart timpeall air agus é ag fás aníos i nGleann an Choire i lár Cho Aontroma, ach cineál Albais nó Lallans agus ní folair nó bhíodh cuid de Ghaeilge Ghleann Aireamh le cluinstin aige ó am go chéile. Bhí roinnt mhaith filíochta á scríobh san Albais seo – ba é David Herbison prímhfhile na linne, agus fuair sé tacaíocht nár bheag ó Ferguson agus óna dheirfiúracha. Mar sin de, ba dhuine é Ferguson a raibh tuiscint aige óna óige do luach cultúrtha canúintí agus teangacha nach raibh meas orthu sna parlúis.

Ba Phrotastúnach é. Ní fios cén uair a thiontaigh sé ón eaglais Phreisbitéireach, nó ar thiontaigh a mhuintir roimhe. Níorbh fhéidir leis scrúdaithe Choláiste na Tríonóide a dhéanamh gan bheith san eaglais bhunaithe. Bhí brú ar leithéidí mhuintir Ferguson tiontú ina nAnglacánaigh, mar chlann a bhí ag iarraidh státas a bhaint amach mar 'gentry' – státas nach raibh dlite dóibh, nó tháinig a gcuid airgid ó chíosa plodcheantair Pháirc an Ghabhann agus Pháirc an Mhuilinn, léas talaimh Shéipéil Mhuire san áireamh. Ní raibh ciall ar bith don ghnó ag athair Ferguson (ná ag duine ar bith dá thriúr mac), agus bhí orthu dul ó áit go háit thart timpeall ar Bhéal Feirste gur shocraigh siad i nGleann an Choire. Rinne Ferguson mionchur síos próis agus filíochta go minic ar na háiteacha inar chaith sé a óige – Gleann an Choire agus deisceart ardchlár Aontroma, Throne agus Carn Muine agus Beann Mhadagain, an Mhainistir Bhán agus Carraig Fheargusa, Oileán Mhic Aodha agus Loch nEachach.

Mar sin féin, ba bheag an iarracht a rinne se fanacht ina cheantar dúchais. I ndiaidh a scolaíochta ar Inst, chaith sé cúpla bliain ar Choláiste na Tríonóide, ach ní raibh an t-airgead ag a mhuintir é a choinneáil ansin go gcríochnódh sé an cúrsa.

Chuir sé eolas ar an traidisiún AnglaÉireannach ann, Swift agus Gandon, Grattan agus Goldsmith agus mar sin, agus (macasamhail Yeats) shocraigh sé go raibh an traidisiún sin oiriúnach dó féin. Fuair sé aithne ar roinnt daoine a chuidigh leis – Butt, Thomas Davis agus mar sin. Ach bhí air dul abhaile go Béal Feirste, aidhmeanna aige a shaol a chaitheamh agus a chuid a shaothrú mar fhear uasal d'údar, ach gan an cur chuige aige. Bhí iarÉireannach Aontaithe, Teeling, arbh aide-de-camp a dhearthár ag Humbert san ionradh a rinne na Francaigh ar Chill Ala, 1798, i mbun irise agus thug sé misneach dó. Theip ar iris Teeling, The Ulster Magazine, ach d'fhoilsigh sé roinnt dánta de chuid Ferguson agus ghríosaigh sin an fear óg le hábhar a chur chuig ceann de na hirisí ba mhó clú sna trí ríocht, Blackwood's Dhún Éidin. Ba iris láidir Phrotastúnach agus aontachtúil Toóaioch í, agus bhí spéis in Éirinn ag úineir/eagarthóir na hirise, William Blackwood, go háirithe sa chaoi a raibh na Protastúnaigh agus Preisbitéirigh uilig, beagbheann ar aicme, ag teacht le chéile chun méadú chumhacht na gCaitliceach, tráth seo na Fuascailte agus ina dhiaidh, a throid. D'fhág sin tionchar ar Ferguson, nó chonaic sé narbh ionann ag Albanach a bheith dílis don choróin agus don reifirmeisean agus a bheith dímheasúil ar chultúr agus ar stair a thíre féin.

Ba do Blackwood a scríobh sé 'A Dialogue between the Heart and the Head of an Irish Protestant' ina bhféachann sé leis an chontrárthacht seo idir tírghrá agus Galldachas a iniúchadh, agus ba é Blackwood a d'iarr air léirmheas mór fada a scríobh ar Irish Minstrelsy James Hardiman, bailiúchán mór d'amhráin na Gaeilge maille le haistriúchán, nótaí agus réamhrá.

D'admhaigh Ferguson gur bheag Gaeilge a bhí aige go fóill – bhí sé i Londain an tráth sin, in ainm agus a bheith faoi oiliúint abhcóide, ach é ag caitheamh formhór a chuid ama ag déanamh taighde ar stair oirthear Uladh, agus é ag foghlaim na Fraincise, na Laidine agus na Gaeilge chuige sin. Dá mba bheag an Ghaeilge a bhí aige, ba mhó an tuiscint ar an fhilíocht agus ar aistriúchán na filíochta a bhí aige ná mar a bhí ag Hardiman agus a chuid fo-aistritheoirí. Nuair a tháinig a léirmheas amach, i gceithre aiste ar an Dublin University Magazine úr, agus léar mór aistriúchán cearta ann mar fhreagra ar Hardiman, ba léir gurbh é Ferguson an duine ba mhó cumais chun filíocht a aistriú ón nuaGhaeilge dá raibh ann go dtí sin. Mar gheall ar an ghlacadh a bhí ina cheantar dúchais leis an Albais mar mheán filíochta níor leisc le Ferguson an Béarla galánta a sheachaint agus, nuair a bhí sé ag aistriú fhilíocht an phobail, Béarla an phobail Eireannaigh sa lá aige féin a úsáid. D'fhág sin an deis aige cuid mhaith de ghramadach na Gaeilge agus roinnt dá rithimí agus dá stór focal féin a úsáid. Ní dheachaigh sé chomh fada agus a chuaigh Synge agus Lady Gregory trí scor bliain ina dhiaidh – ní theann sé chun áiféise leis.

Diomaite de chúrsaí stíle, chuir sé béim ar an chiall, ar an bhrí a bhí sa bhuntéacs a thabhairt isteach san aistriúchán, rud nach ndearna Hardiman. Níor mhinic aige bunbhrí na n-amhrán a chur as a ríocht chun iad a dhéanamh deas go leor do bhlas pharlúis lár na naoú céad déag – d'fhág sé ciall na Gaeilge lom díreach. Lig sé don chultúr Gaelach labhairt chomh díreach agus ab fhéidir sa teanga a bhí a glacadh chucu féin agus a múnlú ag pobal na tíre, agus ar an dóigh sin bhí lámh nár bheag aige i mbuanú an oidhreacht chultúrtha ainneoin an athraithe teanga. Bhain stoiteachas leis an athrú teanga. Laghdaigh Ferguson é.

Cé gurbh iris chostasach don mheanaicme Phrotastúnach a bhí sa Dublin University Magazine, rinneadh athchló go minic ar na haistriúcháin seo, ag díolamóirí Young Ireland ach go háirithe. Bhí meas thar na bearta ag na Young Irelanders ar shaothar seo Ferguson, agus níorbh annamh le leithéidí Gavan Duffy, Mitchel agus Davis féin an tuairim a nochtadh go raibh aistriúcháin seo Ferguson mar thaca láidir dá ngluaiseacht sin, mar spreagadh iontach ag an aos óg a bhí ag cuartú a náisiúntachta. Chuireadh an cineál sin de chaint náire ar Ferguson, a bhí ag iarraidh a bheatha a thuilleamh mar abhcóide gan cairde móra, agus cáil an neamhspleáchais ag bac air obair a fháil on Chaisleán.

Chorraigh an Gorta go mór é. Scríobh sé filíocht agus prós feargach fá mhí-éifeacht an Rialtais agus fá oidhe na nGael agus chuir sé dua le Comhairle Éireann, ábhar Dála nár eisigh aon fhorógra neamhspleáchais. Díreach agus Ferguson ag suirí le saoirse, fuair a athair bás agus chuir sin ar a acmhainn taisteal ar feadh bliana. Nuair a d'fhill sé ar Éirinn, bhí a bhuile curtha de aige, agus níor ghaibh sé le Young Ireland ach mar abhcóide cosanta amháin – ba é a chliantsa an t-aon fhear a scaoileadh saor díobh sin a gabhadh do na trialacha Stáit. Cúpla bliain i ndiaidh an Éiri Amach, bhí Ferguson ar a dhícheall i dtreo na measúlachta, fad mór polaitiúil agus sóisialta idir é agus a iarchairde, an véarsaíocht tréigthe aige, pósadh maith déanta aige (le bean óg de mhuintir Guinness) agus é ag obair go dian mar abhcóide agus ag déanamh cuid mhaith staidéir ar an tseanstair agus ar na heagráin dhátheangacha de litríocht na sean – agus na meán-Ghaeilge a bhí á gcur amach ag na cumainn léannta.

De réir a chéile thosaigh sé ag déanamh leaganacha filíochta de chuid de na scealta seo as na seanfhoinsí Gaeilge, go háirithe iadsin a léirigh, dar leis, seansaíocht Uladh, a luí le hAlbain, a bhá leis na filí agus a ghráin ar an chléir. D'fhág sin nar mhaith le bunaíocht Phrotastúnach Uladh a théamaí Gaelacha agus nar thaitin le náisiúntóirí an chuma chríochdheighilteach, an dath Ultach a chuir sé ar na dánta agus ar na scéalta. Ná níorbh iontaoibh leis an chléir é. Bhí lá na neamhspleách thart agus gan teacht fós, agus níor shásaigh Ferguson ceachtar taobh de shaol an lae sin. Bhí corrdhuine ann a shíl go raibh buanna aige, agus ba dhuine díobh an tAlbanach Larcom a bhí i gceannas na státseirbhíse. Chinntigh seisean ceapachán Ferguson mar phríomhoifigeach san Oifig Taifead Poiblí, an aircíovlann náisiúnta, nuair a bunaíodh sin in 1867. D'oibrigh sé go dícheallach sa phost sin, rinneadh ridire de, agus ceapadh ina uachtarán ar Acadamh Ríoga na hÉireann é go gairid roimh a bhás in 1886. Lean a spéis sa Ghaeilge mar chuid lárnach de chultúr na hÉireann agus bhí sé ar chomhairle Chumann BuanChoimeádtha na Gaeilge nuair a rinne siad achainí ar an Pharlaimint leis an teanga a fháil ar chlár na scoileanna – buaic ghluaiseacht na Gaeilge roimh fheachtas na hOllscoile, 1908.

Níor bheag sin. Ach chomh maith leis sin ba dhroichead é idir an fhilíocht ag Mangan agus Davis agus an mhuintir sin sna 1840í agus lucht an renaissance liteartha sna 90í. Rinne sé sainmhíniú ar chultúr na tíre seo a dheimhnigh páirt na Gaeilge ann. Thug sé le fios gur gnó don fhile an Ghaeilge agus an cultúr a úsáid mar ábhar agus mar ionsparáid. Mhothaigh an Fínín Ó Laoghaire a cháil i bPáras, nuair a bhí Seán Ó hAgáin Young Ireland, Whistler an péintéir Meiriceánach agus Swinburne an critic stíle ar lóistín sa teach chéanna. Nuair a ligeadh don Fhínín filleadh abhaile agus gur thosaigh sé soirées liteartha ina theach, ba mhinic Yeats ar cuairt aige. Ba uaidhsean a fuair Yeats óg a róthuairim (mar a thug Gerard Manley Hopkins air) de thabhacht Ferguson agus dá theachtaireacht agus ba mar aithris ar Ferguson a thosaigh sé ar an chéad stíl aige féin, an stíl Cheilteach sin a d'fhág tionchar chomh mór sin ar smaointeachas na hEireann ó shin – gan trácht ar an stair pholaitiúil.

Ó thaobh an chultúir de, is dócha gurbh é Samuel Ferguson an cathróir is tabhachtaí dá raibh ag Béal Feirste go dtí seo. Bíonn léitheoir an lae inniu míshuaimhneach fá chuid den dílseacht agus den fhrithChaitliceachas atá le braith ar a shaothar, agus ní hannamh tur é. Ach thuig sé gurb í an Ghaeilge eochair ar saíochta agus foinse ar bhféiniúlachta cultúrtha. Ainneoin athruithe uile na tíre lean sé dá saothrú ar feadh an leithchéid, 1830-1880. Thuig sé go raibh cúige Uladh difriúil ón chuid eile den tír agus go raibh sí ag druidim amach léi féin in athuair. Ní raibh iontaoibh aige as ceannas pholaiteoirí Sasanacha ar ghnótha na hÉireann na as bladar bladhmannach na náisiúntóirí míleata. Is beag dá shaothar atá i gcló, ach is fiú dul sa tóir ar roinnt dá phrós cruthaitheach, go háirithe 'Corby MacGilmore' atá lonnaithe ar Bheann Mhadagain, ar a chuid luathfhilíochta cosúil le 'The Fairy Well' agus 'The Fairy Thorn', ar na dánta malla ar fheallmharaithe Pháirc an Fhionnuisce, ar na haistriúcháin ar amhráin an phobail agus ar roinnt dá leaganacha de sheanscéalta na tíre seo. Agus iarrachtaí ar siúl mórtas agus eolas ar an chultúr Ghaelach a spreagadh i measc an phobail uilig, idir Phrotastúach agus Chaitliceach i dTuaisceart Éireann, is mór an trua nach bhfuil teacht go héasca ar bhailiúchán de rogha scríbhinní an údair seo.

22

Denis Henry
'An Irish Catholic Unionist'

A. D. McDONNELL

Denis Stanislaus Henry was born on 7 March 1864, in Cahore, Draperstown, Co. Derry.[1] Denis Henry was the sixth son of a second marriage: his eldest brother joined the Marists, another the Jesuits,[2] two other brothers became solicitors, while two of his sisters entered religious orders.[3] Henry received his early education from the Marists in Dundalk and later with the Jesuits in Mount St. Mary's, Chesterfield, before entering the then Queen's College Belfast, where he read law.[4] After an outstanding academic career, in which he achieved the distinction of winning every available law scholarship possible, Henry was called to the Irish Bar in 1885. He established himself as a successsful figure on the North – West Circuit, becoming a Q.C. in 1898.[5]

Like many in his profession, Denis Henry soon became involved in local politics and at an early stage of his legal career he declared his public sympathy for Unionism. In the July 1895 general election he endorsed the Unionist nominee in the South Derry contest against W.H. Dodd.[6] By strange irony, Henry was to stand later against Dodd in North Tyrone, and eventually capture South Derry in 1916. In the 1895 election in East Donegal, Henry spoke on behalf of the Unionist, E.T. Herdman, earning a scornful rebuke from the *Derry Journal*, which noted with some disdain how

> A star of North-West circuit magnitude...has appeared over the hills of Dark Donegal. Mr. Denis S. Henry, Barrister, has found time in the midst of his brief...to rush from the Derry Assizes to East Donegal to save his country.[7]

Henry attended as a Unionist delegate at the inaugural meeting of the Ulster Unionist Council on 3 March 1905[8] and, in an election speech in 1906, traced his conversion to Unionism as a reaction to a similar conversion namely,

> a reluctance to go with Mr. Gladstone when he took up Home Rule.[9]

Denis Henry's earliest attempts to secure a Westminster seat at North Tyrone in the 1906 general election and in the by-election which arose there the following year, provide perceptive insight not only into his personality and outlook, but also into the manner with with Ulster politics was conducted at a local level. The 1906 contest saw Henry, the Catholic Unionist, stand against the Protestant Liberal, W.H. Dodd, K.C., and lose the election by a mere 9 votes. The *Irish News* described Henry as 'one of that weird class of creatures known as an Irish Catholic Unionist' whose stance would be anathema to Catholics and whose religion would ultimately arouse the worst of sectarian feeling among Protestants.[10]

While the result lent some credence to the former assumption, the overwhelming support of Joseph Chamberlain, Walter Long, H.T. Barrie and local Orangemen disproved the latter.[11] In an election devoid of rancour, 5,954 votes were registered out of a total electorate of 6,174, a remarkable testament to the organisational flair and perhaps the personating ability of both parties.[12] When the result was announced, Henry rejected the advice of his agent, William Wilson, to demand a recount, on the grounds of an administrative error on the part of the presiding officer, E.M. Archdale. Henry congratulated Dodd, praised his professional ability, and promised to continue their amicable relations.[13]

Henry again fought for North Tyrone in 1907, when a vacancy arose following Dodd's elevation to a Judgeship. Standing against another Liberal lawyer, Redmond Barry [who had been Solicitor – General for Ireland], Henry lost by 7 votes in what was 'one of the most stubbornly fought election contests witnessed in the annals of modern electioneering.'[14]

Against the background of the ill-fated Irish Council Bill, the Ulster Liberal Unionist Association met in Belfast and passed a resolution, drawing attention to the throwing of the constitution 'into the melting pot', and affirming that the winning of North Tyrone 'at the present juncture', would materially strengthen the hands of the Unionist party in Parliament'.[15]

As in the previous year, over 90 per cent of votes were cast, with both parties raising ruthless preparations for polling day to the level of an art form: Barryite and Henryite supporters positioned petrol and repair stations at a number of points and had breakdown gangs ready. The aged, infirm and disabled were brought to vote, with outcomes which added elements of tragic burlesque to the proceedings. One man died in the arms of friends while being lifted out of bed, while a blind man who asked the presiding officer to mark for Henry was objected to by Nationalists, the argument raging for an hour before he could proceed. One voter arrived from Buenos Aires to vote for Barry, while at Newtownstewart, brandy was administered to a man who was grateful to live long enough to vote for Henry.[16] Henry suppressed his disappointment at the result and encouraged his supporters to desist from violence, 'if you keep the peace you will please me as much as if you had returned me'.[17]

While the Home Rule crisis 1911 – 14 was at its height, Henry was, at least politically, very much in the background, and concentrated on his legal career. In October 1910 he married Violet Holmes, the third daughter of Lord Justice Holmes.[18] It was a happy marriage, but sadly only lasted for fifteen years.[19]

One of Henry's most noteworthy public appearances during this period occurred in January 1914 when, along with S.L. Brown, K.C., he headed an inquiry into the famous Larkinite demonstrations in Dublin in August 1913, where a confrontation between police and strikers resulted in two deaths and 400 injuries. The final report in February exonerated the police from charges of brutality, though some 20 members were found to have committed unjustifiable assaults.

An opportunity for Henry to redress the disappointments he experienced in North Tyrone came in April 1916 when the South Derry seat became vacant. With a wartime political truce in operation among all the main parties, it seemed that mere endorsement from the local Unionist constituency association would result in capturing the seat. While the final result showed Henry was to be returned comfortably for South Derry, the figures obscure another story. Henry's selection was no foregone conclusion – he emerged only after the third ballot against Lieut-Col. Chichester and D.D. Reid and he found himself having to face an independent candidate who was contemptuous of party truces.[21] The eccentric Dr. Arthur Turnball from Glasgow, a member of the Royal Army Medical Corps, used the election as a platform from which to condemn government handling of the war effort.[22]

The brief campaign which followed offers an appreciation of how Henry's candidature was received by Nationalists. While no doubt benefiting from cross – party embarrassment at Turnball's appearance (he was rapidly and publicly disowned by the respective party associations in South Derry), the tone of Nationalists suggests a mellowing, even welcoming attitude. Among the telegrams of congratulation sent to Henry after his election was one from Rev. P. Convery, PP, VF, St. Paul's, Belfast,[23] (a South Derry man) while a week before the poll a local Catholic clergyman wrote to a newspaper in terms unthinkable, say, ten years before:

> At present it matters not whether a man is a Nationalist, a Unionist, or a Liberal, but to us it does matter very much that he should be a Catholic. And Mr. Denis Henry, KC, is a Catholic. We feel that when our interests, or the interests of our religion are at stake we shall have a supporter in our future MP.[24]

Interestingly, this was the first by – election in Ireland following the Easter Rising, with the poll coming a mere eleven days after the last of the executions and in the midst of ongoing courts – martial. Yet, local politics in South Derry was as yet untouched by these events.[25]

Henry's early parliamentary life was low – key, yet in recognition of his legal abilities he was appointed Solicitor-General for Ireland in November 1918. Henry defended his South Derry seat in the general election a month later against L.J. Walsh, a Ballycastle solicitor representing Sinn Fein and Professor John Conway, a mathematics teacher from Belfast, who stood for the Irish Party.[27] Selected in Kilrea Orange Hall, Henry's candidature, no doubt buttressed by his recent promotion, provides further evidence of the regard with which he was held by Unionists.[28] The *Coleraine Chronicle* referred to Henry as 'that redoubtable champion of Unionism',[29] while a letter from Carson observed that Henry had been

> a most loyal and devoted colleague of mine, and I cannot sufficiently thank you for the help you have given me in fighting the cause of the Union for so many years.[30]

A strong champion and the inevitable split in the anti-Unionist vote combined to give Henry a comfortable majority of nearly 5,000 votes. While in many ways this was an unremarkable contest (in contrast to events in East Down and Derry City), the South Derry election of December 1918 represents the last occasion in which a Catholic won a Unionist seat in Ulster.

Just as he was coming to terms with his new position in the peacetime coalition government, the onset of 1919 brought more promotion for Henry when he became Attorney – General for Ireland, a post which he held until August 1921. While the turbulent events of the period have been well documented, the problems which Henry encountered and the mixed success he enjoyed offer students of the period a different angle on the difficulties facing the administration of Ireland during the Anglo-Irish War. Henry, the able advocate whose mastery of the brief was his hallmark, now found himself in the unfamiliar position of an ill-informed member of an executive grappling with problems which were unforeseen and yet at the same time, of the government's own making.

Henry served two Irish Chief Secretaries: Ian Macpherson and, following the latter's resignation in April 1920, Sir Hamar Greenwood. Throughout, Henry had to respond to persistent and critical questioning on aspects of government policy, notably allegations of misconduct by Crown forces, the revelations of reprisals, and the application of coercive legislation. The burden was enhanced by Greenwood's periodic absences from the House of

Commons and the constant indictments of government from the *Times,
Manchester Guardian* and *Westminster Gazette*.

One of the Henry's major challenges was a
hunger-strike by Sinn Fein prisoners in Mountjoy
Jail, in April 1920. Imprisoned under the Defence
of the Realm Act, the hunger-strikers' demands
included, among others, immediate trial or release.[31]
Henry's lack of conviction in replying to
parliamentary criticism was attributable to the poor
quality of briefing he received and was compounded
by the absence of the Chief Secretary, Greenwood.[32]
Although the Mountjoy protest was a week in
progress, Henry's replies consisted of reading
extracts from Dublin Castle telegrams and a failure
to explain how many of the hunger-strikers had
been remanded, convicted or interned.[33] With the
Times calling for decisive action (the prisoners were
eventually released) Henry, along with Neville
Macready, admitted in cabinet that the whole affair
had been 'badly managed'.[34]

His own problems notwithstanding, Henry
remained unrepentant in his vindication of
government policy, at a time of guerilla attacks
on military personnel, the difficulties of operating
conventional jury trials and the replacement of

Sir Denis Henry, K.C.,
M.P. (1864-1925)
Irish News

British government authority by Sinn Fein Land and Arbitration Courts.
Surveying this pattern of events, Henry told the Commons in February 1920
that Ireland was virtually in a state of war:

> It was not an attack on one party, it is not an attack on the Coalition
> government, it is an attack on your nation. It is an attempt to drive your
> nation out of Ireland.[35]

Thus it was in this manner that Henry defended the War Emergency
(Continuance) Bill, which extended the terms of the Defence of the Realm
Act to Ireland for another twelve months.[36] Undaunted by the subsequent
failure of this Act, Henry endorsed the draconian Restoration of Order in
Ireland Bill which became law in August 1920. The *Irish News* condemned
those provisions of the Act which proposed that courts-martial be supervised
by military authorities with the power of the death penalty, while Joseph
Devlin's protest prompted an outburst that resulted in his removal from the
House following a rebuke from the Speaker.[38] In a heated exchange with

T.P. O'Connor, Denis Henry denied any ill-treatment of prisoners by military authorities, and went on,

> I have been brought up in the belief that free courts ... represent the greatest asset a nation can have...as an Irishman it is a source of shame to me that our Civil Courts cannot function in the ordinary way, as...they did for so many years when I lived in the centre of Dublin.[39]

The government, said Henry, had striven 'for a better state of affairs', and the Restoration of Order Act was a last resort. He regarded those engaged in violent opposition against the administration as 'rebels' and 'traitors', and professed that the government was entitled to deal with them on that basis.[40]

Henry, however, was to find that stridency was an inadequate asset when poorly briefed or when defending allegations of indiscretions by Crown forces. His Commons' response on a violent exchange between civilians and soldiers at Milltown Malbay in April 1920 owed itself entirely to the reading of local military reports, and the phrase 'so my information goes' perhaps conveyed a hint of frustration on Henry's part.[41] In this context, Henry's worst parliamentary performance came in June 1920 when Nationalist and Unionist newspapers referred to violence in Derry in terms of a 'civil war'.[42] Few were impressed by Henry's comment that his thirty-five years in the North-West Circuit had taught him to regard unrest in Derry as an annual event.[43] The *Irish News*, and *Morning Post* were quite critical of Henry's remarks, though the *Belfast Newsletter* noted that responsibility for Derry formed no part of Henry's brief.[44]

Henry's tenure as Attorney-General was more satisfying when parliamentary debate focused on extremely detailed areas of the law. Henry dealt assuredly with various leglislative matters concerning the condition of service of the R.I.C. in Ireland, education and land purchase. His confident explanation of the Criminal Injuries (Ireland) Bill enabled Henry to cope with Joseph Devlin's interruptions with an easy humour 'which brought a smile to the face of the Nationalist member'.[45]

Parliamentary records convey the hectic schedule that Henry faced as Attorney-General, a pressure that was undoubtedly compounded by the presence of an armed dectective when travelling from his Wimbledon home to Westminster. In early 1921, the correspondent of *The Globe* wrote of seeing Henry in Whitehall; Mr Henry, a man of striking appearance, has been working extremely hard lately'.[46] Any expectations of respite for Henry were dispelled when in August 1921, he was appointed as the first Lord Chief Justice of Northern Ireland.

Henry's appointment as head of the new northern judiciary came against the background of the July truce between the British government and Sinn Fein, the 'skirmishing' between De Valera and Lloyd George in order to arrive at a basis for talks, and Craig's determination to assemble the machinery of the new state following Unionist success in the May 1921 elections to the northern Parliament. If the reaction of Nationalists to Henry's appointment was predictable, the subdued Unionist response was surprising. Undaunted by a previously unfounded assertion that Henry would adhere to Westminster rather than ''lead a forlorn hope in Belfast', the *Irish News* expressed a familiar Nationalist theme namely, the 'inherently unworkable' and short-lived nature of the 'Six Counties Parliament':

We now learn that the absurd Northern Judiciary has been given a send off with the elevation to the non-existent bench of Mr Denis Henry, K.C. as Lord Chief Justice...Sir James Craig's Government cannot undertake any work with the degree of permanency attaching to it because they know that there can be no permanency in this partition.[47]

Unionists made little attempt to capitalise on the appointment of a Catholic to the new judiciary, and although the *Londonderry Sentinel* commented on the religion of the Lord Lieutenant [Fitzalan] at the opening of the northern Parliament,[48] the local Unionist press declined any comparable comment on Henry. Perhaps Unionists were concentrating their efforts on disproving the 'impermanency theory' of local Nationalists, a hint of which can be gleaned from the *Belfast Newsletter's* pleasure at the confirmation of Henry's appointment with the remark that

Sir James Craig and his colleagues are going on with the task entrusted to them by the 1920 Act, without troubling themselves too much about the attempt which some newspapers are making to persuade the public that their tenure of office will be short.[49]

Lord Chief Justice Henry was assisted by two Lord Justices of Appeal and two High Court Judges. One of the former was William Moore, Dublin-educated and MP for North Antrim from 1899-1906. His colleague was Justice Andrews, who was thirteen years Henry's junior, educated in Belfast and T.C.D., and who had been standing counsel to many Ulster companies, including the Great Northern Railway Company. The two High Court Judges were D.M. Wilson and T.W. Brown. The son of a Limerick clergyman, Wilson had won the West Down seat in the 1918 general election, was Solicitor-General for Ireland under Henry, before becoming Recorder of Belfast. Brown, from Newtownards, took the North Down constituency in December 1918, succeeded Wilson as Solicitor-General in 1921, and subsequently, albeit briefly, was appointed Ireland's last Attorney-General.[50]

Much of our knowledge about Henry's work as Lord Chief Justice is derived from a detailed, contemporaneous and unpublished account by Lord Justice Moore, who succeeded Henry upon the latter's death in 1925.[51] To the speculation concerning the permanency of the northern state - the Treaty talks began a mere ten days after the judiciary was set in place by Orders in Council - was added the immediate task of curbing lawlessness by means of an efficient well-run judicial system. Damage to property in 1922 was estimated at £3m, 428 people died and 1,766 were wounded between June 1920 and June 1922 and Belfast was to remain under curfew until 1924.

All aspects of assembling the machinery of the new judiciary fell to Henry. A building had to be found to house the Supreme Court and Henry engaged in correspondence and meetings with the Lord Mayor of Belfast and town clerk and was grateful for the intercession of Sir James Craig to procure and equip the County Courthouse, Crumlin Road, Belfast, as this offered the best temporary accommodation.[52] Henry was active in the recruitment of officials to staff the new judiciary and members of the legal and civil service branch of the Four Courts in Dublin could, under the terms of the 1920 Government of Ireland Act, apply for transfer to the Northern Courts. Henry liaised with Dublin Castle, made several visits to meet Sir John Anderson at the Irish Office in London and adopted a policy originated by Craig that, when candidates of equal merit were considered, the deciding qualification should be that the applicant was Ulster-born.[53] As a corollary, the Assistant Registrars, R. McQuitty, J. Breakey and the Assistant Chief clerks, D. McGonigal and A.J. Weir came from Belfast, while F. Redmond hailed from Armagh. Henry himself appointed J.M. Davies from Derry as registrar, invited T.B. Wallace from Dromore, Co. Down, as chief clerk, and selected Barry Meglaughlin from Dungannon as taxing master.

Even the apparently mundane task of acquiring furniture for new court offices came before Henry, who sent Davies to Dublin to select some of the forms used in the late High court from which adapted copies could be produced from the Stationery Office for use in the Northern Courts.[54] Henry clashed with the Treasury over the implementation of the Land Registry Office for N. Ireland[55] and lamented the absence of a Law Library for Bench and Bar, since the Queen's University Library facilities were a mere stopgap.[56]

Between 1918 and 1925, Henry had held the posts of Solicitor-General and Attorney-General for Ireland during the Anglo-Irish War and was Northern Ireland's first Lord Chief Justice in the formative years of the new state. The mounting pressure gradually took its toll on Henry who died on 1 October 1925, at his home, 'Lisvarna', in Windsor Avenue, Belfast. He was sixty-one. The *Times* praised Henry's tenure as Chief Justice and noted that while many important cases had come before the High Court of Northern

Ireland and some had ultimately been taken to appeal in the House of Lords, in no instance was any decision disturbed.[57] The *Irish News* surveyed the 'remarkable career' of an 'eminent Catholic unionist', and concluded that Henry had been

> a fair minded judge...an upright citizen...One of a notable Catholic family...He played an important, though not great, part in the life of this country for the better part of twenty years.[58]

For the *Londonderry Sentinel*, Henry's death meant that

> Ulster loses a brilliant Ulsterman, the Northern Bench a distinguished lawyer and the Northern Government a wise and tactful helper.[59]

23

Irish Catholics in Scotland
from Exile Politics to Integration

TOM GALLAGHER

The ties of faith, language, and kinship, drawing Scotland and Ulster together had been disrupted by the sixteenth century Reformation. Adopted by most of Scotland, resisted by most of Ireland, it was bound to be a major breach since, for a long time to come, the Irish and the Scots would not be alone in interpreting the world in religious, rather than class or nationalistic terms.

By the 1800s, when the first emigrant ships were docking at Glasgow's Broomielaw, there was little common ground left. Scotland had thrown in her lot with a dominant neighbour which enabled her to share in the world's first industrialisation and participate in one of its greatest empires. Meanwhile, Ireland found herself economically destitute and locked in subjugation to the same neighbour with most of her subjects eventually to be won over to the cause of nationalism which the nineteenth century Scot had largely forsaken in favour of a British identity.

The nature of the transition from a harsh but familiar rural society to an alien industrial one was a painful one for Irish immigrants. The personal reception they received from Presbyterian Scots was often cold. In a time of great economic and social upheaval the face of Scotland was being altered more rapidly than at any other moment in the nation's history, before or since. Thus the Scots were acutely unsure of their own identity as they encountered an onrush of immigrants who by 1851 numbered just over 200,000 people.

Like other peoples on the move, the migrating Irish brought with them to Scotland significant numbers of people expounding the religion that was essential for the survival of their cultural identity. The Catholic faith offered an important measure of certainty in the midst of great insecurity and often appalling working conditions.

In Glasgow, the Irish would dominate the unskilled labour market for generations, finding work as casual construction or dock labourers, coal heavers and as sweated labour in the chemicals, textiles, and dyeing works that were badly polluting the city by mid-century. They were an indispensable mobile labour force whose contribution to the prosperity of the 'Second City of the Empire' largely went unappreciated.

Systematic discrimination prevented descendants of the original immigrants from entering the more prestigious areas of the economy. As strangers in a strange land, it is natural for the first waves of immigrants, whoever they may be, to create an enclave insulated from the wider society. The religious divide ensured that the clergy were not going to encourage assimilation into a society that was dominated by Protestant symbols and values. In the second half of the nineteenth century, church activists created a wide variety of organisations designed to absorb the energies of parishioners, young and old. These bodies had distinct religious, recreational, charitable and social functions.

By the 1880s the community was ceasing to be largely Irish-born. But, if anything, the offspring of immigrants often proved to be more Irish than their forebears, thanks to the influence of bodies like the Ancient Order of Hibernians, the Gaelic Athletic Association and the Gaelic League. These had not existed in Ireland when the main migrations occurred before 1860. They were an expression of the nationalist awakening which was reflected in politics by the growth of the Home Rule movement. By the 1880s it had built up an active solidarity movement among the Irish communities in Scotland.

John Ferguson, the foremost Irish nationalist in Scotland, was an Ulster Presbyterian whose solid financial background meant that he was able to devote much of his time to politics. He chaired nearly every Irish meeting of importance in the west of Scotland from 1873 up to his death in 1906 and was famed for his conciliatory talents when factionalism threatened the Home Rule cause. At the height of the struggle against absentee landlordism in Ireland he and his friend Michael Davitt linked up with those in the west Highlands engaged in the same struggle. The moral and material support which the Glasgow Irish extended to the Highlanders as their own land struggle got underway, enabled two sets of immigrants, kept apart by religion and nationality, briefly to make common cause.

However, it was the sporting field rather than the political arena which enabled the community to begin interacting with the rest of Scottish society. Enthusiasm for soccer spread throughout working-class Britain in the last quarter of the century and the Irish in Scotland began to participate fully with the founding in 1887 of Celtic, a name that is as Scottish as it is Irish. When Michael Davitt laid the first sod of the new Celtic Park in 1892, the symbolic links with Ireland were affirmed. But shortly beforehand, the GAA had imposed a ban on soccer and other 'foreign sports' being played by its membership: when enthusiasm for the new sport remained undimmed in Glasgow, it was the first big sign of the community going its own way, rather than falling in with the wishes of those moulding opinion in Ireland.

The successes which Celtic quickly went on to acquire, culminating in six unbroken years as league champions from 1904 to 1910, produced an enormous feeling of pride within a community that had hitherto looked to Ireland for psychological rewards. The worsening rivalry with Glasgow Rangers, a team that made much of its Protestant allegiances, prevented the soccer world being one where the Irish could engage with Scottish society on their own terms. But, contrary to what many outside Scotland think, the sectarian disorders marring football occasions have rarely spilled over into politics even at moments of great tension in Ireland.

Low-level religious hostility between working-class Scots has prevented the mutual regard and trust that might have enabled their leaders to create enduring achievements in the sphere of labour politics or nationalism. But it has never flared up into sectarian disorders on the scale of those seen in the United States or, nearer home, in Liverpool.

By 1914 the Labour Party was acting as a bridge upon which rival members of the working-class could discard most of their ethnic differences. The Irish joined with other downtrodden members of society in a struggle to obtain economic justice from powerful employers and the state. The Labour involvement reconciled them to their place in the British state but, without the Irish Question, it is unlikely that so many unskilled workers would have acquired a degree of political awareness that in time spilled over into British political activity. The most outstanding example is John Wheatley who was responsible for making Glasgow, by 1922, a strong Labour city and who was the most successful reformer in Labour's first government. After 1906, he had emerged unscathed from disputes with the clergy after forming a Catholic Socialist Society. He was always careful to justify his Socialism from the standpoint of radical Christianity, not Marxism. His insistence that 'Capitalism and what it did with people was a destroyer of faith' may have struck a chord with John Maguire, the local archbishop, who had backed trade unionism.

The 1916 Easter rising in Dublin began a number of incident- packed and anxious years before it was clear that the Irish in Scotland were entering a new era. The community gave strong backing to the independence struggle in Ireland but the spectacle of Irishman killing Irishman in the civil war prompted most to throw aside their absorption in exile politics. The Church and the left benefited from the relegation of ancestral ties. Despite the hostility of many priests to socialism of any kind, both struck up an informal alliance. The Church's need for an ally willing to defend an educational settlement which enabled Catholic schools to be financed by the state, while retaining their autonomy, explains the tie-up.

No longer absorbed in the time-consuming task of raising money for Catholic schools, the Church threw its energies into strengthening devotionalism in the community. The Legion of Mary, founded in 1921, grew rapidly in Scottish parishes, as did the vocational guilds formed among Catholic workers and professional men and women so that they could retain a Catholic outlook in their work environment. In 1919 Glasgow was the birthplace of the Knights of St Columba. It was a sign of the times that the Knights slowly displaced the Ancient Order of Hibernians which like them carried out a charitable and welfare role but which was more 'Irish' than 'Catholic' in its orientation.

Irish issues continue to simmer beneath the surface of Scottish life. Here, Rev. Ian Paisley leads a protest march against the Anglo-Irish Agreement in Glasgow, 1985
Irish News

The inter-war decades of Catholic expansion were also ones in which a local press, catering for the immigrant community, flourished as at no other time before or since. The success of the Scottish edition of the Belfast *Irish Weekly* showed that a demand for news from the 'old country' remained even though emigration had slackened off by the 1920s. Michael Fallon (who died in 1991) was Scottish editor of the *Irish Weekly* for 46 years from the glory days in 1936 until 1982 when changes in the structure of the community finally resulted in the title being taken out of circulation.

The signs of change were already evident in the 1940s. Shared wartime experiences and post-war prosperity slowly began to create one community out of rival traditions. The onset of full employment, along with the expansion of state education, and the birth of the welfare state, greatly helped. Tensions and rivalries within the Scottish working-class were much reduced.

It was probably the developers who weakened the identity of the Irish in Scotland more than anyone else. In the 1950s settled inner-city communities were uprooted and their inhabitants banished to distant suburbs miles from traditional centres of activity. The emergence of a new middle class in the Irish Catholic community, less inhibited about reaching out to wider society, also undermined values of community solidarity.

By the 1980s the hallmarks of a distinct Irish community in Scotland were being eroded. The sense of Irishness that had blossomed even among third and fourth generation Scots-Irish was fading with the drying up of immigration to Scotland. The descendants of immigrants celebrated events such as the centenary of Celtic or the 1982 papal visit to Scotland not in isolation but as Scottish occasions. They received fulsome treatment in the mainstream Scottish press, all of which narrowed the scope for the *Irish Weekly* and similar Irish papers to offer a distinctive voice.

If today Scots are becoming more aware that their ties with Ireland are much deeper and significant than the appearance of marching bands on certain days of the year, the Scottish edition of the *Irish Weekly* certainly deserves recognition for keeping alive the memory of more durable Scottish-Irish links during most of this turbulent century.

24

Sport in the North of Ireland
from the 1890s

PETER FINN

Organised sport, both as a participant and spectator activity, is now a most important element of modern popular culture in the north of Ireland. In order to understand the role of sport in our society it is necessary to regard it first and foremost as a social phenomenon; a major consumer and producer of news for the mass media, a specialist sector of the economy and an element of life inextricably interwoven into our political culture.

The coverage of sport by the *Irish News* since 1891 is a valuable historical record which helps us to comprehend why sport is such a dominant social phenomenon in the collective psyche of the population. If our understanding is to proceed beyond the bare bones of a chronological narrative, it is necessary to consider the primary factors involved in the historical development of sport since 1891: the changing nature of work, urban and industrial development, rising levels of affluence, better education and literacy, mass production, improving transport and communications, better diet and public health and the changing place of young people in society. In a short review of the history of sport in the north of Ireland 1891-1995 it is only possible to sketch out some important historical trends, note significant sporting achievements and give pointers as to how games move in step with society.

As in many other parts of Europe, sport in the mid-nineteenth century was divided between the equestrian and hunting pursuits of the rich and the traditional rural games of the poor. However, within the lifespan of a single generation in the latter half of the nineteenth century, there was a dramatic transformation of recreational activity and this is clearly reflected in the *Irish News*.

On Saturday 2 July 1892 the *Irish News* reported on horse racing from Kempton and Newmarket, a cricket match between Oxford and Cambridge, rifle shooting organised by the Belfast Rifle Association, and an *Irish News* cycling tour. What is significant about this sports coverage? The existence of organisations to promote sport points to sport being viewed as a noncasual activity, now requiring rules of competition. The emergence of organised sport also displayed a class dimension with cricket, cycling, rugby, rowing, hockey and, to some extent, athletics being the preserve of the middle and upper classes. The first athletics club in the north was formed for 'gentlemen' at Queen's University in 1872.

Rugby football made its way to Belfast from Trinity College Dublin, with the founding of NIFC (North of Ireland Football Club) in 1868. The game developed quickly in Belfast and the larger towns and became almost exclusively associated with a professional and educated elite. New clubs such as Queen's, Instonians and Collegians reflect this. The Schools Cup, first played for in 1876 and won by Armagh Royal School, became almost an institution in its own right and can now proudly boast to be the second oldest rugby cup competition in the world. The purchase of land at Ravenhill by the Ulster Branch of the then IFU acted as a great spur to the game, attracting as it did many international games in the early days.

Cricket was the other sport to enjoy widespread development after 1891 and, whilst still associated with a largely professional elite, it had wider appeal particularly in the rural towns associated with textiles such as Armagh, Sion Mills, and Lurgan. Some of the great names of Ulster cricket are R. M. 'Bob' Erskine, William 'Willie' Andrews, Oscar Andrews and James Macdonald.

Rowing went through a period of expansion in the north of Ireland in the 1890's and early years of this century and again reflects a strong class dimension to sport. In the rather exclusive world of Ulster rowing the Bann RC Coleraine and Belfast Commercial Boating Club produced oarsmen who competed with success both in Ireland and Britain. Amongst their number were Tom Glenn (Bann RC) Thomas V McCormick (Belfast) and T. Forde Hall OBE (Belfast).

The early years of sports coverage in the *Irish News* reflect the values of the time, a Victorian ethos of sport – the amateur dream of sport for gentlemen which spawned the Olympic movement. This was only part of the process, however, as other factors were leading to what could be described as a democratisation of sport, opening it up to the working classes.

Popular Sport

At a more popular level modern sport also replaced old village games, and we begin to see the end of communal and regionalised sport. A notable exception to this, however, is the survival of road bowls (bullets) in County Armagh. The forces of industrialisation, urbanisation and improved transportation had a dramatic impact on the demography of the north and, with it, attitudes to sport. Village games came to be codified and new organisations sprang up to 'control' sport. Gaelic sports, association football and boxing became particularly popular.

Soccer

Association football (soccer) spread most rapidly in the working class districts of Belfast. The first leagues were local and primitive but with the formation of Cliftonville Football and Athletic Club in 1879 the sport became much better organised and attracted large numbers of spectators. A senior league comprising Cliftonville, Linfeld, Glentoran and Distillery began to draw the

George Best, the soccer icon of the 1960s and early 1970s
Irish News

interest of the *Irish News* and by 1898 soccer was big news. Football clubs were also the focus of other sports providing grounds for boxing contests, athletics meetings and pony trotting.

Readers of the *Irish News* became well accustomed to the famous exploits of Belfast Celtic between 1891 and 1949. This club was formed to tap the mine of sporting talent that existed in the Falls area. Celtic Park was opened in 1897 with the club having been admitted to senior football a year earlier. Belfast Celtic captured the hearts and minds of the people of west Belfast and names such as Jimmy McAlinden, Billy McMillen, Charlie Tully, Paddy Bonnar and Johnny Campbell have become legendary. Success on and off the pitch gave pride to a people for whom life was hard in many ways. It was a binding force for the area from where it drew its support.

Belfast Celtic has the distinction of being the first Irish Club to play in Europe. The disgraceful attack on Celtic players by a section of the Linfield crowd at Windsor Park on

26 December, 1948 led to a decision of the directors of the great club to withdraw its membership from the IFA and disband.

Soccer became the most popular sport in the north. Its rapid development was assisted by the simplicity of its rules, the fact that it could be played on a range of surfaces and a revolution in personal mobility brought about by the motor car. Newspapers also fuelled soccer's pre-eminence in the sports culture by encouraging ever greater crowds to attend games. A significant development in soccer this century has been its geographical spread from Belfast out into provincial towns, thus sustaining its popularity. Like other sports it has had its political problems; the 1921 split in the IFA, the Belfast Celtic incident, problems with Derry City and the existence of an undercurrent of sectarian tension. As the most popular sport played by both communities in our divided society, such problems are not to be unexpected. All over the world sporting allegiance has manifestations beyond the physical activity. The popularity of the game has manifested itself most obviously at international level with a record of success far in a way superior to what could be expected from a relatively small population. One major reason for this has been the tradition of 'exporting' local talent to the top teams in Scotland and England. Danny Blanchflower and Pat Jennings are only two examples of this, but the most outstanding and celebrated player to leave the north was George Best. Best's exploits with Manchester United are now legendary and in no small way contributed to the status of Northern Ireland soccer.

Athletics

Athletics is a sport which has suffered from division throughout its entire history in the north of Ireland. The division of athletes into the camps of the Irish Amateur Athletics Association and the GAA was settled for a decade by the formation of the National Association of Cycling and Athletics in Ireland in 1922 to which all northern athletic clubs affiliated. The *Irish News* in August 1926 reported that a special train was organised to bring spectators to the national championships in Croke Park, Dublin, at which the northern clubs like Willowfield, North Belfast, and Queen's competed freely with southern clubs. It was a rather strange phenomenon that the partition of Ireland actually led to the creation of a united athletic body.

Irish athletes experienced a decade of international success after 1922, including Olympic successes in Amsterdam (1928) and Los Angeles (1932). Internal squabbling in the north put an end to athletic unity. The creation of the NIAAA in the early 1930s laid down the conditions for a more or less nationalist/unionist split in the sport which was not finally settled until as late as 1987. The main activities of the NIAAA from the 1930s have centred around the Greater Belfast area where a large network of clubs developed.

Athletics was a much more popular sport in the past than it is today, with NIAAA fixtures drawing large crowds to venue such as Paisley Park. The eligibility of Northern Ireland to compete in the Empire and later Commonwealth Games has proved a great international incentive for athletes. The crowning glory of athletics in the north of Ireland must be the success of Mary Peters in winning the gold medal for Pentathlon in the 1972 Olympic Games in Munich.

The split in the sport of athletics was acrimonious and created a situation where athletes for generations were unaware of their peers in the other 'camp'. The NACAI allied itself closely to the activities of the GAA and organised athletics in a wide geographical area of the north, mostly of a rural character.

'Rinty' Monaghan a legend in Irish boxing
Irish News

The resolution of conflict within the sport is most welcome to participants and spectators alike and an indication that strongly held positions can be reconciled by goodwill on all sides. Cycling, a very popular minority sport over the years, suffered the same fate as athletics and this has taken away some of the shine from a great tradition (both rural and urban) of road racing in the north. Ballymena rider Billy Kerr was one of the north's most successful riders ever.

Boxing

The only sport which could rival soccer for passionate support is boxing. As in all poor societies, the 'ring' represents a window of opportunity for the brave and talented fighter. Ulster and the city of Belfast, in particular, has produced many great boxers and the King's Hall is an arena which is known and feared by the boxing fraternity worldwide. The first outstanding success of Northern boxing was the little flyweight 'Rinty' Monaghan. It was Belfast promoter Bob Gardiner who pulled off a scoop by securing the fight at the King's Hall for the undisputed world title in March, 1948 between 'Rinty' and Jackie Patterson of Scotland. On that night, Rinty Monaghan became the first home-based Irishman to win a world title. On his death in 1984 Fred Heatley wrote in the *Irish News*: 'In the death of John Joseph 'Rinty' Monaghan, Belfast has lost not only a former great boxer, but one of the outstanding citizens of our generation'.

Other great fighters were to emerge over the following decades. In the 1950s it was the Kellys, John from Belfast and 'Spider' Billy from Derry. They were followed by Freddie Gilroy and John Caldwell, both Belfast men, both champions who fought out a raging battle at the King's Hall in 1962. Danny McAlinden was a colourful and exciting performer from Newry and the first Irishman to win the British heavyweight title. The 1970s and 1980s saw the likes of Des Rea, Hugh Russell, Paddy Maguire, Charlie Nash and Davy Larmour. The night of 8 June, 1985 is a major landmark in Irish sport, a night when Barry McGuigan defeated a modern great in Panama's Eusebio Pedroza for the WBA featherweight title. The tradition continues with former world champion Dave 'Boy' McAuley, Eamonn Loughran and Wayne McCullagh.

Rugby

Since its arrival in the north of Ireland in 1868 rugby football has opened itself up to all sections of society and has enjoyed considerable success as both a spectator and participant activity. Its real strength lies in the existence of well supported clubs (often associated with schools) which cater for a wide range of ability. Senior club rugby took on an All-Ireland structure in the 1990-91 season following many years of a highly competitive senior league in Ulster.

Rugby is a sport which has always displayed a very strong international dimension and, to their credit, Ulster rugby clubs have a fine tradition of 'touring' and offering hospitality to touring club sides. At representational level, Ulster has an enviable record of inter-provincial success and has also produced some of the great names of international rugby in Jack Kyle, Willie John McBride and Mike Gibson.

For a small geographical area the tradition of sport which has emerged from the class-conscious days at the end of the nineteenth century is immensely rich and diverse. This is precisely because sport is so much part of the popular culture. A positive benefit to this society has been its role in bridging class as well as sectarian barriers – this is not to say that snobbery and sectarianism do not exist in Ulster sport. What is significant is that to list great sports people from the north of Ireland evokes a feeling of pride from all sections of society: Mary Peters, Willie John McBride, Alex Higgins, Denis Taylor, Joey Dunlop, George Best .....

Modern sport in the north of Ireland is now very diverse, with clubs for virtually any sport one would care to mention, and as such is reaching out to even greater numbers of participants. The last two decades has also seen the increased role of government in the promotion of sport through the activities of the Sports Council and the local district councils and with this an increasing standard of facilities. The sports culture of the north is a valuable resource in an increasingly international world where contact and openness are so important.

An examination of the history of sport in the north of Ireland 1891-1995 reveals a number of things: a common European heritage where sporting trends are mirrored in other geographically distant regions, a rich local tradition reflecting the special characteristics of this society and a record of competitive success in a range of sports of which we can all be proud.

Loose ball...
England's Jonathan Webb and Will Carling tussle for possession with Ireland's Eric Elwood and Ciaran Clarke during a Five Nations Championship game at Lansdowne Road, March 1993
Irish News

25

The GAA in Ulster since 1891

BRENDAN HARVEY

1891 was the year in which the Gaelic Athletic Association in Ireland started to decline. In the north it fell apart.

After the initial enthusiasm which followed the setting-up in 1884, matters came to a head when the main founder, Michael Cusack, was removed from his post as secretary in 1886. Then there were the controversial congresses of 1887 and 1889 in which the I.R.B. representatives vied with the Catholic clergy for control of the infant body. The 'American Invasion' of 1887 of athletes and hurlers was also a financial disaster.

In 1889, the Catholic Primate, Cardinal Logue, thought 'that the Association was a demoralising influence and young men were enjoined to avoid it'. Then, in 1890, the Parnell scandal broke. Like the rest of Ireland, the GAA broke into pro- and anti- Parnell sections. In October 1891, Parnell died. The political split took a decade to heal.

In the decades 1891-1901 in Ulster, the GAA was almost defunct. Very few clubs stayed in existence, county boards did not function and no Ulster delegates attended any GAA congress in this period. But the United Irishmen centenary celebrations in 1898 and the growth of the Gaelic League started to bring a change as the new century dawned. The new century saw the first flowering of the GAA in Ulster. Much of this new enthusiasm stemmed from the large number of young men who had joined the Gaelic League. They had become imbued with the national spirit and found a natural home in the GAA which gave them an outlet in the physical pastimes of football and hurling.

The Tyrone history of the GAA in dealing with this period records 'the generous coverage of all aspects of the national revival' in the newly formed *Ulster Herald*. Its first editor was Tim McCarthy, a Cork man and later editor of the *Irish News*. Another man who epitomised this new awakening in both language and games was Michael Victor O'Nolan, the father of the writer Myles Na Gopaleen. A noted hurler and referee he was both Tyrone and Ulster chairman during 1904-1908. In 1903 he organised the *Feis Mór* in Strabane – the first of its kind in that area.

The North Antrim GAA look upon the hurling final, played at the initial Glens Feis on July 5, 1904, as their first 'big day'. This tie-up between GAA games and Feis cultural events was also evident in Co Down. Sheila McAnulty, in her Down history *O Shiol go Blath* , recounts how the inaugural *Feis an Duin* in 1902 featured a hurling game between two Belfast teams. In 1903, an *aeridheacht* on Easter Sunday, run by Down Gaelic League, was the spur which established the Down County GAA committee.

The formation of the Ulster Council in 1904 saw some order introduced into GAA affairs in the north. The county which prospered most was Antrim. They already had an inbuilt advantage in hurling, but football also prospered in Belfast with the influx of many good players from southern counties. Antrim won six Ulster football titles in a row from 1908 to 1913. They contested two All Ireland Finals in the 1912 calendar year, having beaten one of the best Kerry teams in the 1912 semi-final by 3-5 to 0-2.

The onset of World War I and the formation of the Irish Volunteers in 1913-14 affected all aspects of life in Ireland including the GAA. Then came the terrible awakening of Easter 1916. The aftermath of the rising was more far-reaching. A new nationalism was abroad. On the smaller stage of the GAA in the north, the names of new or reconstituted clubs in Co. Tyrone in 1917 and 1918 tell their own story, viz:- Trillick McDonaghs, Fintona Pearses, Galbally McDermotts, Pomeroy Plunketts and Clonoe O'Rahillys.

The years 1920 and 1921 brought their share of trouble and strife. The 1920 Ulster senior football championship was played but 1921 was a year of confusion. Eoin O'Duffy had been elected secretary of the

A hurling match at the first Glens' Féis, at Glenariffe, Co Antrim, 5 July, 1904
Ulster Museum

Ulster council in 1913. By 1920 he had become deeply involved in the 5th Northern Brigade of the IRA. He went on to become a TD for Monaghan, Chief of Staff of the Free State Army and Chief Commissioner of the Garda and eventually leader of the Blueshirt movement. O'Duffy kept his official connection with the Ulster council until 1923. The Ulster president, Seamus Dobbyn, was also interned during this period. It is easy to see why the sport's administration was non-existent.

After these years of the 'Troubles' and subsequent inactivity on GAA fields in the north, a second revival was attempted. The Ulster Council held reorganisation meetings in 1923 and 1924. But the revival was slow as organisation in some counties was sketchy and in Tyrone, Fermanagh and Down no county board at all existed.

However as time progressed, things improved. The Tailteann Games in Dublin, in 1924, were a major attraction. The Ulster football championship, with seven or eight teams competing, took place regularly. The Anglo-Celt Cup was presented in 1925 and the Dr McKenna Cup was played for in 1927. But probably the biggest boost to Ulster footballers was the introduction of the Railway Cup inter-provincial competition. Ulster featured in the first game of the competition. The All-Kerry Munster selection shaded them by 1-8 to 3-1. In that first Ulster selection, of team and substitutes, only Fermanagh was not represented.

The 'feathers in the cap' for Ulster football in the 1920s were the wins by Armagh in 1926 and by Cavan in 1927 of the All- Ireland Junior Championship. In 1928, Ulster made it to the final of the Railway Cup football and Cavan appeared in their first All-Ireland senior final. They were beaten by the then dominant Kildare outfit by 2-6 to 2-5.

Despite all the setbacks of the earlier years prospects, especially in football, were good. The 1930s were to be the prosperous years for the leaders of Ulster football. All through the '30s and indeed the '40s, Cavan's footballers reigned supreme in Ulster. On the national scene they won Senior All-Ireland titles in 1933, 1935, 1947 and 1948. They won minor titles in 1937 and 1938. Naturally, Ulster football teams did tremendously well in the Railway Cup competition. It was initially won in 1942, again in 1943, 1947 and 1950. Cavan players such as the two O'Reillys (John Joe and Tom), Simon Deighnan, P J Duke and Tony Tighe backboned these teams. They had their 'last hurrah' when they won another senior All- Ireland (against Meath) in 1952.

A contentious issue arose in 1938. The patron of the GAA, Dr Douglas Hyde, in his capacity as first President of Ireland, attended an international soccer match. The then president of the GAA was Padraig McNamee – the first Ulsterman to occupy that office. He ruled that Dr Hyde had thereby ceased to be a patron of the organisation. It was a controversial issue then and, indeed, continued to be so between the Irish Government and the GAA. This 'ban' or Rule 27, banning soccer, had been part of the GAA constitution from the beginning of the century. The ban was in the main a positive expression of loyalty to one form of Irish culture. With the establishment of the Irish Free State in 1922, various people strove to remove it but this was always resisted. The majority in congress supported Michael Collins' view of the Association as 'the one body which never failed to draw the line between the Gael and the Gall'.

In the north, especially in urban areas like Belfast and Derry, the application of the ban cut through communities and even families. It is cited as a reason why Derry city, except for a minority, has not since the early heady days of 1890 been involved in Gaelic games. In fact, in Derry soccer is king. But long-held attitudes do change. In the 1960s, with the advent of TV coverage, the pressure to change mounted. Rule 27 was abolished at the GAA Congress held at Queen's University in April 1971. Rule 15, which bars membership to the police and Crown forces, is still with us.

For most people, however, the enjoyment of playing or watching the games was the main thing. As the years went by, the number of members participating in Ulster grew.

During the days of Cavan's dominance, several counties attempted to play 'David' to their 'Goliath'. Monaghan succeeded in 1930 and 1938 and were always in contention during the 40s. Armagh contested six finals in the 30s. They came closest in 1938. After beating Cavan in the semi-final, they went down to Monaghan in the final.

The 1940s saw a variety of counties put it up to Cavan. In 1940 and 1942 (at the unusual venue of Dundalk), Down were the finalists. In 1945, for only the second time since 1914, Fermanagh graced the Ulster final at Clones. It was 1982 before a Peter McGinnity-led squad made it back to Ulster final day.

Then, out of the shadows, burst an exciting Antrim outfit. Led by George Watterson, and starring such talent as Kevin Armstrong, Sean Gibson, Pat O'Hare and Joe McCallion it was to beat Cavan in the decider of 1946 by 2-8 to 1-7. Kerry, in a controversial game, put a stop to Antrim's gallop. Cavan came back with a vengeance to win the next two All-Irelands back to back – the 1947 final being played in the Polo Grounds, New York. Antrim had another Ulster title in 1951. Students of Gaelic football regarded these two Ulster titles as small reward for such an exciting team.

Then, in 1953, a rejuvenated Armagh went all the way to the All-Ireland final. Before a record crowd of 86,000, they were beaten by Kerry in what became known as the 'missed-penalty' final. Another new team emerged in

1955. It was the Jim McKeever-led Derry squad and they pushed Cavan very close in the Ulster final. The next year, Tyrone broke through. They had several of their 1947 and 1948 All-Ireland Minor winning teams and they overcame an ageing Cavan squad by 3-5 to 0-4.

The pairing in the Ulster final of 1957 was unusual – Tyrone v Derry. Tyrone came out on top by 1-9 to 0-10. This Tyrone team, with stars Iggy Jones, Jody O'Neill and Jim Devlin, went close against the eventual All-Ireland winners of '56 and '57, namely Galway and Louth.

Came the 1958 final, came another challenger! It was the emerging Down team. But Derry saw them off by 1-11 to 0-10. Derry went on to contest an exciting All-Ireland final against Dublin, having beaten Kerry in the semi-final. But it was the beaten finalists, Down, who were bound for glory.

Hurling

An account of the GAA in the north over the past hundred years has to consist mainly of the story of Gaelic football. However, if one reads the various county histories, the initial chapters all refer to a tradition of some form of stick and ball game. In Donegal, football only came into vogue in the 1920s. The earliest GAA trophy still existing in Co. Derry was the Hurling Championship Cup won in 1891 by St Patrick's of the Waterside. Yet the present picture of Gaelic games in the north is one of football being played right across Ulster but hurling is only widely played in Counties Antrim and Down and to a lesser extent in Counties Derry, Armagh and Tyrone.

If one delves into a biography of Michael Cusack, the main theme of his founding efforts was to 'bring back the hurling'. In the Glens of Antrim, the Ards of Down and other 'islands' in Ulster some form of hurling or camanacht had been played down through the years. The local name for the primitive form of the game was 'Shinny'. Historical accounts of games and contests in bygone years liken it to its cousin 'Shinty' or Camanach in Gaelic Scotland.

Because of its geographical isolation from the hurling strongholds of the south, the north has always experienced a difference in standards and skills. But this has always been a challenge to the hurling folk of Antrim and Down. The story of All-Ireland successes is limited but all the sweeter for that. Down won the All-Ireland Junior championship in 1964. Antrim were All-Ireland Intermediate champions in 1970. The latter had their moments of glory in contesting the All-Ireland Senior finals of 1943 and 1989. But one of the most promising aspects was the appearance of Derry in the All-Ireland Minor Hurling championship semi-final against Cork in 1990.

On seeing the efforts being made to establish a 'compromise rules' game between Gaelic football and Australian Rules, one is tempted to propose that a true compromise game would be possible between shinty and hurling. They have a common history and are both parts of a shared culture.

Down

Switching back to football, the spotlight shifted to the county of Down, whose team during the '60s set not only the north but the whole country alight. They won their first Ulster title in 1959. From 1960 to 1969, they contested every Ulster football final, winning six of them. In the four which they lost, Cavan were the victors. But whereas Cavan seemed to have lost their All-Ireland touch, Down in 1960, 1961 and 1968 went on to become All-Ireland champions with players of the calibre of the McCartans, the O'Neills, K Mussen, Paddy Doherty, Joe Lennon and Leo Murphy.

The Seventies saw a levelling-off of football standards in the north. Six of the nine Ulster counties won the Anglo-Celt cup – Donegal for the first time in 1972 and again in 1974. Derry won three titles and Tyrone, Armagh and Down all had their spell as Ulster champions. A welcome reappearance among the Ulster champions was made by Monaghan in 1979, after a break of 41 years. But missing from the roll of honour were previous title holders, Cavan and Antrim. Although Cavan have occasionally contested Ulster finals since their last success in 1969, Antrim's lone appearance was in the 1970 final. How the once mighty have been relegated!

The turbulence of the northern scene extended into the Eighties. But the well-worn path to the Ulster final was trodden by those counties with hopes of All-Ireland glory. A new face appeared in 1982. A Peter McGinnity-led Fermanagh squad beat Derry and Tyrone before going down in the final to Armagh. Monaghan came through again in '85 and '88. Armagh won in '80 and '82. Donegal came out on top in '83 and '90. Tyrone were the most successful, winning in '84, '86 and '89. In '86, they led Kerry for most of the All-Ireland final before going down to an onslaught from that great Kingdom team.

Although Ulster teams at minor and under-21 levels performed well at national level, success eluded all northern aspirants at All- Ireland senior level during the 70s and 80s. Was this due to the unsettled conditions of life in the north during this traumatic period? The difficulties are the obvious ones of disruption of normal life and travel – the harassment of teams or individuals and the blatant sore of the occupation of the St Oliver Plunkett grounds in Crossmaglen.

But in 1991, Down brought the All-Ireland trophy back north after a blistering final with Meath. It was a record fourth win for the county, which has never lost in an All-Ireland final appearance. The old doubts had evaporated. This 1991 Down win broke the mould. The ambitious Ulster

Down's Mickey Linden backed up by Peter Withnell storm Meath's defences in the 1991 All-Ireland final

Irish News

counties responded. In 1992, Donegal brought 'Sam' back to the 'hills'. Then in 1993, Derry made it a three-in-a-row for Ulster. All this time, Down were waiting in the wings. They responded to the challenge by regaining the All-Ireland trophy in 1994 – beating Dublin in the final. In 1995, however, a valiant Tyrone side were pipped by a point by Dublin in an exciting All-Ireland final.

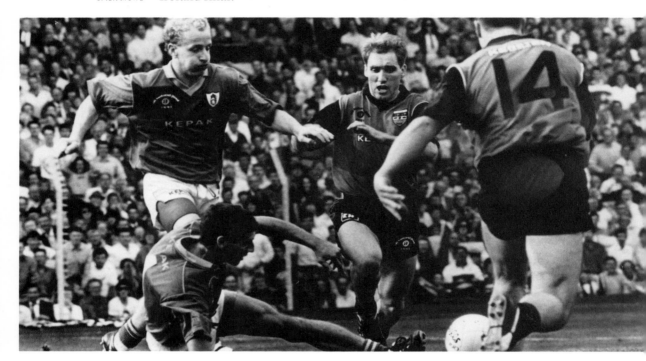

These achievements on the playing fields have been paralled in the day-to-day world. Both B.B.C. (N.I.) and U.T.V. have striven to present the Ulster (and All-Ireland) championship on the Sunday evening T.V. screens. The venue for the Ulster final – St Tiernach's Park in Clones – has had a major face lift. Sponsorship from the commercial world is now an important part of the County finance. And the GAA in general and the Ulster council in particular have joined with government agencies in funding and running coaching and leisure schemes.

The involvement of the GAA with the Sports Council of Northern Ireland has been another new development. The position of the Association in dealing with local government councils on matters such as the provision of grounds and facilities for Gaelic games call for a more open and outward attitude from the executive officers of the GAA in the north.

Conclusion

In the light of this new found confidence, it came as no big surpise that a motion to do away with the old rule 15 (barring membership of GAA to police and crown forces) was proposed at the 1995 annual congress. The ceasefire, which had been called the previous September, had created a suitable atmosphere. The motion was, however, deferred. Since then, a top GAA delegation, led by the President, Jack Boothman, has met the Secretary of State, Sir Patrick Mayhew at Hillsborough Castle to discuss this matter among others.

And so the question is often posed, especially in the divided society of the north of Ireland: Is the GAA a sports organisation or is it a national movement? As far back as 1895, the first patron said: 'As far as he knew – and he had been a patron for years ... the Association was purely an athletic body and that alone'. But the sweep of history has placed it into the position of the 'openly nationalist fostering of native Irish games'. So one can reasonably answer the above question by stating that it is a unique blend of both.

But one could go even further. With its tradition of having played its part in saving Irish games, it has improved the social life of Ireland (especially rural). It did cut across class boundaries and instilled qualities such as good teamwork and discipline into the management of its games. In the north of Ireland of the future the GAA, with its base so solidly established in its own community, can surely build bridges with opposing cultures. With such potential it must rise to the challenge of a new Ireland, of a new harmony.

26

A Glimpse at Fashion in Ulster
in the 1890s

FRANCES GARBUTT

In 1891 women in Ireland were obsessed with clothes. The trouble was that keeping up with fashion was even more expensive than it is today. Shoes were a luxury that many could not afford. Working women were often to be seen sporting the latest dress styles over cold bare feet. In contrast, the general prosperity of the middle classes generated a demand for large wardrobes of rich and elaborately decorated costume. Aniline and chemically-based dyes had been developed which introduced a whole spectrum of vivid colours to the fashion textile industry.

The newly invented sewing machine had dramatically increased the rate at which styles changed from season to season, while the establishment of Charles Worth's couture house in Paris meant that new ideas were never in short supply. Many middle-class women would spend their time visiting their dressmaker, ordering new clothes from Derry or London, selecting trimmings from pedlars and viewing the latest collections of fabrics and ready-made dresses from their local shops.

The fashion silhouette in 1891 was dominated by the tightly laced corset. An ideal waist measurement of 16 inches could be achieved by sheer force if the corset was long and strong enough; hence the most popular design of the year was made from whalebone and covered 22 inches from below the bust down to the thigh. Some women were even wearing full body and foot corsets in bed to obtain the perfect tiny proportions.

The bustle, which had been another essential undergarment for decades, disappeared in the 1890s. Consequently the slimmer silhouette led to a reduction in the amount of underwear worn. This would consist of a fine linen or silk chemise next to the skin, linen or cotton drawers and two petticoats which were pleated or gored with a drawstring at the waist.

Outer garmets were slim fitting to enhance the 'hour glass' figure but were richly and elaborately adorned. A dinner gown praised in the *Irish Society* journal is typical of the ornate style which was so fashionable at the time:

It is made of a rich duchesse satin of a deep orange tint and beautifully hand embroidered in jet in a design of large shamrocks round the hem and up the left side of the waist. Here the skirt is open in curves showing a graduating panel, almost to the knee, of orange-tinted *mousseline de soir* covered with narrow frills of the same gauze-like material. The bodice, with embroidered shamrocks at the right side and slightly drawn into folds at the left is draped with a pointed berthe of exquisite Honiton lace. Three large ostrich feathers entirely hide the small left sleeve of orange chiffon, while the longest plume falls down over the arm. The other sleeve is composed of chiffon frills caught up with one large jet shamrock.

This lavish concoction would have been worn with flesh coloured or white silk stockings, high-heeled kid leather or silk court shoes with pointed toes, long fine suede gloves with twenty or thirty tiny buttons and an elegant sufficiency of jewellery. She may also have been carrying a huge ostrich feather fan – a popular accessory at the time which doubled up as first aid for women who wore their corsets too tight.

In the summer, fresh flowers were added to evening gowns in the form of a nosegay, or were threaded into the hair. Some women even had real flowers sewn directly onto their dresses by their designer or seamstress immediately before they made their grand entrance.

Daywear for middle-class women in 1891 was only slightly less extravagant. Irish lace, heavy silks, linen and velvets would be worn most frequently and the most fashionable colour this year was bright sunflower yellow. Outfits and undergarments were changed frequently during the day according to the very strict dress code which existed in Ireland until well into the twentieth century.

The illustration shows a typical summer afternoon ensemble which would have been worn for a stroll in the garden or for informal entertaining at home. Although one of the main functions of the corset was to thrust the bust forward, necklines were high and concealed beneath a yoke of ruched tulle or fine lace.

Leg o'mutton sleeves, which were popular earlier in the century, made a comeback recently. Like all fashions in the Victorian era, it was taken to the extremes, with some sleeves reaching such a size that cushions were

The elegant dress of an upper class lady in the 1890s
Illustration by Frances Garbutt

required to hold them in place. The bodice was cut on the cross so it could be pulled tightly to mould to the tiny waist and was always highly decorative with flounces, frills and bows. In contrast, the skirt was rather simple at the front; tight at the hips, straight and slim-fitting to the ankle where it would flare out into a gathered floor-length tier of lace or embroidered self fabric.

The train at the back, although shorter than it had been in previous fashions, became a point of controversy in the 1890s. Newspapers across Ireland began to campaign for shorter skirts to be worn, following a statement by the Chief of Police in Venice who banned sweeping trains because he believed they spread disease by trailing in street dirt. Alas, their words were to no avail and the hemline of genteel ladies was to stay at the ground until the beginning of the 1920s.

But for less genteel ladies of the period the bicycle was proving popular and with it came a new freedom of dressing in the form of bloomers. The baggy calf-length knickerbockers had been introduced in the 1850s by American women's rights campaigner, Amelia Bloomer, who believed that the fashions of the day were too restrictive and that it was time for a change. However her prediction in the *Dublin Evening Post* that 'it takes time to revolutionise one's wardrobe as well as one's opinions' certainly came true; bloomers caused widespread outrage and were ridiculed in the press and condemned from the pulpit. It was not until the 1890s that the fashion really took off and, even then, bloomers were only accepted for cycling.

The new enthusiasm for outdoor sports and activities such as camogie, horse-riding and tennis made it necessary to wear more rational garments in general. A typical sporting outfit would consist of bolero jacket and full-length tailored skirt in a dark coloured heavy fabric such as Donegal tweed or homespun cloth. This would be worn with a white starched 'shirtwaister' with a high stiff collar and tie and lace-up or buttoned leather ankle boots. The masculine effect would be completed with a top hat or a straw boater, worn at a rakish angle over netted short hair.

The strict dress code of the time also applied to menswear. Lounge suits were worn for informal occasions and were generally of dark blue serge or subtly patterned tweed. One new fashion was to team these with brightly-coloured fancy waistcoats, although the *Tailor and Cutter* journal issued a warning in 1891 that 'gentleman with abdominal convexity should use discretion in the employment of hues and patterns calculated to draw attention to the unromantic formation'. Trousers were off the peg – top variety and some dashing young men had begun to wear them with turn-ups, although the practice was generally frowned upon. Central creases had also become important since the introduction of the trouser press in 1890.

The demand for well-fitting shirts meant that there were many new establishments making shirts to measure. William Tillie's factory in Derry pioneered a complete industry for the region producing machine and handmade shirts from fine Irish linen and calico in plain or subtle striped designs. These were beautifully made but hardly comfortable, as the fashion in the 1890s called for extremely high, stiff collars which almost choked the wearer.

Out of doors, the most popular overcoat for stylish Irish men was the 'Ulster' designed by John Getty McGee of Belfast. Promoted as 'The best storm-defier ever produced', it was made from lined frieze (a course wool felt) and was a three-quarter length double-breasted style with a short detachable cape and lots of pockets. A fashionable man-about-town would wear his Ulster with one of two new hat designs – the Homburg, which was introduced in 1890, or the very latest for 1891, the trilby. Country dressing would usually combine a Norfolk jacket, which was a high buttoned single-breasted tweed, with matching knickerbockers, a deerstalker, woollen stockings, high-buttoned boots and gaiters.

In total contrast, working-class men in Ireland had little time for money or clothes. They wore basic homemade garments made from homespun cloths such as baínín (untreated white wool) and heavy tweed and the priorities were warmth and comfort – fashion for most was irrelevant.

Working women, on the other hand, were generally fashion conscious, although they had to make do with the little that they could afford from the shops and rely on their own skills of weaving and hand sewing. Those who earned a shilling a day could afford to buy ribbons and trimmings to dress up and modernise old styles and would sometimes save to buy ready-made fabrics from pedlars or the local market.

Aprons were usually worn and were looped up, along with the hem of the skirt to expose the petticoat beneath which would be plain or striped cotton or linen. In the 1890s, full skirted ankle length petticoats were favoured in deep red or red and blue stripped fabric. Feet would be bare, protected by the traditional soleless stocking known as trioghtíní, while those who could afford shoes would wear them only on special occasions. Married women in Ireland would also wear a plain white cotton cap indoors and a linen cap out of doors, while in the winter this would be covered by a soft hand-woven woollen headscarf.

The shawl, originally from Scotland, was an item of outerwear adopted particularly by women in the north. Mill workers took to the fashion so readily that they came to be known as 'shawlies'. It was usually made from brightly coloured coarse wool and the loose weave meant that it was lightweight and, above all, warm. In the winter, the shawl would be kept on all day and at night it would double up as a blanket.

Such was the gulf between the rich and poor in nineteenth-century Ireland that it was possible to tell a person's social class from a distance of a hundred yards. Not so today where an infinite variety of clothes are available in every fashion for everybody.

Notes

CHAPTER 1

1 (Henry S. Kennedy), *The Irish News and Belfast Morning News* (*Irish News*, 1935). The circulation of Belfast newsletters in 1856 was as follows:
Morning News - 7,080
Northern Whig - 1,795
News-Letter - 916
Mercury - 864
Ulsterman - 726
Banner of Ulster - 654

2 *Ibid*; T.J. Campbell, *50 Years of Ulster 1899-1941* (Irish News, 1941), pp 6-7

3 W.P. Ryan, *The Irish Literary Revival* (London, 1894), pp 154-8

4 Devlin to Dillon, 5 Oct. 1891 (TCD, Dillon Papers, 6729/1)

5 F.J. Whitford, 'Joseph Devlin' in *Threshold*, 1959, pp 24-26

6 *Irish Weekly*, 11 July 1936 (interview with P.J. Kelly, RM, first editor of the *Irish News*)

7 Prospectus for 'New Catholic and Nationalist Journal for Ulster', Belfast, 27 Apr. 1891 (Irish News Library)

8 *I.N.* 'Articles of Association' (30 Apr. 1891)

9 *I.N.* 15 Aug. 1891 (first edition)

10 Kennedy, *ibid*, pp 12-13

11 Campbell, *ibid*, p. 6

12 For *Irish Weekly*, see Michael Fallon article in *Irish News Centenary Supplement* (Part 2), (1992), pp 27-28

13 In a letter to John Dillon on 11 August 1894, Joe Devlin complained at the Healyite tone of the paper and the way in which its London editor, Vesey Knox MP, 'is using his position to sow distrust...in the minds of the people'. (Dillon papers, 6729/14).

14 Devlin to Dillon, 26, 29 July 1897 (Dillon papers, 6729/39,/40)

15 F.J. Whitford, 'Joseph Devlin and the Catholic Representation Association of Belfast 1895-1905', (QUB Library), *passim.*; 'Joseph Devlin: Irishman and Ulsterman', M.A., University of London (1959), Ch. 1

16 *Northern Whig*, 1 July 1905

17 *Ibid*, 5 July 1905; I.N., 5 July 1905

18 Kennedy, *ibid*, pp 14-15; See *I.N.*, 29 Dec. 1921 for obituary of William McCormick

19 See *I.N.*, 8 Nov. 1923 for obituary notice of Daniel McCann, JP. McCann, as secretary of the Parnell Leadership Committee, helped to bring Parnell to Belfast in May 1891

20 T. McCarthy to William O'Brien, MP, 28 Aug. 1897 (University College Cork, William O'Brien papers, AH65); interview with Mr Paddy Scott, Oct. 1990

21 Memo on *Irish News* by former directors and addressed 'To shareholders of *Irish News*', 14 Oct. 1907 and Legal Opinion of T.M. Healy, KC (Down and Connor diocesan archives, Belfast)

22 *I.W.*, 5 Jan. 1929 for McCarthy's obituary; Kennedy ibid, pp 15-16; McCarthy to O'Brien, 8 Mar. 1897 (O'Brien papers, AH19)

23 *I.W.*, 5 Jan. 1929

24 Cited in F.X. Martin (ed.) in *Clogher Record*, v VI, no. 1 (1966) p. 24

25 *I.N.*, 1 May 1916

26 *Ibid*, 24 June 1916 welcomed the result under the headline, 'Ulster Faithful and Unselfish'; *I.N.*, 25 July 1916 condemned the 'Affront to the Nation' by Lansdowne and the British Government

27 E. Phoenix, *Northern Nationalism: Nationalist Politics, Partition and the Catholic Minority in Northern Ireland 1890-1940* (Belfast, 1994), pp 23-56 for political developments in north-east

Ulster after 1916 and the role of the press.

28 *I.N.*, 24 December 1920
29 *I.N.*, 9 January 1922
30 *I.N.*, 31 Mar. 1922
31 *I.N.*, 14 Oct. 1924
32 *I.N.*, 25 Jan. 1923
33 Interview with T. McCarthy in 'Report on Visit to Belfast and Derry' by H.A. MacCartan, 20 Mar. 1923 (UCD, R. Mulcahy papers P7/B/287); memo by Kevin O'Shiel (Free State Government's Northern expert), Jan. 1923 (State Paper Office, Dublin, S2027)
34 MacRory to McCarthy, 15 Mar. 1927 (Armagh Archdiocesan Archive, MacRory papers)
35 James Kelly Memoir, p 59; interview with Mr James Kelly, October 1989; *I.N.*, 5 May 1938 for obituary of William (Billy) Duggan.
36 Interview with Mr P Scott, October 1990
37 James Kelly Memoir; letter from Mrs Alice Hill to Cahir Healy, 25 Jan. 1929 on the future of the *Irish News* (PRONI, C Healy papers, D2991/A/9A and 9B)
38 Interview with Mr J. Kelly,
39 *I.N.*, 28 Oct., 9, 17, Nov. and 29 Nov. 1932
40 Interviews with J. Kelly and Mrs S. Hennessey; correspondence concerning Healy's dismissal from the board of the *Irish News*, 1938-9 (See Healy Papers, D2991/B/142)
41 'Hiawatha', *Lays of an Ulster Paradise and Other Poems (Irish News)*, 1960, p. 85
42 *I.N.*, 18 Sept. 1936
43 *I.N.*, 4 Sept. 1939
44 *I.N.*, 15 May 1941
45 Interview with Seaghan Maynes, Nov. 1991; profile of S. Maynes by John Hunter, *I.N.*, 19 Feb. 1991
46 *I.N.*, 27 Dec. 1956
47 *I.N.*, 15 Nov. 1945
48 Obituary by B. Kelly in *Irish Printer*, July 1989
49 Interview with T. O'Keeffe, 29 Jan. 1980
50 *I.N.*, 9, 10 Oct. 1968

51 *I.N.*, 29 May 1974; interview with Mr Edward Gallagher, Aug. 1991
52 *I.N.*, 16 Nov. 1985
53 *I.N.*, 23 Feb. 1995
54 Article by R. Greenslade in *The Guardian*, 27 Feb. 1995; *I.N.*, 24 Feb. 1995; Interview with Mr Tom Collins, 7 Apr. 1995. The *Irish News* circulation figure compares with 34,000 for the paid-for edition of the *News Letter*

Abbreviations
I.N.   Irish News
I.W.   Irish Weekly

CHAPTER 22

1 *Londonderry Sentinel*, 3 October 1925
2 *Irish News*, 2 October 1925.
3 *Londonderry Sentinel*, 3 October 1925.
4 *Ibid*, 3 October 1925
5 *Ibid*, 3 October 1925
6 *The Times*, 31 July 1895
7 *Derry Journal*, 29 July 1895
8 R. McNeill, *Ulster's Stand for Union* (London 1922) p.35
9 *Londonderry Sentinel*, 9 January 1906
10 *Irish News*, 9 January 1906
11 *Londonderry Sentinel*, 6 January 1906
12 *Derry Journal*, 22 January 1906
13 *Londonderry Sentinel*, 23 January 1906
14 *Ibid*, 9 March 1907
15 *Ibid*, 2 March 1907
16 *Ibid*, 9 March 1907
17 Ibid, 12 March 1907
18 *Interview with Sir James Henry, on 29 July 1980, in London*
19 *Ibid.*
20 *Irish News*, 16 February 1914
21 *Tyrone Constitution*, 28 April 1916
22 *Londonderry Sentinel*, 16 May 1916
23 *Irish News*, 24 May 1916
24 *Cuttings File in Possession of the Henry Family*
25 Though R. Kee nominates the W. Cork contest of November 1916 as 'the first by-election fought in Ireland after the rebellion', in *Ourselves Alone*, (London 1982),   p.16
26 *Nationality*, 28 September 1918
27 *Northern Constitution*, 7 December 1918
28 *Ibid*, 23 November 1918
29 *Coleraine Chronicle*, 7 December 1918

30 *Northern Constitution*, 14 December 1918

31 D. Macardle, *The Irish Republic* (Dublin 1951) p.348

32 C.J.C. Street, *The Administration of Ireland* (London 1921), p.233

33 *5 HC Deb 127, (12 April 1920), 1487*

34 T. Jones, *Whitehall Diary - Vol. III, Ireland, 1918-1925*, Ed. by K. Middlemas. (London 1971), p.15

35 *5 HC Deb (19 February 1920) 1171*

36 *Ibid*, 1169-1170

37 *Irish News*, 7 August 1920

38 *5 HC Deb 132 (6 August 1920) 2909-2914*

39 *5 HC Deb 141 (25 April 1921) 2406*

40 *Ibid*, 2407

41 *5 HC 128 (19 April 1920) 189-190*

42 *Belfast Newsletter*, 23 June 1920

43 *5 HC Deb 130 (22 June 1920) 2126*

44 *Belfast Newsletter*, 23 June 1920

45 *Daily Chronicle*, 6 November 1920

46 *Cuttings File in Possession of Henry Family*

47 *Irish News*, 6 August 1921

48 *Londonderry Sentinel*, 9 June 1921

49 *Belfast Newsletter*, 6 August 1921

50 *Belfast Telegraph*, 1 October 1921

51 *CAB6/57*: Publication of Memorandum on Supreme Court of Judicature, by Lord Justice Moore, 1 October 1921-31 July 1922. (P.R.O.N.I.)

52 *CAB 6/57: Ibid*, p.3

53 *CAB 6/57: Ibid*, p.7

54 *CAB6/57: Ibid*, p.9

55 *CAB6/57: Ibid*, p.11

56 *CAB6/57: Ibid*, p.29

57 *The Times*, 2 October 1925

58 *Irish News*, 2 October 1925

59 *Londonderry Sentinel*, 3 October 1925

Further Reading

CHAPTER 1

Campbell, T.J.   *Fifty Years of Ulster* (Irish News, 1940)
Oram, Hugh   *The Newspaper Book: A History oif Newspapers in Ireland* (Dublin, 1983)
Kennedy, H.   *The Irish News and Belfast Morning News (Irish News, 1935)*

CHAPTER 2

Kelly, James   *Bonfires on the Hillside: An Eyewitness Account of Political Upheaval in Northern Ireland* (Fountain Publishing, 1995)

CHAPTER 3

T.W. Moody and   *Ulster Since 1800*
J.C. Beckett (eds.) (i) *A Political and Economic Survey*;
                     (ii) *A Social Survey* (London, 1955, 1957)
T.W. Moody and   *The Course of Irish History* (Mercier Press, 1994 (ed.)
F.X. Martin (eds.)
Buckland, Patrick   *Irish Unionism 2: Ulster Unionism and the Origins of Northern Ireland, 1886-1922* (Dublin, 1973)
Buckland, P.   *James Craig*, (Dublin, 1980)
Laffan, M.   *The Partition of Ireland* (Dundalk, 1983)
Bardon, J.   *A History of Ulster* (Belfast, 1992)
Phoenix, Eamon   *Northern Nationalism: Nationalist Politics, Partition and the Catholic Minority in Northern Ireland 1890-1940* (Ulster Historical Foundation, Belfast, 1994)
Stewart, A.T.Q.   *Edward Carson* (Dublin, 1981)
Gwynn, D.   *The Life of John Redmond* (London, 1932)
Miller, D.W.   *Church, State and Nation in Ireland, 1890-1921* (Dublin, 1973)
Holmes, R.F.G.   'Ulster Will Fight and Ulster Will be Right': The Protestant Churches and Ulster's Resistance to Home Rule, 1912-14' in W.J. Shields (ed.), *Studies in Church History*, vol. 20, pp 321-35

CHAPTER 4

Andrew Boyd   *Holy War in Belfast* (Anvil, 1969)
G.B. Kenna   *Facts and Figures of the Belfast Pogrom 1920-1922* (Dublin, 1922)
W.A. Maguire   *Belfast* (Keele, 1993)
                     Capuchin Annual (1943), pp 283-361
Report of Cameron Commission, 1969
Report of Lord Scarman's Inquiry, 1970

CHAPTER 5

Buckland, P.   *A History of Northern Ireland* (Dublin, 1981)
Buckland, P.   *The Factory of Grievances: Devolved Government in
                      Northern Ireland 1921-39* (Dublin, 1979)
Harkness, D. W.   *Northern Ireland Since 1920* (Dublin, 1983)
Farrell, M.   *Northern Ireland: The Orange State* (London, 1976)
Faulkner, Brian   *Memoirs of a Statesman* (London, 1978)
Fisk, Robert   *In Time of War: Ireland, Ulster and the Price of Neutrality
                      1939-45* (London, 1980)
Kelly, H.   *How Stormont Fell* (Dublin, 1972)
Laffan, M.   *The Partition of Ireland* (Dundalk, 1983)
O'Neill, Terence   *Autobiography* (London, 1972)
Phoenix, Eamon   *Northern Nationalism: Nationalist Politics, Partition and
                      the Catholic Minority in Northern Ireland 1890-1940*
                      (Ulster Historical Foundation, 1994)

CHAPTER 6

Bob Purdie   *Politics in the Streets - The Origins of the Civil Rights
                     Movement in Northern Ireland* (Belfast, 1990)
Conn McCluskey   *Up Off Their Knees* (Dublin, 1989)
Frank Curran   *Derry: Countdown to Disaster* (Dublin, 1986)
Patrick Buckland   *A History of Northern Ireland* (Dublin, 1980)
Michael Farrell   *Northern Ireland: the Orange State* (London, 1976)

CHAPTER 7

*Agreement between the Government of the United Kingdom of Great Britain and
Northern Ireland and the Government of the Republic of Ireland.* HMSO London,
Cmnd. 9657. (The Anglo-Irish Agreement).
Aughey, Arthur   *Under Siege - Ulster Unionism and the Anglo-Irish
                     Agreement*, Blackstaff, 1989.
Bardon, Jonathan   *A History of Ulster*, Blackstaff, 1992.
Fitzgerald, Garret   *All in a Life - An Autobiography*, Gill and Macmillan, 1991.
Hadden, Tom and   *The Anglo-Irish Agreement - Commentary, Text and Official
Boyle, Kevin   Review*, Sweet and Maxwell, 1989.
Kenny, Anthony   *The Road to Hillsborough: The Shaping of the Anglo-Irish
                     Agreement*, Oxford 1986.
Lee, J.J.   *Ireland 1912-1985 - Politics and Society*, Cambridge 1989.
O'Leary, Brendan and *The Politics of Antagonism - Understanding Northern
McGarry, John   Ireland*, the Athlone Press, 1993.
O'Malley, Padraig   *Northern Ireland - Questions of Nuance*, Blackstaff 1990.

CHAPTER 8

T.P. Coogan   *Michael Collins, A Biography* (Hutchinson, 1990)
John Bowman   *De Valera and the Ulster Question 1917-1973* (Oxford,
                     1982)
Brian Farrell   *Sean Lemass* (Dublin, 1983)
Eamon Phoenix   *Northern Nationalism: Nationalist Politics, Partition and
                     the Catholic Minority in Northern Ireland 1890-1940*
                     (Ulster Historical Foundation, 1994)

CHAPTER 9

Akenson, D.H.	*The Irish Education Experiment. The National School System in the Nineteenth Century* (1970)
Akenson, D.H.	*Education and Enmity. The Control of Schooling in Northern Ireland 1920-50* (1973)
Atkinson, N.	*Irish Education: a history of education institutions* (1969)
Campbell, J.J.	*Catholic Schools: A Survey of a Northern Ireland Problem* (1964)
Coolahan, J.	*Irish Education: History and Structure* (1981)
Corkey, W.	*Episode in the History of Protestant Ulster 1923-47* (1965)
Magee, J.	*The Teaching of Irish History in Irish Schools* (1970)
Murray, D.	*Worlds Apart. Segregated Schooling in Northern Ireland* (1985)
O'Connell, M.	*Education, Church and State* (1992)

CHAPTER 10

Alison, R.S.	*The Seeds of Time* (Belfast, 1972)
Bardon, J.	*Belfast: An Illustrated History* (Belfast, 1982)
Barrington, R.	*Health, Medicine and Politics in Ireland 1900-1970* (Dublin 1987)
Blaney, R.	*Belfast: 100 years of Public Health* (Belfast, 1988)
Carnegie United Kingdom Trust	*Report on the Physical Welfare of Mothers and Children*, vol. 4, Ireland (ed.) E. Coey Bigger (Dunfermline, 1917)
Farrell, Michael	*The Poor Law and the Workhouse in Belfast 1838-1948* (Belfast, 1978)
Froggatt, Peter	'Industrialisation and Health in Belfast in the Early Nineteenth Century', in David Harkness & Mary O'Dowd (eds), *The Town in Ireland*, Historical Studies XIII (Belfast, 1981)
Gribbon, S.	*Edwardian Belfast: A Social Profile* (Belfast, 1982)
Gordon, Isabel	Countess of Aberdeen (Ed.) *Ireland's Crusade Against Tuberculosis. Series of Lectures delivered at the Tuberculosis exhibition, 1907*, vols 1-3 (Dublin, 1908-9)
Marshall, Robert	*The Royal Victoria Hospital Belfast*, 1903-1953 (Belfast, 1953)
Russell, George [AE]	'The Food in Ireland', Irish Homestead, (Dublin, 1906). Extracts found in H Summerfield (ed.) *Irish Homestead*, vol. 1 (Gerards Cross, 1978)
Russell, George [AE]	'Food Values', *Irish Homestead*, (Dublin, 1913). Extracts found in H. Summerfield (Ed.) Irish Homestead, vol. 1 (Gerards Cross, 1978).

CHAPTER 11

P. Bew	*Land and the National Question in Ireland, 1858-82* (Dublin 1978)
R.D. Crotty	*Irish Agricultural Production: Its Volume and Structure* (Cork, 1966)
J.S. Donnelly, Jr.	*Landlord and Tenant in Nineteenth Century Ireland* (Dublin, 1973)

L. Kennedy	'The Rural Economy, 1820-1914', in L. Kennedy and P. Ollerenshaw (eds.), *An Economic History of Ulster 1820-1939* (Manchester, 1985)
J.M. Mogey	*Rural Life in Northern Ireland* (London, 1947)
B.L. Solow	*The Land Question and the Irish Economy, 1870-1903* (Cambridge, Mass., 1971)
W.E. Vaughan	*Landlords and Tenants in Ireland, 1848-1904* (Dublin, 1984)
M.J. Winstanley	*Ireland and the Land Question, 1800-1922* (London, 1984)

CHAPTER 12

Kennedy, L. and Ollerenshaw P	*An Economic History of Ulster 1820-1939* (Manchester, 1985)
Maguire, W.A	*Belfast* (Keele, 1993)
Bardon, J.	*A History of Ulster* (Belfast, 1992)
Kennedy, L.	*The Modern Industrialisation of Ireland 1940-1988* (Dundalk, 1989)

CHAPTER 13

| C.H. Barnes | *Shorts Aircraft Since 1900* (London, 1967) |

CHAPTER 14

Emmet O'Connor	*A Labour History of Ireland 1824-1960* (Dublin 1992) Gill & MacMillan
Austen Morgan	*Labour and Partition: The Belfast Working Class 1905-23* (London 1991)
John W. Boyle	*The Irish Labour Movement in the Nineteenth Century* (Washington D.C. 1988, Catholic University Press of America)
Graham Walker	*The Politics of Frustration, Harry Midgley and the failure of Labour in Northern Ireland* (Manchester 1985)

CHAPTER 15

M. Wallace	*Northern Ireland: Fifty Years of Self-government* (Newton Abbot, 1971)
H. Calvert	*Constitutional Law in Northern Ireland* (Stevens, 1968)
Walsh, L.J.	*On My Keeping and in Theirs* (Dublin, 1921)

CHAPTER 16

L. Kennedy and	*An Economic History of Ulster 1820-1939* (Manchester, 1985)
P. Ollerenshaw	*Banking in Nineteenth Century Ireland: the Belfast Banks 1825-1914* (Manchester, 1987)
Padraig McGowan	*Money and Banking in Ireland* (Dublin, 1990)

CHAPTER 17

E. Gallagher and S. Worrall	*Christians in Ulster* 1968-1980 (Oxford, 1982)
J.C. Beckett	'Ulster Protestantism' in T.W. Moody and J.C. Beckett (eds), *Ulster Since 1800* (London, 1957)
J. Bardon	*A History of Ulster* (Belfast, 1992)
John Barkley	*Blackmouth and Dissenter* (Belfast, 1991)

CHAPTER 18

	The Catholic Directory (Dublin 1891-1995)
Canning, Bernard J.	*Bishops of Ireland 1870-1987* (Ballyshannon, 1987)
Fulton, J.	*The Tragedy of Belief: Division, Politics and Religion in Ireland* (Oxford, 1991)
Gannon, P.J.	'In the Catacombs of Belfast', *Studies*, vol. 11 (1922), pp. 35 47
Kenna, G.B.	*Facts and Figures of the Belfast Pogrom, 1920-22* (Dublin, 1922)
MacManus, F. (ed.)	*The Years of the Great Test* (Cork, 1967)
McElroy, Gerard	*The Catholic Church and the Northern Ireland Crisis* (Dublin, 1991)
Miller, D.W.	*Church, State and Nation in Ireland 1898-1918* (Dublin, 1973)
Rafferty, O.P.	*Catholicism in Ulster, 1603-1983* (Dublin, 1994)
Rogers, Patrick	*St Peter's Pro-Cathedral Belfast, 1866-1966* (Belfast, 1966)
Whyte, John H.	*Interpreting Northern Ireland*, (Oxford, 1990)

CHAPTER 19

Sam Hanna Bell	*The Theatre in Ulster* (Dublin, 1972)
Terence Brown	*Northern Voices: Poets in Ulster* (Dublin, 1975)
Terence Brown	*Ireland: A Social and Cultural History 1922-79* (Fontana, 1981)
Sheila T. Johnston	*Alice: A Life of Alice Milligan* (Omagh, 1994)
Kate Newmann	*Dictionary of Ulster Biography* (Belfast, 1993)

CHAPTER 20

Blaney, Roger	*Presbyterians and the Irish Language* (Ulster Historical Foundation, forthcoming)
Ó Buachalla, Breandán	*I mBéal Feirste Cois Cuain.* An Clóchomhar Tta. Dublin, 1968
Ó Fearaíl, Padraig	*The Story of Conradh na Gaeilge.* (Clódhanna Teo. Dublin, 1975)
Ó Snodaigh, Pádraig	*Hidden Ulster.* Clódhanna Teo. (Dublin, 1973)
Coiste Ceanntair Bhèal Feirste Glór Uladh	*Féile Leath-chéad an Chonnartha, 1893- 1943.* (Belfast, 1943)
Ó Cuív, Brian (edit.)	*A View of the Irish Language.* (Oifig an tSoláthair. Dublin, 1969)
Ó Casaide, Séamus	*The Irish Language in Belfast and County Down, 1601-1850.* M.H. Gill and Son, Ltd. (Dublin, 1930)
Martin, F.X. and Byrne (eds.)	*The Scholar Revolutionary: Eoin MacNeill, 1867-* F.J. *1945*, and *The Making of the New Ireland.* (Irish University Press. Shannon, 1973)
Fox, Charlotte Milligan	*Annals of the Irish Harpers.* (John Murray. London, 1911)
Belfast Gaelic League	*An Craobh Ruadh.* (A High-class Literary and Art Magazine, devoted to the promotion of the Irish Language, Arts and Industries). Ard-scoil Ultach. (Belfast, 1913)
Mac Airt, Seán (ed.)	*Fearsaid* (Jubilee Journal of the Queen's Gaelic Society). Cumann Gaelach, QUB. (Belfast, 1956)
Ryan, Desmond	*The Sword of Light: From the Four Masters to Douglas Hyde 1636-1938.* (London, 1939)

CHAPTER 21

Ó Dúill, G.	Samuel Ferguson (Dublin, 1993)

CHAPTER 22

J. Biggs-Davison and   *The Cross of Saint Patrick: The Catholic Unionist Tradition*
G. Chowdharay-Best   *in Ireland* (Kensdal Press, 1984)

CHAPTER 23

T. Gallagher   *Glasgow: The Uneasy Peace - Religious Tension in Modern*
                        Scotland, 1819-1940 (Manchester, 1989)
J.E. Handley   *The Irish in Modern Scotland* (Cork, 1947)
R. Swift and S. Gilley (eds.) *The Irish in Britain* (London, 1989)

CHAPTER 24

Patrick Myler   *The Fighting Irish* (Dingle, 1987)
Mary Peters   *Mary P.: Autobiography* (London, 1974)
Mark Tuohy   *Belfast Celtic* (Belfast, 1978)
Malcolm Brodie   *Linfield, 100 Years* (Belfast, 1985)
Edmund Van Esbeck   *Irish Rugby Scrapbook* (London, 1982)
                         Irish Football Association: 100 Years (Belfast, 1980)

CHAPTER 25

Marcus de Burca   *Michael Cusack and the G.A.A.* (Dublin, 1989)
Padraig Puirseal   *The G.A.A. and its Timer* (Dublin, 1982)
Sile Nic an Ultaigh   *An Dún: The G.A.A. Story (Down)* (Newry, 1990)
C. Short   *The Ulster G.A.A. Story* (Monaghan, 1984)

List of Contributors

DR EAMON PHOENIX is Senior Lecturer in History at Stranmillis College, Belfast. He is the author of *Northern Nationalism: Nationalist Politics, Partition and the Catholic Minority in Northern Ireland, 1890-1940* (Ulster Historical Foundation, 1994) as well as numerous scholarly articles on modern Irish history.

JAMES KELLY, the doyen of Irish journalism, joined the *Irish News* as a young reporter in 1929. Until his retirement in 1983, he was for fifty years Northern Editor of *Irish Independent* Newspapers. His autobiography, *Bonfires on the Hillside* is to be published shortly.

ANDREW BOYD is a well-known journalist, broadcaster and historian. He has written a number of books on Northern Ireland affairs including *Holy War in Belfast* (1969) and *The Rise of the Irish Trade Unions* (1972 and 1985).

DR BOB PURDIE is a lecturer in Politics at Ruskin College, Oxford. He is the author of *Politics and the Streets − the Origins of the Civil Rights Movement in Northern Ireland* (Blackstaff Press, 1990).

MARTIN O'BRIEN is news intake editor with BBC Northern Ireland. He was editor of the *Irish News* from 1982 to 1984. He was awarded the Irish Association's Montgomery Medal for his Master's dissertation on Mrs Thatcher's Northern Ireland policy.

TIM PAT COOGAN is a former editor of the *Irish Press* and a historian, broadcaster and commentator. His books include important biographies of Michael Collins and Eamon de Valera, as well as his latest work, *The Troubles, Ireland's Ordeal 1966-1995 and the Search for Peace* (Hutchinson, 1995).

The late JOHN MAGEE (1914-93) was formerly Principal Lecturer and Head of History at St. Joseph's College of Education, Belfast. He is the author of several books including *Northern Ireland: Crisis and Conflict* (London, 1984) and *A Journey through Lecale* (1991). The chapter in this book was written shortly before his lamented death.

DR. E. MARGARET CRAWFORD is Senior Research Officer at the Department of Economic and Social History, Queen's University, Belfast. She is the editor of *Famine: the Irish Experience*, 900-1900 (Edinburgh, 1989).

DR. FRANK THOMPSON is Head of History at St. Mary's College, Belfast. His book on the land question in Ulster in the late nineteenth century will be published shortly by the Ulster Historical Foundation.

DR. PETER COLLINS is Cultural Traditions Fellow at the Institute of Irish Studies, Queen's University, Belfast. His doctoral thesis was on Belfast labour history. His books are *The Making of Irish Linen* (Belfast, 1994), *Nationalism and Unionism* (Belfast, 1994) and *Sources and Resources for Ulster Local History* (forthcoming).

JOHN F. LARKIN was Reid Professor of Criminal Law, Criminology and Penology at Trinity College, Dublin from 1989 to 1991. He is currently in practice at the Northern Ireland Bar. He has written extensively on Irish Law and Irish legal history. His works include *The Trial of William Drennan* (Dublin, 1991).

DR. PHILIP OLLERENSHAW is Principal Lecturer in Economic and Business History at Bristol Polytechnic. He is the author of *Banking in Nineteenth Century Ireland: the Belfast Banks 1825-1914* (Manchester, 1987) and co-editor of *An Illustrated History of Ulster 1820-1939* (Manchester, 1985).

REV. PROFESSOR JOHN M. BARKLEY is a distinguished ecclesiastical historian and former principal of the Presbyterian Assembly College, Belfast. His publications include *A Short History of the Presbyterian Church in Ireland* (Belfast, 1959) and his autobiography, *Blackmouth and Dissenter* (Blackstaff, 1991).

OLIVER P. RAFFERTY, S.J., is a native of Belfast and the author of *Catholicism in Ulster 1603-1983: An Interpretative History* (Dublin, 1994). A regular contributor to *The Tablet* and other journals, he is presently researching Anglo-Irish relations at Oxford University.

JOHN GRAY is librarian of the Linen Hall Library, Belfast. He is the author of *City in Revolt, James Larkin and the Belfast Dock Strike of 1907* (Belfast, 1985) a study of the Belfast Dock Strike of 1907, as well as numerous articles on local and cultural history.

DR ROGER BLANEY is a former Head of the Department of Community Medicine and Medical Statistics at Queen's University, Belfast. He is the author of *Belfast: !00 Years of Public Health* (1988). His book, *Presbyterians and the Irish Language* is to be published shortly by the Ulster Historical Foundation.

DR GREAGOIR Ó DÚILL is a Dublin-based writer also grew up in Whitehead, Co Antrim. A former teacher and archivist, he is the author of a biography of Sir Samuel Ferguson in Irish. He has written five collections of verse in Irish and is editor of *Filíocht Uladh*, an anthology of contemporary Ulster poetry.

DR. A.D. MCDONNELL is Head of History at Abbey Grammar School, Newry, Co Down. His doctoral thesis deals with the career of Sir Denis Henry and the 1918 election in Ulster.

DR TOM GALLAGHER is Reader in Peace Studies at the University of Bradford and author of *Glasgow, The Uneasy Peace, 1889-1940* (Manchester, 1989), an account of the Irish in Scotland.

PETER FINN is Senior Lecturer in Geography at St. Mary's College, Belfast. A former international athlete, he is engaged in research on the historical development of Irish sport in a European context.

BRENDAN HARVEY is Head of Mathematics at St. Malachy's College, Belfast. An authority on the development of the G.A.A. in Ulster, he is researching a history of the Association in County Antrim.

FRANCES GARBUTT has a degree in fashion and textile design. A former fashion editor with the *Irish News* and broadcaster she has designed for Weatherall and Marks and Spencer and now specialises in fashion illustration.